Fundamentals of
Investigative Report
Writing Second Edition

Gary Guthrie

cognella® | ACADEMIC PUBLISHING

Bassim Hamadeh, CEO and Publisher
Kassie Graves, Director of Acquisitions and Sales
Jamie Giganti, Senior Managing Editor
Jess Estrella, Senior Graphic Designer
Mary Jane Peluso, Senior Specialist Acquisitions Editor
Brian Fahey, Senior Licensing Specialist
Abbey Hastings, Associate Production Editor
Bryan Mok, Interior Designer

Fundamentals of
Investigative Report Writing

TABLE OF CONTENTS

APPENDIX B:

Preface and Acknowledgments

Based on my twenty-five years of experience in law, I appreciate the purpose, importance and value of a well-written and complete investigative report. That practical opinion and appreciation has expanded now that I'm employed to teach adults how to prepare for careers that require good investigative documentation. I wrote this book because, as a classroom instructor, I was frustrated in my attempts to locate a textbook covering realistic, foundational investigative report writing. Although my peers produced many good products, I felt each fell instructionally short in some area or other.

This textbook was designed to reflect a practical, sergeant's approach to investigation and documentation. I believe each chapter is a relevant reflection of the basics the students need to begin their respective report-writing journeys. The information presented is based on nearly thirty-one years of investigating, writing, and subsequently defending reports in a variety of official venues.

I want to thank my wife and family for their understanding and flexibility through the 'cop years' as I learned the difficult and hard lessons that ultimately provided the basis for this textbook. I also want to thank all the unnamed "teachers" in my life who generously offered their time to develop my skills.

Finally, I want to express my gratitude to two true friends and mentors who have helped me make the challenging transition from street cop to college instructor. I am grateful to Paul Azevedo, who actually hired me, then generously invested time and effort to minimize the embarrassment of his decision. And my unconditional gratitude to Gary Creason, who for years daily exercised interest and patience in his direction of me to develop instructional skills, which enabled me to become a vested instructor.

The Man in the Arena

"It is not the critic who counts; not the man who points out how the strong man stumbles, or where the doer of deeds could have done them better. The credit belongs to the man who is actually in the arena, whose face is marred by dust and sweat and blood; who strives valiantly; who errs, who comes short again and again, because there is no effort without error and shortcoming; but who does actually strive to do the deeds; who knows great enthusiasms, the great devotions; who spends himself in a worthy cause; who at the best knows in the end the triumph of high achievement, and who at the worst, if he fails, at least fails while daring greatly, so that his place shall never be with those cold and timid souls who neither know victory nor defeat."

– Theodore Roosevelt

Theodore Roosevelt, "The Man in the Arena," *Citizenship in a Republic*. Copyright in the Public Domain.

The thoughts, experiences, and instruction shared within this book are offered to those who knowingly accept risks to "enter the arena" to accomplish the dangerous, the difficult, and the distasteful tasks others summarily reject.

The "Man in the Arena" is a portion of a 1917 speech in which Theodore Roosevelt mocked those that stand on the sidelines and watch, often only to find fault and point boney fingers in unrealistic criticism of those rare and brave individuals who willingly place themselves in positions of risk, and who do so in the most difficult times, to ensure order and safety, and reassure the vulnerable.

Theodore Roosevelt was the twenty-sixth president of the United States. He recognized the efforts of the special "warriors" as he too was a man of many endeavors; soldier, statesman, naturalist, author, and reformer who knew a few things about being that human in the arena. He believed that it's extremely easy to speak strong opinions and critique others; that going out there and doing it is the difficult part.

As in Roosevelt's speech, the author attempts to encourage, empower, and bestow honor to those in the arena and to their loved ones, who willingly and routinely sacrifice themselves for often unnoticed deeds and for worthy causes.

Introduction

It is not an exaggeration to say that valued investigative report writing will not fall out of fashion anytime soon. Few work products used by our various systems of government or institutions of commerce mean as much to the efficiency of operations as the value of a quality investigative report.

Whether the investigation and subsequent documentation is a determination of why Mary is frequently late to work, or personnel performance evaluations, or the determinations as to why an aircraft failure occurs, it is the investigative report that determines and documents factual relationships that explain the present event and fuel future strategies.

The task may at times seem insurmountable to the new report writer. To the experienced writer, the obligation to a good investigative report may never actually feel achieved. And the truth remains that a writer may never know the significance or value of a good report.

Reports are often like a baton passed from one investigator to another, over time and job assignments, with initially only a hazy resolution, and the real significance revealed in the next generation, or the one after that.

But most commonly, a writer will immediately suffer the ill recognition and unkind consequences of a poorly crafted or insufficient report. Lacking reports simply don't get the job done; they tend to provide additional hurdles to those ultimately tasked with resolving the issue.

In our law enforcement training strategies, there appears to be an uneven emphasis on officer safety, highlighting firearm practices and defensive tactics. I believe those focused strategies are potentially myopic when considering all the personal threats to the officer.

Based on my career observations, an insufficient report that represents a poor investigation, or inadequate documentation, represents a significant threat to the individual officer and his employer. And as we function and exist in a time of seemingly rampant litigation, the threat to long-term financial stability is real.

Finally, it is important to highlight that punitive damage awards are paid by individual named officers, not their departments. Therefore, a good, professional, well-written police report is the best defense to such a threat, and a protection that should not be underestimated.

My current job has afforded me the chance to review numerous report-writing textbooks available on the market today. No offense to my peers, but I feel the current offerings are lacking.

I feel they are inadequate as basic foundational instruction to the new vocational investigative report writer. And as report writing is actually a commitment to a lifelong skills development process, the new writer needs to securely establish the foundation on which to build over the remainder of their career.

I am a former officer, detective, supervisor, and now educator with more than three decades of practical experience. I've investigated, documented, and eventually defended the written products of my experience and skills.

Through these very real experiences and lessons, I understand first hand and appreciate the value of a quality investigative report. I feel an obligation to encourage urgency for new writers to capture the correct attitude, develop a solid foundation, and accept relevant information in order to develop their skills.

The purpose of this book is to offer instruction and examples of how a beginning investigative report writer can build a solid, basic foundation on which to build expertise.

1

Attitude and Ethics

Chapter Summary

Investigative report writing can be a complex and challenging task. It requires the accomplished author to have a dedicated, success-driven attitude that includes a focus on individual accountability to continually develop, improve, and produce error-free work.

   The proper attitude also includes a writer's focus on ethical considerations. Incomplete or inaccurate work tends to diminish respect for and confidence in the author, the author's workplace, and the author's profession at large.

Chapter Learning Objectives

Discuss the purpose of an investigative report.

Explain the community's expectation of the purpose of an investigative report.

Describe the reality of the varied purposes and agendas of a report's readers.

Understand the challenges of report writing: A writer must adopt the proper attitude.

Discuss how the process of developing into an accomplished report writer is career long.

Understand how the development process requires honest self-evaluation by the author.

Describe the proper attitude for achieving mistake-free work.

Discuss the ethics of mistakes, intentional or unintentional, and the benefits of proofreading.

Understand that unbiased and objective reporting is an obligation of the writer.

The Importance of Attitude and Ethics

Wouldn't it be nice if people always got along handsomely and never disagreed? Or if people followed all rules exactly as the design of the rules intended? Or if there were no occasions on which we needed to determine what went wrong with some practice, design, or equipment?

Nice thought, but we know these ideals will never be completely met. Therefore, there will always be a need for some sort of an investigation. Although the majority of investigations tend to be informal and don't require written documentation to review the issues, others do.

This book was designed to offer considerations to support a foundation for the beginning investigative report writer. This is less an academic exposure to writing and more an exploration for the vocational investigative report writer. Although throughout this text I will often refer to the police report, the principles offered could easily be applied to a variety of other types of investigative documentation.

What is the purpose of an investigative report? An investigative report's purpose is to produce a document that is a fair and objective review of issues and an unbiased evaluation, in order to arrive at a determination of the issue(s).

Law enforcement's role in society is, in short, to preserve peace and order, uphold and enforce laws, protect citizens, and apprehend criminals. Ultimately, law enforcement represents the community's will and must maintain the community members' trust through transparent, professional, unbiased review, cooperating within reasonable actions and accountable behavior.

The community requires reassurance that the authority it extends to the police is not abused, the use of force is reasonable, police actions are justified, investigative conclusions and determinations are reached without prejudice, and the ideals of the design of our government are followed and supported. Community representatives monitor these concerns primarily through investigative reports.

In a corporate setting, the goal of the investigative report is to credibly establish facts, behaviors, and actions to determine if those circumstances meet the intent of the company's policy and/or procedures. It also provides data to determine whether other strategies should be considered.

Accuracy

The purpose of the investigative report is to provide an accurate written account of the event, the participants' actions, and observations, in order to document relevant and related evidence, capture statements, and, in some cases, provide facts and analysis for a conclusion.

Often, the author must swear to the report's accuracy and, in many cases, defend the investigation and the report to a cavalcade of evaluators.

To be sure, investigative report writing is a critically important function that serves many purposes, needs, and agendas. Among other possibilities, a single report has the potential to affect an individual, the population of an organization, a community, or entire professions; prompt a change of law; or modify society's foundational institutions.

When a writer considers the potential effects of a report, the number of readers, and the vast variety of their agendas—and then adds the critical requirements to be complete, unbiased, and accurate—the prospect of investigative report writing can seem overwhelming. All considered, it is a task that can be challenging and complex.

It has been said that those employees with the least amount of experience accomplish the most significant tasks. For example, the recently graduated, academy-trained officer is assigned to a brief field training and then pronounced ready to operate in the "real world."

As the new officer steps into this world, it is incumbent on them to possess the tools and skills to find immediate success in this challenging function. Talk about zero to sixty in nothing flat!

The truth is that learning to create a good investigative report is a lifelong endeavor. The honest writer at any level of experience must write with the appropriate attitude. The investigative report writer should maintain the perspective that improving their ability to communicate in writing is a journey and not a destination.

Attitude Is Key!

To succeed in this challenging journey, you must possess and apply the correct attitude! You must invest yourself to the maximum each and every time you write. And to be clear, this commitment includes all forms of written communication, from detailed, complicated investigative reports to routine office emails.

The most realistic perspective might be to view today's work not only as an accomplishment, but also as a reminder and a continuing challenge to seek to improve. Today you are at this stage of the journey, with much more to learn and accomplish.

Each time you write, reread and evaluate what you just wrote. Make sure the first sentence is complete, articulate, unbiased, and fair. Then apply the same analysis to the next sentence, and so on. To put the correct attitude into action, you must honestly evaluate your attitude and work.

You should remember that your report will have multiple readers, each with different disciplines and agendas; each searching for different themes or information in a single narrative. This reality presents a challenge to the writer to consider how to use language carefully, make clear the objectiveness of the investigation, provide extensive detail, and consider a multi-faceted application.

Accept that your written work offers the clearest and most immediately obvious representation of you. Your writing exhibits your attitude, skills, and, ultimately, your professional commitment. To apply the correct attitude, always be honest in your frequent, routine self-evaluations and be committed to improving.

Those who pursue the many careers that require professional documentation, such as law enforcement, presumably hold the long-term intention to gain a job and keep a job.

I can tell you with all certainty that the career you want will remain yours only if you produce competent and professional work on a regular and routine basis. Although it can be said in different ways, it boils down to this: Your future employers won't *hope* you write decent reports; they will *insist* on it!

Your renewed, dedicated, and focused attitude can help fuel your success. Your focused attitude and actions can help you accomplish your goal to develop into a valuable and respected professional. In many circumstances, the quality of your attitude and investment may be the only factor that you exclusively control.

You Must Self-Evaluate

As you self-evaluate to determine the proficiency level you currently occupy, think about how you can better yourself. Always consider the level you are at today a temporary level—one deserving of improvement. Remember that report writing is a journey on which you must challenge and cultivate yourself or else you stagnate and become ineffective.

A critical component of the proper attitude is to refuse to allow in your writing the chance for mistakes. You, the author, are solely responsible for your work, and you must adopt the attitude and mindset that mistakes simply will not materialize in your report narrative at all!

Here's just one justification for that thought: If you are accepting compensation for employment, you are responsible for the work for which you are paid. If you allow mistakes to happen, other people will be forced to pay again for those mistakes with additional work investments.

The process of someone else finding and fixing unnecessary mistakes is a truly wasteful imposition on always-limited work resources. The additional "repair" investments and efforts are definitely noticed by others, and tend to construct negative opinions of your professionalism.

I recommend you take each mistake discovered by someone else personally—as in, never to occur again! Never allow yourself the "whatever" attitude that leads to being seen as undisciplined or lazy.

Look to identify and repair those mistakes before the report is passed on. Personally review your work and then ask a peer for a "fresh eyes" review. This buddy system practice is not a sign of weakness; it is common in the workplace.

Although I will discuss this concept later in this chapter, I want to offer another thought now: There are ethical considerations attached to mistakes in written communication. Simply stated, you are being paid for work that you have not provided. I have witnessed discussions that parallel mistakes in written reports with employee theft of pay (for both the pay lost to the author and the cost of the document's repair).

Seemingly careless or routine mistakes tend to damage people's general opinion of all investigative reports. Avoidable mistakes can cast a negative global shadow on your employer and on the profession your employment represents. Many people think errors reveal ignorance, a lack of dedication to work investments, intellectually dull practitioners, undisciplined efforts, and/or simply dishonest professionals.

Personal and professional respect is earned, not given. You must have the desire to earn that respect by producing quality, mistake-free, thoughtful, and valuable work. By doing so, all involved maintain and grow the respect of others.

When your clients respect your professionalism through disciplined demonstrations, such as quality written work, that confidence tends to produce a working relationship of trust and invites cooperation. The client is not suspicious of your dedication or wary of your professional abilities or aptitudes. Instead, they are reassured, they anticipate professional behavior, and they are confident in your subsequent work.

Let me provide something of a parallel example. Should you ever require delicate surgery, would you accept without reservation the surgical services of a doctor or hospital that has a mistake-laden reputation? Or would you prefer to be cut by a surgeon at a hospital that has a mistake-free reputation?

Then, would you hold the mistakes of a surgeon only against that individual surgeon, or would you tend to be suspicious of his workplace or begin to question the abilities of all surgeons?

And finally, the surgeon that does make mistakes—has he violated an ethical oath and diluted a foundation of trust by allowing his mistakes to occur in the first place?

Take Responsibility to Avoid Mistakes

If the investigation or report has mistakes, those mistakes cast a shadow of suspicion on the quality of the entire investigation. The thought is, if some of the information reported or presented in a professional piece of work is not accurate, all other facts presented can only be viewed with a questioning eye.

Luckily, you possess the gift of proofreading. I highly recommend you use that gift multiple times and as often as possible. The expectation of professionalism DEMANDS an objective, accurate, and unbiased investigation and report.

There is simply no excuse for misspelled words with today's technology. Misspelled words are mistakes that can easily be eliminated. Don't make them.

Other types of mistakes, such as sentence structure errors, are owned by the author alone. It is the sole responsibility of the writer to identify and fix improper writing practices. Other issues, such as having English as a second language, while understandable, are not professionally acceptable or excusable; writing ability must be improved to successfully operate in a professional environment where English is the primary language.

During one author's recent book-signing event, an admirer asked the author, "How can I write better?" The author responded, "To write better, you must read more." Good advice. When readers routinely expose themselves to correct sentence, paragraph, and narrative construction, they naturally assimilate good writing structures and habits.

Let me offer a final realistic perspective regarding mistakes. Even if you somehow survive in a job while submitting mistake-laden work, you can be sure others' confidence in your dedication and professionalism will diminish. Their reduced opinions will affect their confidence in your competencies for special assignments or promotions.

Decision makers often base decisions on their confidence in your abilities and reputation. Those who read your work, from report reviewers to investigators to court personnel to supervisors, know your reputation by simply reading your name.

It is also true that they implement strategies when they note the report author's name; they consider the author's professional reputation. Work to earn a good reputation.

You must continually re-invest yourself with the proper attitude and strive to focus on the investigative report–writing abilities and proficiencies that you need to improve. With the appropriate attitude, focus, and disciplined good habits, you can refine and reinforce quality documentation skills and abilities.

With the correct attitude, you realize and accept that you are bound to a clear ethical standard. Your obligation is to be simply an objective fact finder, fact gatherer, and fact presenter—not an editor of convenient fact or opinion.

The Ethics of Report Writing

You have an ethical duty to remain objective and neutral. You are not to take sides because you believe or identify with one side more than another. It is unethical to lean your investigation and/or report to one side or the other. You have the ethical responsibility to present the gathered information in your report in a professional, balanced, and deliberate way.

Yes, we are human and we have feelings. Often we have been raised to acknowledge, respect, and trust our feelings. Admittedly, sometimes it is hard to completely remove them from our writing, but you should at least refocus those feelings.

Refocus to dedicate yourself to produce a complete, well-written, and professionally objective piece of work. If you reveal your feelings in your writing, the result will reveal a bias, dilute the perspective of professional objectivity, and ultimately weaken the value of your efforts.

Intentionally lying in an investigative report is always ethically wrong, is likely illegal, and is professionally unacceptable. It is just as unethical to lie in degrees, or hedge to shadow the facts. It is also lying to serve a personal manipulative or vindictive purpose through written inflection; do not editorialize or colorize words or phrases to illustrate or emphasize your feelings or opinions.

The reason you are in a job that requires investigative reports is because you are likely of the character to want to do something to help the community. You likely want to stop the wrongs of a violator and make sure the breakdown of rules never happens again. Objectivity will serve this goal.

Always Remain Objective

While those personal and/or professional goals are highly honorable, you achieve those goals ultimately through a fair, objective, factual, accurate, and professional piece of work. Focus on true issues presented in your work in which others can trust and have confidence.

We don't find measurement rulers adjusting the lines and marks to fit the ruler's individual opinions or prejudices. Instead, we expect the ruler to objectively and accurately provide the dimensions for the viewer to analyze and draw an appropriate conclusion.

Always write with precision and emotional neutrality. Investigative report authors must remain objective, and not appear in any way to become the persuasive beckoner.

The investigative report writer should investigate to collect true and relevant facts, assemble those relevant facts professionally, and produce them in the anticipated professional format, allowing readers to digest truth so they can reach conclusions as they see fit.

Confidence in your presentation of factual, non-prejudicial information is necessary to allow the reader to trust the information and have a credible foundation from which to analyze and make decisions.

The value or the righteousness of the investigative systems demand that representatives, on any side of the investigative document, operate with conduct and behaviors devoid of passion or prejudice. All must maintain the attitude of professional objectivity and honesty.

In the context of investigative report writing, you must focus on providing the system with work that fits an almost scientific methodology and that includes complete, ethical, unbiased, and professional investigation and report writing.

Ultimately, when you provide the appropriate information, you must trust that the appropriate intellectual evaluation, relevant debate, and realistically appropriate, systematic conclusions will follow.

These are the essential attitude and ethics found in the successful and accomplished investigative report

writer. You must possess these qualities as a foundation in order to develop into a respected professional.

Chapter Questions and Writing Scenario

Chapter Questions

1. Please explain the purpose of an investigative report.
2. Investigative report writing can be a challenge to accomplish. Please provide three reasons it is challenging and explain why those reasons must be considered.
3. Please explain how mistakes potentially affect the author's individual reputation and options for the future.
4. Mistakes are of significant global ethical and professional concern. Please explain how mistakes exert an effect on ethical and professional levels.
5. Briefly describe the global detriments of "colorizing" the facts.

Writing Scenario 1

You are a new law enforcement officer. This is your first week on the job and you are assigned to respond to a domestic violence call at a residence on your beat. A neighbor heard the incident and doesn't know the occupants of the apartment where the incident occurred.

You arrive to find that the defendant is a fellow officer from your academy class who has not yet been hired by another agency but is currently in background investigations as a pre-employment requirement process. You understand domestic violence is a mandatory arrest situation, and the manner in which you handle the situation will have an effect on your academy mate's ability to get hired.

The victim, his wife, tells you he punched her in the mouth. The punch broke the skin on her upper lip, but doesn't appear to have caused serious damage. The wife insists that nothing be done, repeatedly stating, "I started this and I deserve the smack!"

Ethically, explain how you handle this call and what you should do.

Your assignment is to provide a brief explanation, in narrative format, of how you would handle this situation, with correct grammar, spelling, and mechanics. Your response should be typed on separate paper, with no fewer than three paragraphs, and no longer than one page.

Fuel your attitude! Fuel your success!

Image Credits

Back in the day …

There was a time, before computers or word processors, when police reports were not simply pecked out on the police vehicle's Mobile Data Terminals unit or on a laptop computer. In those days, reports were laboriously handwritten: word by word, sentence by sentence, and paragraph by paragraph. If you forgot something that needed to be added later, you couldn't simply thumb the space bar a few times to insert a paragraph in the middle of a page.

Any spell check was routinely conducted by a reference to a paperback dictionary you carried within your "war bag." Officers were required to write the entire report in ink. Because erasable ink was not available, whenever you made a mistake, you relied on a brand of paper paint to white-wash and cover the goof!

So, right next to the dictionary, the portable AM radio, and the CPR mask stored in your "war bag" was a series of precisely colored paper paint containers, taped together in a "six pack" fashion, at the ready to paint over your errors.

Sounds like a great solution, doesn't it? However, most supervisors would allow you fewer than five total paint jobs before they required you to re-do the entire report. And who wants to re-do any report for any reason?

Therefore, the field officers back in the day focused on being mistake-free report writers and/or excellent paper painters. And eventually, we became most appreciative of word processing technologies.

2

Investigation and Note-Taking

Chapter Summary

In order to produce a valuable investigative report, it is critical to establish and keep in mind the objective of the investigation. The objective can be focused upon by reviewing the specific elements of the violation being investigated. Behaviors are precisely described in detail, and then measured against the elements of the violation. Investigative note-taking is a valuable method by which to provide accurate details in the construction of the final documentation, and can provide appropriate imagery for the investigation participants.

Chapter Learning Objectives

Discuss the two basic purposes of investigative reports.

Be able to identify an investigation's objectives.

Identify and address the elements of the relevant law or policy.

Detail the violator's behaviors as they relate to the elements of the law or policy.

Be able to measure those behaviors against the elements of the law or policy investigated.

Understand how to take notes during the investigation and how notes are used to construct the final report documentation.

Explain other values of report note-taking.

Purposes and Objectives of an Investigative Report

The first stage of investigative report writing is to conduct the investigation. Although the purpose of this text is to present foundational report-writing skills and techniques, we should address some basic investigation considerations. An understanding and application of basic investigative concepts will help develop report writing. Whenever you accept the responsibility to write a report, the first question to ask is, "What is the purpose of this report?" When you identify an investigation's purpose clearly, you can begin to determine the best strategy for directing the investigation.

In this chapter, we will consider two basic purposes for a routine investigation. The first is to document relevant issues of a criminal violation, when there is a law and there are behaviors that are outside the letter and intent of the law. The second is to determine whether someone or something has behaved outside of a policy or intended function. These kinds of investigations look into whether Mary is routinely late to work, or whether a particular piece of equipment works as it was designed and built to. These administrative investigations measure behavior against policy.

Briefly, the objectives of a criminal investigation are essentially as follows:

- Identify the *corpus delecti* or specific elements of the crime being investigated.
- Detect, establish, and document the occurrence of crime.
- Capture details to assist in crime reduction strategies.
- Locate and identify suspects and evidence.
- Locate, identify, and document criminal methods.
- Recover and return stolen property.
- Prepare sound criminal cases for legal consequence.

The objectives of an administrative investigation are essentially as follows:

- Identify the *corpus delecti* or specific elements of the policy being investigated.
- Reinforce the elements of administrative policy.
- Identify and document the employee or subject behavior.
- Measure the behavior against the policy.
- After measurement, determine if the behavior is outside of policy.
- Assess the degree to which it is outside of policy.
- Make recommendations as to an appropriate resolution.

Know the Elements of the Violation

During your review of the lists above, you'll notice the first item on each list indicates that the writer must become very familiar with the specific elements of the crime or policy that is being investigated.

For example, let's say you have accepted the responsibility to provide an investigative report about an auto theft. Your first obligation is to be familiar with the actual elements of auto theft. Here is the California Vehicle Code definition of auto theft, 10851 VC:

10851. (a) Any person who drives or takes a vehicle not his or her own, without the consent of the owner thereof, and with intent either to permanently or temporarily deprive the owner thereof of his or her title to or possession of the vehicle, whether with or without intent to steal the vehicle, or any person who is a party or an accessory to or an accomplice in the driving or unauthorized taking or stealing, is guilty of a public offense and, upon conviction thereof, shall be punished by imprisonment in a county jail for not more than one year or pursuant to subdivision (h) of Section 1170 of the Penal Code or by a fine of not more than five thousand dollars ($5,000), or by both the fine and imprisonment.[1]

When we break down the basic elements, we find the following:

- Element # 1: "Any person who drives or takes a vehicle not his or her own"
- Element #2: "Without the consent of the owner thereof"
- Element #3: "With the intent to either permanently or temporarily deprive the owner thereof of his or her title to or possession of the vehicle"

For a valid auto theft to occur where 10851 VC is the law applied, the defendant's behavior and actions must, at some level, involve each of these elements. Therefore, your investigation should identify those defendant behaviors that clearly demonstrate first that the defendant drove or took a vehicle not his or her own.

Although there might be more than one way to do so, you essentially investigate to establish that, at the time of the "acquisition and possession of the vehicle," the vehicle actually belonged to someone other than the defendant—as in, it was registered to another person, and that other person owns the vehicle; therefore, the registered owner is the victim.

The next element is that the car was taken "without the consent of the owner." You would need to establish that the defendant had possession of the car and was in possession without the consent of the owner. In other words, the owner did not loan the vehicle to the defendant.

Now consider the third element. How might you investigate the defendant's "intent" to deprive the owner of the "title to or possession of the vehicle"? As you investigate to determine whether the defendant's actions were consistent with the elements of the law violation, you then document those behaviors in detail—sufficient detail that anyone who reads your report will agree that the defendant's behaviors matched the elements of the law the defendant is accused of violating.

You can see that the elements provide a "road map" for your investigation. As you gain experience, you will become more familiar with crime codes and their respective elements, and perhaps no longer need to research the elements for the road map. In the beginning, however, that research can be essential to precisely capture and investigate the crime.

It is the same for an administrative investigation. Let's say you are to provide an investigation of whether an employee has violated an administrative policy at work. For illustrative purposes, let's say it is a policy regarding violence in the workplace.

In this policy, any expression of violence, specific or implied, is not permitted or considered acceptable. And in this example, Mary, in a fit of frustration, has told a coworker, "You are so stupid; I hope you die."

When you conduct the investigation, you first need to obtain and review the specifics of the written policy. Then you need to exactly define and establish Mary's actions as indicated by her statements and other behaviors, such as voice inflections, hand gestures, and so on.

---

1 California Legislative Information, V C Section 10851: Theft and unlawful taking or driving of a vehicle (2011), https://leginfo.legislature.ca.gov/faces/codes_displaySection.xhtml?lawCode=VEH&sectionNum=10851

When you have identified and documented ALL of Mary's relevant behaviors, then you measure those against the specific wording of the policy to determine whether Mary did violate the intentions of the policy on violence in the workplace. Each step of this determination and measurement process must be documented in your report.

Although it might be essentially true and factual to write your report by saying, "Saw crook; arrested same," this is clearly insufficient. Always remember you will eventually be placed in a position to defend your report. Begin to defend it even as you write it by insuring the defendant's behaviors are clearly documented and then honestly measured against each of the elements of the law or policy.

Avoid Writing Conclusions as Your Descriptions

With the idea of defending your report as you write it in mind, here is another very important concept for you to consider and address in your investigative reports: Do not simply write down conclusory statements—conclusions that you have drawn or assumptions you have made. For example, do not just say, "Defendant Brown was drunk." Your readers may not agree with you; you must provide the specific exhibited behaviors as the proof that led you to the conclusion that Defendant Brown was drunk.

A mental checklist process is valuable in addressing real-life processes in general, and it is a *must* in your report writing. For example, I was once involved in a radio call where the officers responded to a store employee's request to assist a "drunken" customer who had passed out on a shopping cart. The officers approached the nearly unconscious customer and automatically began a drunken person protocol.

Thankfully, at an early point of the contact, one of the officers noticed no odor of an alcoholic beverage on or about the subject and realized the "drunken" customer was in fact suffering from physical and mental processing distortions created by a diabetic episode.

Even though you know the subject was "belligerent," "uncooperative," or "resistive" because you were there to witness the subject's specific behaviors, your readers were not. You must describe the multitude of relevant exhibited behaviors that led you to your conclusion in order to enable the reader to understand and agree with it.

You must always support your conclusions with the data you analyzed or used to reach them. In math class, good instructors require students to show the work that they have used to reach the correct answer. The same concept applies to written conclusions within your investigative report documentation.

Next, think about what you are investigating. Think about what is relevant to include in your report, then provide that relevant information and, if necessary, explain why that information is relevant.

Let's say you are to investigate and document a nighttime car burglary. The victim left the car parked and locked in the street in front of his house and was awakened by the sound of glass breaking. The victim ran to the front window of his house to see a burglar pulling the car's stereo through the broken car window.

Would you agree it would be important to consider and determine the source of illumination the victim used to see the burglar in the darkness? Considerations such as street light location or the presence of other light sources, such as a porch light, that the victim used to see the burglar are significant. The accuracy of the victim's observations is relevant to both the investigation and the subsequent prosecution of the defendant. Remember, you will be in a position to defend your investigation, so begin to defend it from the start by providing all relevant facts.

Consider Related Evidence

We haven't discussed evidence just yet, and the discovery and documentation of evidence is a significant issue for you to focus upon. Be assured, we will address the basic concepts in more depth later in this text. That said, as you begin your investigation, you need to also consider those physical items and statements that relate to the issues of your investigation. Some of the physical items may include hard property items such as weapons, drugs, photo documentation, fingerprints, and so on. You should also consider the interview or interrogation statements you collect in your investigation as physical evidence.

To properly handle evidence related to your investigation, you must indicate in your documentation the first moment of discovery for each item, along with what happens to it from that point onward. This process may include photo documentation, testing, measurements, collection, and final submission of the evidence to the property vault. This necessary step-by-step documentation of evidence is called the *chain of custody*.

Your investigation should discover and reveal many facts. As you collect and organize the facts that you intend to consider and perhaps eventually include in your report, the information gathering, evaluation, organization, and storage is a process in itself. This investigative process is another challenge you must consider. So let's finish this chapter with a few words about note-taking.

Note-Taking Is a Necessary Skill

Simply stated, note-taking is the most accurate and simple way to remember and organize the information used to construct your report. I've found that very few people have the exact same method for collecting and organizing notes—or even the same fashion for putting those notes on paper. However, I know that successful investigative report writers all use some form of personalized note-taking within their initial investigation process.

Notes assist your memory when you later construct the report. Notes help organize first things in your report first, and then serve to remind you of the next thing, and so on. Notes will capture easy-to-forget or easy-to-distort details, such as names, measurements, and a multitude of other detailed facts. Notes will help make sense of witness or victim locations and will separate and clarify multiple statements collected from multiple witnesses or victims.

In some investigations, it may be helpful to write your notes on separate pages so you can literally follow page by page to accurately review, and then retell, the detailed steps and information of your investigation.

Consider Using an Outline

You also may find it beneficial to use your notes to create a basic outline—a sort of bare-bones skeleton of your report. This is particularly beneficial when the report is excessively detailed or convoluted with factors that are seemingly unrelated or disconnected until the end of the documentation.

A skeleton provides the basic support for a body. Outlines made from your notes can provide the basic support for the body of your report. Once you've identified the basic "bones" of your report, you simply add in the details and facts to complete the story.

I have also seen field investigators draw a quick sketch to refer to later. They "scratch" a representative drawing, adding items or details to refer to as they write from the memories the drawing revives. Whichever method you use, I highly recommend you take notes as a standard, routine practice.

Remember, your notes are part of the investigation and therefore may be a part of the discovery process. Always be professional and remember that your notations can be studied by the jury. For this reason, I recommend you keep business notes completely separate from any personal information.

Don't Use Your Personal Cell Phone

If you decide, in today's technological world, to use your personal electronic devices to take quick pictures or capture your investigative thoughts, just know that ALL the information stored on that device can be reviewed and even supplied in open court to the jury.

DO NOT USE YOUR PERSONAL CELL PHONE TO TAKE PICTURES OF EVIDENCE! If you do, your personal photos, including Aunt Effie's eightieth birthday party or your family's visit to the local amusement park, can also be reviewed.

For specific details regarding your note-taking, storage decisions, and practices for handling your investigative notes after you have completed the report, invest the time to contact your employer or your local prosecutor for suggestions—or both. Some kinds of investigations require your notes to be included in the case file. Other kinds of investigations do not. It is imperative that you know the requirements and options.

We've just discussed how note-taking can help you to organize the report and ensure its accuracy and completeness, but that's not the end of the benefits note-taking offers.

Remember that Appearances Can Be Important

There is an undeniable customer service component in the professionalism of your work. In most investigative documentation circumstances, the victim and sometimes the defendant hold the opinion that whatever you are assigned to investigate is a significant event in their lives.

Because it is important to them, they expect the investigator to be dedicated to accuracy, completeness, and professionalism.

Consider the impression an investigator taking notes makes against the image of an investigator who attempts to commit significant details to memory, taking no notes at all. While these may be just images, which one would you prefer conducting the investigation of a significant event in your life?

The image of an officer taking notes is significant to those involved; it offers a measure of reassurance of the investigator's interest and professionalism, if not the actual value of the final product.

If you accept the community-oriented policing concept and models for efficient policing, maintaining a partnership with the community is an important long-term yet fragile process. Seek to enhance and reinforce those goals whenever and however you can. Making the investment to take notes is beneficial to you as an investigator and report writer, and it also supports the goal of strengthening the partnership with the community.

Chapter Questions and Writing Scenario

Chapter Questions

1. Please identify and explain two basic purposes for conducting an investigation.
2. Please identify and explain the elements of a violation of law and/or a policy.
3. Explain how the investigator must address these elements in the investigation.
4. Provide an example of how the investigative report writer compares the elements of the violations against the violator's behaviors to establish whether a violation has occurred.
5. Provide two examples of conclusory words, and then provide observations (data) to explain how those conclusions were reached.
6. What is the chain of custody? Provide an example, starting with the writer's observation of a piece of evidence, documentation, and collection.
7. Explain the potential problem of collecting investigative notes on the investigator's personal electronic devices.
8. What are common perceptions of the investigator's act of taking notes?

Writing Scenario 2

Watch your favorite (or any convenient) law enforcement television show or film. During the show, collect pertinent storyline details as the story unfolds. Do not pause or rewind—there is no remote control for real-life experiences, so practice collecting the information you think may be important as it unfolds. Do not collect the information electronically; record the story in some fashion of handwritten and readable notes. Then organize your notes into a typewritten report outline.

Provide your handwritten notes from watching the television show along with your more organized, typewritten outline.

Measure the subject's behaviors against the elements of law or policy.

Always provide the data you used to reach your conclusions.

Outlines are like a skeleton; they can provide the bare-bones support to structure the report.

Image Credits

Photo 2.1: Copyright © Depositphotos/
    londondeposit.
Photo 2.2: Copyright © Depositphotos/
    SergeyNivens.
Photo 2.3: Copyright © Depositphotos/
    AndreyPopov.

You Never Know Who Is Looking ...

Among the things I have suggested for you to consider as you plan your investigation and write a precise report are the varying agendas of your anticipated readers. If you can formulate a clear idea of the reader's interests and expectations, you can construct a more targeted report.

But to understand the extent of your readership might be a daunting task! Just take a quick look at the chart illustrating the congressional oversight of the Department of Homeland Security. Imagine if you were to be assigned to undertake an internal investigation and to produce a report of an item of interest to both the US House of Representatives and the US Senate.

In this case, I can only recommend you do your best and ask for a substantial raise in rank, benefits, and salary!

3

Utilizing Standard Report Formats

Chapter Summary

It is common for industries to use standard report formats. When report formats are standardized, writers and readers alike become familiar with the document layout and can quickly navigate through the format to either provide or access the information within the document. Standard forms allow writers and readers to confidently complete and review reports efficiently and accurately.

Chapter Learning Objectives

Discuss the foundational purpose of standardized report writing formats.

Explain the importance of a writer recognizing, understanding, and appreciating how to use the report format for the writer's circumstance.

Establish and define the various divisions of the standard report format to be used in this text.

Define the purposes of the various divisions found within the standardized format to be used in this text.

Understand why the writer must construct his report to fit the report format.

Order Is Useful

People are most comfortable when they know where things are routinely placed in their surroundings. Have you ever lost something, and although you have looked for it in the spot where the item is "always" stored and not found it, you later return to search that same area one more time?

Although one might wonder about the logic or wisdom behind rechecking a place already checked, it is human nature to expect to find something where it is "supposed to be." Understanding the order of things can also serve to develop confidence in handling a new set of circumstances or in accomplishing an unfamiliar task.

Knowledgeable people, such as those at the Braille Institute, appreciate the concept of order as they train people to function independently with little or no sight. Trainees that have diminished sight are taught to

become familiar with their new sight-challenged circumstances by organizing routine surroundings or activities into a known order. One such routine function is feeding one's self via the use of standardized food locations on the plate; using them helps people remain independent.

The student is taught to divide the plate as if it were a face of a clock, and then arrange food in a specific configuration, such as meat at six o'clock, vegetables at nine o'clock, and so on.

When we accept the concept of placing an important thing where someone knows to find it or where it belongs, we have acknowledged the value of order, or format. Report writing has such order, which we will refer to as *standardized report writing format*.

Standardized Report Format Purpose

Most, if not all, industries have a standardized format for their reporting responsibilities. Additionally, each industry likely has its own codes, jargon, forms, and other day-to-day operational particularities. Many times, these operational functions are similar from industry to industry; sometimes they are not.

Investigative report writing is no different. The standardized formats change from institution to institution, from agency to agency, and region to region. Essentially, a report writing format is a sort of map to familiarize writers and readers so that all can quickly access a specific reporting function and find the information at an expected location in a report.

Format includes divisions, which are the sections where the writer should include certain information and a reader can locate specific information. Let's take a look at one of the standardized report formats.

The following section headers are from the San Diego County ARJIS 9 Report Form. A brief explanation of each section's purpose follows its header.

SYNOPSIS:

Concise explanation of incident in past tense.

ORIGIN:

Source of incident—radio call, observation, investigation assigned.

INVESTIGATION:

Basic and foundation elements of the general investigation.

BACKGROUND:

Relevant information leading to crime, arrest, or incident, such as prior arrests or contacts. Current investigation information listed here in chronological order.

STATEMENTS:

Statements of Suspects, Witnesses, and so on. Investigation continued.

EVIDENCE:

Chain of Evidence documentation information, or "None."

INJURIES:

Injuries that are documented in the incident report, or "None."

PROPERTY DAMAGE:

Property damage that is documented in the incident report, or "None."

FOLLOW UP:

Details of "follow-up" report that need to be accomplished, or "None."

RELATED REPORTS:

Reference of related reports, or "None."

WITNESS LIST:

A list of Witnesses that are/were involved in the investigation.

Reviewing this format, you can see how efficiently and quickly a knowledgeable reader can find specific information regarding witnesses, evidence, injuries, property damage, or any other part of the investigation by being familiar with the format.

Additionally, the standardized format offers the new report writer a visible reminder of the components of an investigation that the writer may wish to investigate, address, and/or include in the report.

This Is the Format We're Going to Use!

The standard format I require students to use for classwork has fewer sections than the one previously shown. The one we will use requires basically the same information included in the previous format, but ours seeks to assist the new writer in developing a natural narrative flow instead of halting the narrative's rhythm (as mandated by the many section headers of the ARJIS 9 Report Form).

The format I require is called the "1, 2, 3" format, or "Synopsis, Evidence, Narrative." In my view, this format is the most appropriate for our instructional purposes because it is used by many law enforcement departments.

Additionally, it is a format that is often mildly amended for use in corporate applications. By changing the first section heading from "Synopsis" or "Summary" to "Executive Summary," the format transforms into a standardized business reporting document.

The typical format used in my instructional venues to complete assignments is as follows:

Table One

SYNOPSIS:

Sometimes labeled "Summary." Concise explanation of incident in past tense.

EVIDENCE:

Chain of Evidence description, documentation, and/or other evidentiary information, or "None."

Although compliance with the requirements of the Evidence section can typically be satisfied using the example within Table One, displayed above, the writer can also simply write the evidence line by line in paragraph form. (There will be more discussion about this topic later in this chapter.)

This section enables the writer to provide the reader with a quick overview of the number of evidence items, descriptions, locations discovered, by whom they were discovered, the method by which the item was recorded or collected, where the item is archived, and finally the tag number of the item in the vault.

When the Evidence section is properly completed, the information provides complete, summarized, "at a glance" chain of custody evidence description. With this basic chain of custody reporting function accomplished, the written narrative can focus on explaining the exceptions or the items that require additional consideration.

NARRATIVE:

This section *always* begins with the Origin as the first paragraph. The Narrative section will include all the other basic investigative functions, such as background, issue elements, statements, injuries, and so on, indicated in the ARJIS 9 Report Form.

Let's break down the "1, 2, 3" or "Synopsis, Evidence, Narrative" format so you can familiarize yourself with this format's functions and what is expected from the report writer who uses it.

Synopsis

The first heading in the "1, 2, 3" format is Synopsis (or Summary). This section includes only the briefest of information to advise the reader on what the original circumstances were and what to expect in the report document.

The Synopsis often times is critical to the reader. For example, in law enforcement, an investigator may be assigned literally dozens of reports each month on which he must accomplish follow-up investigations. That task can involve a tremendous amount of information for the investigator to organize, memorize, and manage. It can be a challenge just to quickly access one report needed out of the stack assigned.

Therefore, it is beneficial to the follow-up investigator to have a way to quickly scan a report section, such as the Synopsis, to become familiar with the report or to identify the particular issues that are detailed later in the report.

This is also why the Executive Summary is useful in corporate circumstances. It provides the executive with the opportunity to efficiently review the basic issues of the investigation without a commitment to reading the entire document.

The Synopsis or Summary provides the reader with a relevant yet quick thumbnail account of what the report is about, without obliging them to read the entire narrative. Most Synopsis texts include only *basic*, *relevant* facts and/or statements.

Remember, the Synopsis is a concise explanation of the incident that is written in the past tense. Here is an example of a Synopsis.

SYNOPSIS:

Known Defendant displayed physical objective symptoms consistent with being under the influence of a controlled substance. Defendant was arrested. Search incident to arrest revealed a personal use amount of methamphetamine concealed in his pants pocket. Defendant was charged with personal possession and being under the influence of a controlled substance.

You'll notice that the Synopsis example above does not include details such as date, time, location, names, or specific descriptions such as the defendant's objective symptoms. Those important and necessary facts will be detailed with other critical information in the report's Narrative section.

The Synopsis provides only the relevant and basic information so the reader has an overview and can anticipate the detailed account of investigative issues provided later in the Narrative section.

Evidence

The second section heading in the "1, 2, 3" format is labeled "Evidence." The purpose of the Evidence section is to summarize and quickly provide the chain of custody information for evidentiary items involved in your investigation. As writers, we present it this way and at this point in the report so that the reader can see an overview of the evidence without reading the complete narrative to determine all the contextual considerations.

Specifically, the term chain of custody essentially requires a writer to document each step of an evidence item's journey, from initial discovery through any processing, such as photographing, to collection and, finally, to secured storage. This information is critical to the determination of issues such as the evidence's relevancy and possible contamination.

A writer can present the chain of custody information in a narrative form; however, that process is typically labor intensive. It requires an inordinate amount of writing; the same basic information can be presented in a summarized chart form.

All evidence-reporting methods include a chain of custody statement to explain the process. For example: "I located, collected, documented, and later logged all evidence into SWCPA [Storage vault location] under [Reference or] Property Tag Number C-12341."

Take a look at the following example.

EVIDENCE:

I located, collected, documented, marked, and later logged all evidence into SWCPA under Property Tag Number C-45678.

In this section, the writer provides the reader with a quick reference as to the number of evidence items, their descriptions, where they were found, who discovered them, how they were recorded or collected, where they are archived, and, finally, the numbers that are needed to retrieve them.

Let's review a completed evidence chart from a crime report of a store robbery.

At a glance, the reader can see the documentation of the chain of custody in this example. While this will tend to reduce the writer's work because it summarizes the evidence, the items and their particular relevance to the investigation may still need to be addressed later in the narrative.

If the report writer decides to not use a table, the writer still has an obligation to provide written text that provides all the information that the table headings require: the item description, location found, who found, how marked, where archived, and number for retrieval. The obligation can be often satisfied by the following written statement:

Officer Boyd located, documented, collected, and marked all evidentiary items w/ "AB 10/08/15." All items were later logged into evidence into SWCPA under Property Tag Number C-2341 by Officer A. Boyd.

Item 1: 3-Latent fingerprint cards w/ collected latent print. Latent prints were removed from the interior of the right entrance door by Officer A. Boyd.

Item 2: 1-compact disc containing photos of the interior of the store, the cashier's position, and evidence collected. The photos were taken by Officer A. Boyd.

Item 3: 1-A handwritten demand note given to the cashier by the suspect. The demand note was collected from the victim cashier by Officer A. Boyd.

Often, the writer may still wish or need to provide additional written explanations of exactly where and/or why the fingerprints were collected from the interior of the right door. For example, during the investigation, it was determined that the defendant touched the door at the location the prints were later collected.

The summarized evidence section or table often satisfies most chain of custody concerns quickly and efficiently, and it saves the writer a laborious written task.

Narrative

The third and final section heading in the "1, 2, 3" format is labeled "Narrative." The purpose of the Narrative section is to provide a complete, detailed story of the investigation. This is the opportunity to explain all that the writer feels is necessary and relevant to the investigation.

The story, told in *first person past tense* in chronological order, brings the reader from first things first to last things last. The writer offers to the reader every relevant observation, item of evidence, and statement that has been collected. The writer does this accurately, fact by fact, objectively, and without prejudice or bias. The writer allows the reader to consider, analyze, and balance all the information presented so that the reader can reach appropriate conclusions or opinions. (In some cases, such as in a policy or equipment review, the writer may *additionally* be charged with the responsibility of summarizing the components of the investigation

in order to provide a professionally considered conclusion or other final determination. However, even in reports where a writer is required to present a conclusion or judgment, the writer must still provide all the relevant, specific information used to form that conclusion.)

The first paragraph in the Narrative section is *always* the Origin. This is a paragraph that explains to the reader how or why you came to be the investigator. The Origin's intent is to introduce your purpose and motivation for conducting the investigation; it also demonstrates your objectivity.

The Origin is critical to illustrating why and how you participated—as if to say, "This is an investigation I was assigned or an investigation I took the initiative to begin." The Origin sets the objectivity expectation early, and it can develop an immediate trust between the writer and the reader.

Essentially, there are four basic statements of origin, and they are as follows:

- On 09/11/15 at approximately 2134 hours I was driving eastbound in the 1400 Block of Fourth Avenue when I observed a tan Ford sedan ...
- On 09/11/15 at approximately 2134 hours I received a radio broadcast to respond to the 1400 Block of Fourth Avenue to investigate a citizen's report of possible "shots fired" ...
- On 09/11/15 at approximately 0900 hours, I was assigned to conduct the formal Administrative Investigation of an incident involving Officer Jones, which occurred on 08/11/15 ...
- On 09/11/15 at approximately 0900 hours, I was assigned the follow-up investigation of a commercial burglary report, which occurred on 08/11/15 ...

Once you've identified the reason you began the investigation, then you can offer the step-by-step chronological story that details your investigation. I know—easier said than done!

To best understand the contents of a typical written report and determine what to include, consider the many functions of writing as a means of communicating and maintaining records:

1. Provide a written record and a readily accessible memory bank of police, facility and/or business information.
2. Refresh a writer's memory for testimony; support further investigation and/or clarify administration concerns.
3. Provide a means of controlling or facilitating institutional communication throughout the organization, or other institutions, and/or their associated agencies.
4. Provide a database of information for solving or reducing crime, or policy violations.
5. Furnish a base of accurate statistical information for issues such as resource management, allocation and policy.
6. Aid in identifying criminal or institutional behavioral concerns; to stimulate the development of prevention or intervention plans.
7. Aid in assisting the effectiveness of management strategies, and overall agency operations.
8. Assist in identifying unusual or periodic intra-agency inefficiencies or problems.
9. Assist to document operational needs, justify budgets, requests, etc.
10. Produce statistical information to supplement relevant databases.
11. Provide a vital tool for an agency to meet its goals and objectives.
12. Provide a source of accurate, detailed and succinct information to prosecute a criminal, or manage a policy or policy violation.[1]

Chapter Questions and Writing Scenario

Chapter Questions

1. Please identify and explain the three major sections of the standardized report format that will be used in this text.
2. Explain the chain of custody and which information about evidence is required in a report.
3. Please provide the wording of the first paragraph of the Evidence section of the standardized report format and explain why it is important.
4. When should the author include an explanation of evidence, evidence collection, or evidence relevancy in the report Narrative?
5. What is the first paragraph of the Narrative section? Explain why it is important to include that paragraph.
6. What information should the author include in the report Narrative?

---

1 Berg, B., G. Gibbs, and M. Miller, *Report Writing for Police and Correctional Officers* (McGraw-Hill, 2013), highered.mheducation.com/sites/dl/free/0078111463/945394/Ch01.pdf. Page 5.

Writing Scenario 3

Workplace Accident Investigation

Mr. Robert Gonzales is employed by Star Enterprises, works the swing shift, and is assigned to refuse collection at a local office building. Last Tuesday, he was working alone while wearing his commercial assigned uniform with unapproved footwear.

During his shift, Gonzales was pushing the assigned custodial cart in the hallway on the third floor. While pushing the cart, he apparently did not apply sufficient attention to the path in front of him, and he walked into a large pool of water that had collected on the tile floor. He slipped and fell onto his back, injuring his spine and the back of his skull.

After the fall, Mr. Gonzalez lay on the floor for an estimated twenty minutes until the Shift Supervisor, Mr. John Smith, discovered Gonzales and summoned emergency medical resources. Because of the severity of his head injury, Mr. Gonzales is currently in a drug-induced coma at Sharp Hospital.

As the workplace investigator, you must consider other relevant information that might be important to investigate and document. For example, consider all relevant civil liability aspects as in percentage of blame considerations—for example, a description of the source of the water on the floor or the type of shoes Mr. Gonzales was wearing. There are no camera recordings or eyewitnesses to the accident.

In your report, please briefly identify and add at least two *other* factors that might be relevant to address in your investigative report, and why they are relevant to the investigation. Consider issues such as poor hallway lighting or other facility deferred-maintenance issues.

Required: You are to utilize the standard Synopsis, Evidence, Narrative format discussed earlier. Be sure to provide the "who, what, where, when, why, and how" of documentation, collection, and safekeeping.

Optional: You may create other names and businesses if the direction of your narrative requires. If you wish, you may also use pictures, diagrams,

When One Strays from the Standardized ...

One of the themes of this chapter has been to highlight the benefits of becoming familiar with and using the standard report format. Similar benefits accrue when an author follows other standardized investigation and reporting procedures and formats.

At first, you may question why many aspects of investigation and report writing are based on standardized processes. Some of today's standardized procedures and report formats are based on legal and, occasionally, medical precedents. One criminal investigative arena that has been tried and tested many times is in the area of driving under the influence (DUI).

While nearly all DUI operational forms are printed to the specifications that match standardizations tested and challenged many times, the actual standardized "impairment evaluation" has been also tested. And there may be no other criminal issue more challenged than the "routine" DUI!

Consider this, from the website DUI Authority:

What is the difference between standardized Field Sobriety Tests and non-standardized Field Sobriety Tests? Simply put, non-standardized tests have not been validated by any organization, including NHTSA [National Highway Traffic Safety Administration]. For standardized tests, NHTSA has employed several studies to show that someone who shows several clues in performing those tests are most likely under the influence and too impaired to drive. No such studies have been done on non-standardized tests so or any other illustrations you feel would help paint your evidence or situational picture.

Additional Thoughts and Reminders

What other factors should you consider relevant to investigate and address in your report? One might be the water's source:

- How did the water get on the floor?
- Who is responsible for the water on the floor?
- Should you consider and document the leak's source?
- How would you investigate the leak's source?
- Would you document or collect the water leak's source?

Another factor might be Mr. Gonzales' responsibility:

- Conduct an initial assessment of his awareness: Was he impaired? Somehow distracted?
- He was wearing incorrect shoes, right? Did he know the shoes were incorrect? If so, how did he know? If not, did anyone else know before the incident?
- Should you photograph the shoes? Should you collect them for further analysis or review?
- When he is able, should you interview Mr. Gonzales?

Your goal is to *completely* investigate and document the event and its background in order to answer all questions regarding this accident.

the accuracy of testing sobriety is anyone's guess.[1]

Even standardized tests can be compromised if they are not administered in a consistent way. For instance, officers must provide verbal explanations or physical demonstrations of the tests in a standard order.

Defense attorneys argue that non-standardized tests, administration, and documentation are not reliable and therefore should not be used. Those arguments are convincing when there are no studies to refute them.

Therefore, there are often numerous reasons to stay consistent with a standardized investigative and reporting format.

1   E. Beall, "Field sobriety tests: The non-standardized tests," *DUI Authority* (2014, February 27), http://www.duiauthority.com/non-standardized-test/.

Chain of Custody (aka Chain of Evidence)

Chain of custody refers to the chronological documentation or *paper trail*, showing the seizure, custody, control, transfer, analysis, and disposition of evidence, physical or electronic.

Because evidence can be used in court to convict persons of crimes, it must be handled in a scrupulously careful manner to avoid later allegations of tampering or misconduct.

Table 3.1

Item #	Item Description	Location Found	Found By	How Marked	Disposition	Property Tag #
1						
2						
3						

Table 3.2

Item #	Item Description	Location Found	Found By	How Marked	Disposition	Property Tag #
1	3-Latent fingerprint cards w/ collected prints	Interior of right entrance door.	Boyd, A. #05806	Written "AB" 10/08/14	Impounded at SWCPA	C-2341
2	Compact disc (CD) containing 12 digital pictures	Photos of interior of store, cashier's position, evidence collected.	Boyd, A. #05806	Labeled "AB" 10/08/14	Impounded at SWCPA	C-2341
3	Handwritten "Demand Note"	Cashier's counter position.	Boyd, A. #05806	Envelope w/ written "AB" 10/08/14	Impounded at SWCPA	C-2341

Image Credits

Photo 3.1: Copyright © Depositphotos/tashatuvango.
Photo 3.2: Copyright © Depositphotos/elenathewise.
Photo 3.3: Copyright © Depositphotos/librakv.

4

Becoming Familiar with the "Always" Rules

Chapter Summary

To satisfy the requirements needed to produce a valuable professional report, many foundational mandates need to be considered and addressed. These mandates will be referred to as always" rules and applied in the construction of each investigative report document.

Chapter Learning Objectives

Identify the benefit of identifying and accepting foundational always rules in life.

Discuss the purposes of the foundational always rules of report writing.

Explain the importance of writing with the right attitude.

Understand the importance of addressing the elements of the law or policy.

Be able to detail the violator's behaviors as they relate to the elements of the law or policy, and then compare those behaviors to the law or policy.

Understand and apply the always rules when writing and revising a report, including how to write with particularity and in a clear, concise, and complete manner.

Understand and apply the use of reference materials when writing reports.

The Always Rules of Life

As we successfully operate on planet Earth, we become familiar with and develop respect for some foundational conditions: always rules. When we recognize, understand, and appropriately apply these natural laws, they provide a foundation for healthy and successful living.

We have to look no further than the scars on our knees and elbows to remind us of our brief and often painful momentary failures to appreciate one of Earth's always rules: gravity. Our correct understanding and application of the principles of gravity means we will avoid most unpleasant impacts and abrasions and the unsightly scars that result.

The Always Rules of Report Writing

So it is with our understanding and application of always rules in report writing. When we correctly apply the foundational rules, our reports do not suffer the routine "abrasions" of mistakes or omissions. Therefore, it is imperative to respect and understand the always rules and consistently apply them in the construction of the investigative report.

To begin with, a basic foundational statement might include the following thoughts:

> An investigative report must be written clearly, completely, and concisely. It must contain a description of the necessary elements of the crime or violation, provide descriptions of behaviors of the relevant participants, and present information in a way that permits a prosecutor, evaluator, or other decision maker to determine whether there is reasonable belief the violation did occur and the accused did in fact commit the violation.

Broad statements are often helpful in a generalized conversation, but this one is likely not specific enough to be of real value to the developing writer. How does a new report writer translate this broad statement into the particular techniques, tools, and tips that can help the writer create a successful report? Let's break down the lofty goal into specific things the writer can do and look closely at specific always rules.

Following the always rules shows readers the writer's attitude and ability to convey the thoroughness and accuracy of the investigation. A few of these rules are already familiar to you from earlier chapters. Because of their significance, they will be routinely reinforced throughout this book.

Briefly, here are some writer's *behaviors* and *practices* that reveal the best investigational *attitudes* and *efforts*:

- Report only the relevant facts, *accurately*! Seek to discover and present *all* relevant information, free from errors and inaccuracies.
- Report only in chronological order.
- Eliminate reputation-busting mistakes, such as misspelled words, inconsistent verb tenses, or too many repetitions of the same connective word, such as "then." Your writings represent you.
- Don't distract the reader with confusing sentence structure or unorganized paragraphs. Make your report straightforward and easy to read!
- Invest in the value of reporting. Understand what it does—and what it *can* do when it is done well.

- Don't offer conclusions without supporting observations or evidence. Never assume the reader will agree with any conclusion you offer unless you provide the observations that led you to the conclusion.
- KNOW that you will be challenged on any opinion. Therefore, be sure that any conclusion you offer is based on valid logic; critical thinking; and solid observations, data, or evidence.
- Reread and edit your own writing. Proofread, proofread, and proofread again. Consider it a gift to your reputation!
- Take every opportunity to improve your writing skills: Read other people's well-written works to absorb their structure, organization, and rhythm. Ask others to read your work in order to analyze how your own written communication can be made clearer and easier to read. And when you have to read someone else's repetitive, unclear, or gap-filled narratives—or even just one confusing, twisted-up sentence—try to figure out what's wrong with it and how the writer could make it simpler, clearer, and more accurate.

Initially, this all may seem a bit overwhelming to you as a new writer. Take solace in the undeniable fact you are not the first person to walk this path. Many have walked it before you, felt overwhelmed, gradually improved, and become successful. Remember: Proper attitude breeds confidence, and a developing writer needs confidence to succeed and grow.

When you are assigned a challenging report, be confident that you will succeed when you apply the always rules. These rules provide the correct foundation and the initial direction an investigative report writer can successfully rely on, even when confronted with new or complex assignments.

Identify the Report's Purpose

ALWAYS begin by reminding yourself of the report's intended purpose. Be it a policy investigation, criminal investigation, or equipment malfunction, identifying the purpose of the investigation will help you define an investigative and report strategy.

Want more thoughts regarding that point? Consider an example: You are to investigate and document whether a particular piece of equipment operated properly.

First, establish the proper operational expectations. Then determine and document the actual operational events. When you have sufficiently established both the equipment operational expectations and actual equipment performance, you are then ready to write your comparisons (and, if it is part of your assignment, your concluding determination).

Know the Elements of the Violation

In criminal or policy violation investigations, ALWAYS refer to the specific policy or law's elements to focus your investigational direction. If you're unclear about what the elements are, it is worth your time to look up the policy or law and break it down into its component parts.

With the elements of the violation in mind, you can be clear about the relevant issues. You have the insight to investigate and document those behaviors that are either within or outside the parameters of the policies or laws.

Specifically describe those behaviors that are outside of the issue's elements. Don't assume anyone will agree with any unsupported "conclusions" you offer. You should describe the behaviors with such

particularity that anyone who reads your report will clearly understand them. Then they can measure the described behaviors against the known elements of the policy or law, and any violation becomes obvious.

Never assume you will gain agreement just because you have declared a conclusion. The readers need to see your detailed descriptions to measure the behaviors you have observed, statements you have gathered, and evidence you have collected against the rule's standard to reach their own conclusions.

When a report makes a conclusory declaration such as, "The defendant was under the influence," without offering a detailed description of the defendant's exhibited behaviors or physical symptoms, readers have no way to analyze the circumstances. Many readers will not trust such a statement; they may lose trust in the rest of the report, as well.

But when you provide a description of objective symptoms exhibited by the defendant, such as "watery eyes, rapid and disconnected speech, dilated pupils, rapid heart rate, unsteady gait," and so on, you then enable the reader to see what you observed, compare those behaviors to the standards, and reach appropriate conclusions.

Answer the Who, What, When, Where, How, and Why

ALWAYS answer the six basic questions of who, what, when, where, how, and why. When you finish each initial draft narrative, reread it to confirm whether these six component questions have been answered. If not, it is likely you have omitted some relevant information. If your rereading reveals you have not answered the six questions, revise your work to do so.

It is not realistic to assume every report will immediately produce a quick resolution. You may not resolve the crime, or you may not achieve a final determination at the conclusion of your report.

In that sort of circumstance, ALWAYS consider the other purposes for your investigative reports. Investigative report writing is seldom for entertainment, but it is to record an objective, considered, professional presentation of facts.

Maintain the enthusiasm you need to offer your maximum effort even when there is no immediate satisfaction of resolution. Other reasons for investigative report documentation outside of speedy resolution are to

- record facts in a permanent record;
- coordinate follow-up investigation leads;
- determine efficiency in order to ensure quality work;
- provide statistical data for follow-up analysis; and
- assist in the apprehension, prosecution, or defense of offenders.

As you take responsibility for your work, become adept at note-taking. Maybe you have an incredibly detailed memory, but at this juncture, ALWAYS take notes. (See Chapter 2 for more on taking notes.)

Consider Your Words

ALWAYS avoid redundant terms, such as "verbal argument," "physically hit," "same identical," "repeat again," "unexpected surprise," "unintended mistake," "usual custom," and "still remains." Reread and revise to clear out the unneeded words.

ALWAYS seek to minimize repetition of connective terms, especially the words that begin the next event or report component. For example, as you write a sequence of events, it is not acceptable to begin every line with "then we," "then he," "next he said," or "next she said." Reread and delete or vary these repeated words.

ALWAYS reread and slice away at these redundant words, gradually eliminating them. When they remain in your finished reports, they take up readers' time and become a distraction; having too many of them will refocus readers' thoughts on your wordy style, which is less important than the real substance of your report.

ALWAYS be reluctant to use common industry codes, abbreviations, or acronyms, and if you do ALWAYS explain the meaning. For example, a patrol officer might install the following sentence in a report: "My MDT (Mobile Data Terminal) advised me that the Defendant had active felony warrants for his arrest." By including the explanation of what the acronym MDT means, the writer makes readers aware that it is likely the patrol car's computer.

There often is no reason to include police codes in the report narrative; when done, it tends to be disruptive for the readers who are unfamiliar with the jargon.

Follow Standard Formats

ALWAYS follow the prescribed industry format; doing so will remind you of the necessary order for presenting information. For example, the format will direct you where to insert information such as the evidence. It can also provide a map for the reader to find the specific information they seek.

ALWAYS write in chronological order. Chronological order means you tell the first things that occurred first, second things second, and keep the events in the order in which they actually unfolded to ensure the reader isn't confused.

ALWAYS write as you actually speak and not in a fashion that indicates you've seen every crime drama episode ever shown on television. You should already have a conversational style that reveals a proper education and appropriate professionalism. Maintain that style and level of communication in your writing.

Avoid officious tones, pompous words, and complicated sentence structures. Using them tends to convey a disconnected and unrealistic perspective. It can also reduce readers' trust in your reports (as readers wonder what the overblown language is trying to hide or make up for).

A knowledgeable friend once explained that, as writers, we should always write with words our mothers understand. If your mom isn't familiar with the words you use, then it's best to avoid them or explain them in your narrative.

Break Up Run-On Sentences and Big Paragraphs

ALWAYS break apart run-on sentences and big paragraphs. They take time and effort to untangle and can be a real distraction in your reports. As a general rule, single sentences that contain fifteen or more words are too long and need refinement. Paragraphs that are six or more sentences generally need to be divided.

ALWAYS write in a first person, active voice. Avoid abstract words and use concrete terms. We'll talk more about this in Chapter 5.

Design Your Report for Success

Finally, ALWAYS focus on making your report the "Three Cs"—clear, complete, and concise. Thoughtfully select your words and organize your paragraphs to precisely accomplish your purpose. Design the overall construction of your report. This is called documentation precision!

Focus on "building" your report to be:

- Clear (free from jargon, passive voice, and unnecessarily complicated or long sentences)
- Complete (with all relevant facts to answer all relevant questions)
- Concise (avoiding redundancies and big paragraphs to minimize reader overload)

Construct the report in a professional, efficient fashion that doesn't require the reader to suffer the pain of distracting grammatical errors, invest in filling in the blanks of missing details, or decipher your code to capture your true meaning.

Use Reference Materials

ALWAYS have reference materials at your disposal. If possible, have copies of similar reports available to refer to during your investigative report processes. These collected examples of successful previous reports can assist you throughout the entire process—from investigative considerations to report organization to final report construction.

Reference materials can also include cheat sheets, such as bulleted reminders and checklists. Maybe you'll find the following checklist helpful.

The "Three Cs" Checklist

Always Be Clear

- Provide objective details to support situational conclusions, such as descriptions of the behaviors that led you to believe a person was "suspicious," "drunk," or "resistive."
- Avoid redundancies, such as "verbal argument," "physically hit," and so on.
- Make your report easy to read! Don't tire the reader with routine errors or jargon.
- Report only the relevant facts, *accurately*!
- Report only in chronological order.
- Write in a first person, active voice.
- Reread, revise, and proofread often.

Always Be Complete

- Follow the prescribed report format.
- Know the elements of the violation and ensure that you address each element by providing sufficient detail to the reader about the offender's behavior as it relates to each element.
- Answer the who, what, when, where, why, and how questions.
- Provide all relevant facts, details, descriptions, and information; consider both (or multiple) sides of the issues.
- Don't offer conclusions without a complete description of the facts that led to your conclusions; never assume the reader will agree with any conclusion you offer unless you provide the details that led you to it.
- KNOW that you will be challenged on any opinion. Therefore, be sure that your conclusions are based on professional, valid, critical thought and observations.
- Reread, revise, and proofread often.

Always Be Concise

- Address each element of the law or policy by providing focused yet sufficient detail to illustrate the offender's behavior as it relates to each element.
- Eliminate unnecessary words. Don't duplicate information—but if you do, be accurate!
- Reread your work. Delete or change words that you repeat often. Make sentences shorter and simpler. Break up paragraphs that are long.
- Reread, revise, and proofread often.

Chapter Questions and Writing Scenario

Chapter Questions

1. Why should a writer identify the report's purpose at the start of the writing process?
2. Why is it important for the writer to be familiar with the elements of the violations they have been charged to investigate and report?
3. Please provide three methods offered in the text that a writer can use to consider the use of words within a report.
4. What does it mean for the author to write in chronological order?
5. Please explain the Three Cs of writing.
6. According to the guidelines, please explain how many sentences should be in a standard paragraph.
7. What is the value of frequently proofreading one's work?

Writing Scenario 4

In Writing Scenario 2, you were assigned to watch your favorite (or any convenient) law enforcement television show or film to collect pertinent storyline details in handwritten notes. You were also instructed to organize your notes to produce a typed report outline.

Writing Scenario 4 now requires you to use the handwritten notes and typed outline to write a complete report that conforms to the Synopsis, Evidence, Narrative format explained in Chapter 3.

You are encouraged to apply the always rules. Be sure to proofread to correct all mistakes. When you submit this assignment, include your handwritten notes, your typed outline, and the completed (and also typed) Synopsis, Evidence, Narrative report.

Design your report to be clear, complete, and concise.

Image Credits

Photo 4.1: Copyright © Depositphotos/iqconcept.
photo 4.2: Copyright © Depositphotos/firea.
Photo 4.3: Copyright © Depositphotos/jamesgroup.

It's About the Total Package ...

I know this chapter is about writing to meet a bunch of rules! The thing is, once you practice them enough to routinely and correctly apply them as you write, revise, and proofread, you will never have to look them up or learn them again.

Your professional reputation will be positive, and a major component of your career responsibilities will be easier to read, more effective, and a POSITIVE credit to your reputation.

Let's take as an example the investigator who completes a fantastic, time-consuming investigation to proficiently dig out the real concerns and data that can answer the questions that prompted the investigation in the first place. I mean—this investigator completes a quality investigation!

Then the same investigator puts the story on paper, ignoring some, if not all, of the always rules of quality report writing. The communication is so poorly written that the readers are confused as to the investigator's actual meaning. It is difficult to tell what the investigator did and found.

The readers, including supervisors and those who are forced to live with the ramifications of the poorly written document, have no idea how much hard work went into the investigation and how thorough it was simply because the report does not convey that.

There are major gaps in the investigator's professional report writing skills.

Learn and apply the always rules to exhibit your great investigation and communicate *exactly* what you intend to communicate!

5

Writing with Precision

Chapter Summary

An investigative report author needs to write with *precision*, which includes both clarity and particularity. The precision goal is met through familiarity with and application of a few foundational writing practices. An author who routinely focuses on precision will produce a valued investigative report.

Chapter Learning Objectives

Identify the benefits and necessity of producing investigative reports with precision.

Explain what it means to write with particularity.

Be able to write in the first person, active voice, and understand why and how that contributes to precision.

Discuss how to write in the subject-verb-object sequence.

Explain the difference between an extrinsic and intrinsic writing focus.

Detail the difference between using concrete and abstract words.

Apply the techniques for improving precision, including using extrinsic, concrete, and piece-by-piece descriptions; using the past tense consistently; and constructing sentences in subject-verb-object order.

Why Improve Our Precision?

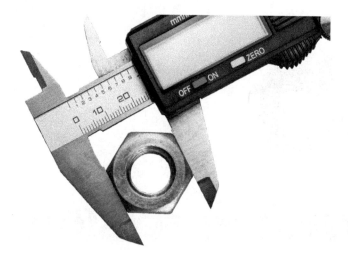

I anticipate that the reason you invest the fleeting moments of your life to study investigative report writing is that you have a desire to make life better for others. You want to be a positive influence on others and perhaps uphold and support the rules and values of your community.

You wish to hold the line against those that violate the rules, and to encourage a safe and enjoyable life for all. You are to be congratulated for not only holding this focus but also for now actively investing yourself to achieve these goals!

I also know the experiences and understanding you gain from learning good investigative report-writing techniques will benefit you in the future, even outside of formal investigation. As a parent, voter, juror, cop, or business professional, the principles you are learning will support your awareness; your critical thinking, analysis, and evaluation skills; and your actions.

Write with Precision to Hit the Goal

If we wish to accurately hit our targets to meet our goals, then we must be precise in our aim. In investigative report writing, we hit our target when we write with precision. While passive constructions and generalizations can color small talk or entertainment communication, they hold no place in investigative report writing.

Investigative report writing is not designed to be entertaining. By necessity, investigative report writing is precise, exacting, and written with design and particularity. It is not acceptable to write in the style of "it was a dark and stormy night."

Professionals who practice law understand they are held to a level of precision in communication that the courts have described as "with particularity." Ideally, this term means that nothing is left available to interpretation. In investigative report writing, this means that descriptions, facts, and all other components of an investigative report are specific, clear, and precise.

Precision investigative report writing is the most effective tool to achieve the altruistic goals of professionally protecting the community, making life safer and more efficient. You must precisely aim to hit the target, or you will likely miss. An outcome outside of your target is most often inefficient for your purpose and is sometimes completely unacceptable.

Use the First Person and an Active Voice

In Chapter 4, we briefly discussed how the investigative report writer should always write in the first person, active voice. Let's address this concept in more detail.

First person, active voice sentences are necessary to accurately and efficiently define who did what to whom. Active voice takes the form of an action-expressing verb that tells *the subject who performed the action*. The first person, active method of writing is preferred.

Here are some examples of first person, active voice:

- "I found the knife on the hallway table."
- "I measured the tire skid marks on the roadway."
- "Mr. Brown unlocked and opened the door into the garage."

Active voice sentences such as "I opened the box" are efficient, clear, and need no additional explanation. Let's compare that one to a passive voice construction: "The box was opened by me." The active voice statement, "I opened the box," has four words. The passive voice version, "The box was opened by me," has six words. The active voice is more efficient, requiring two fewer words.

There are a number of sources that agree that active voice is more efficient. One source explains:

> To achieve both economy of word usage, and the vigorous, confident style which characterizes good business writing, use the active rather than the passive voice. If you count the number of words, you will see that the active voice uses fewer words than the passive voice. Moreover, the active voice is a more efficient means of conveying information because the agent and action are identified first.[1]

The passive voice involves turning the object of the verb (the thing that was acted upon) into the subject of the sentence. Don't do it.

Here are some examples of the passive voice:

- "The knife was found on the hallway table."
- "The tire skid marks were measured on the roadway."
- "A garage door was unlocked and opened."

When you read these passive voice examples, you can't tell who performed any of the actions described. Who found the knife? Who measured the tire skid marks? Who unlocked and opened the garage door?

When a sentence is written in the passive voice, the "doer" of the action is left unnamed (or tacked on at the end in a "by" phrase, such as "by Mr. Brown"). A passive construction requires the writer to later supplement it with additional information—or else the inefficient sentence is left with a descriptive hole. It is incomplete, takes readers longer to understand, and is often confusing.

Active voice sentences use "I," "me," and "we" generously. This keeps the doers of actions clear. The active voice tells who exactly did what to whom (or what), where, and when.

---

1   Sandra Cleary, ed., *Communications: A Hands-On Approach* (Lansdowne, South Africa: Juta, 2009), 126.

Use the Subject-Verb-Object Sequence

Additionally, construct most of your sentences in the order of subject, verb, object. Your choices for completing these sentences are mostly confined to the first or third person, and singular or plural.

So what does that mean, that first/third and singular/plural thing? Essentially, the writer needs to plan how sentences are constructed. When a sentence is written and you are ready to revise it, recognition of the sentence's structure helps you decide whether to add or subtract information so that the finished product is precise.

For example, take a look at these subject-verb-object sentences:

- "I arrested Brown." (first person, singular, past tense)
- "We arrested Brown." (first person, plural, past tense)
- "He arrested Brown." (third person, singular, past tense)
- "They arrested Brown." (third person, plural, past tense)

Can you identify the subject, the verb, and the object in each sentence? Which ONE of the above declarations does not need additional clarification? Which ONES do? Now that you see the questions that first/third and singular/plural constructions can raise for the reader, you have an obligation to add or subtract information in the sentences to precisely tell the story.

It is most appropriate when you tell a story, when speaking or in writing, to generally refer to yourself as "I" or "me," and not in the third person. Do so in your reports!

Write in a Conversational Style

Writing reports with precision also requires you develop a conversational style that is realistic. Write in a rhythm and with sentence structures that resemble how you speak professionally. Do not write in an officious, grandiose style in your reports.

Here is an example of a report that makes the reader ask, "Who talks like this to their friends or co-workers?"

> The undersigned officer exchanged the information of driver #1 with driver #2 in a manner consistent to restrict individual interaction and contact. Under the circumstance, it was decided a restricted contact was best.

The writer can convey the same events with the following:

> Due to the highly emotional situation, I decided to provide each of the drivers' information to the other so that they would remain separated and at a distance.

When you write with precision, you don't expect the reader to wade through pretentious, unnecessary, and verbally cluttered nonsense. Your professional intention is to surgically make each word meaningful.

Seek to efficiently convey facts and thoughts; don't make readers waste time trudging through the mud of unnecessary words.

And never write, "I, Officer Brown, was driving southbound on Fourth Avenue." It's highly likely that your name is somewhere else on the report and extremely likely the reader already knows who you are. Spare the reader the unnecessary restatement of your name.

Provide Precise, Extrinsic Descriptions

Have you ever attempted to buy a used item from someone? Were you shocked to hear how much they valued the item? The basis of this circumstance brings us to the next stage of developing techniques to write with precision.

When the seller of the used item offered you an estimate of market value, he or she likely included a sentimental component. The part of the value above the external market realities included *intrinsic* considerations that you don't share with the seller. You are only willing to pay the value of what the item means to you. And although you may understand the seller's emotional attachment to the item, that seller's intrinsic value component is not valuable to you. You may not mind hearing the stories, but you are probably not willing to pay extra for a six-person tent because of the many fun camping trips the seller had in it—or above market value for a house because of the seller's nostalgic childhood memories.

Similarly, it is not realistic to expect that our investigative report reader will hold the same intrinsic understanding that we have when we communicate. In other words, it is risky to expect them to understand our value system, as indicated in our intrinsic descriptions, and to fill in the blanks of our descriptions.

Recognize that although you intrinsically feel something, your reader may not feel the same way, and thus they may not automatically understand an intrinsic statement. The opposite of intrinsic is *extrinsic*, and you must write in an extrinsic fashion.

Your feelings about something are intrinsic and conceptually abstract. They are from within you, and you intimately understand them. When you describe anything in terms of how you feel about it, you can only use abstract and intrinsic words. This practice is dangerous because readers may not understand intrinsic and abstract descriptions the way that you mean them. You must provide concrete and extrinsic descriptions to be precise.

Intrinsic Description	Questions Raised in Readers' Minds
It was getting dark.	How dark? Can't-see-anything dark?
He was drunk.	How drunk? What behavior revealed it?
She was belligerent.	What is belligerent behavior?
He was acting suspiciously.	What is suspicious behavior?

Through the above list, it's easy to see that not everyone will immediately understand or agree with the intrinsic description unless extrinsic detail is also provided.

Furthermore, a writer who utilizes the intrinsic method of writing defines others' behaviors by their own internal definitions. When writers use the extrinsic focus, they do not assume that their conclusions are the only interpretation of external events. Nor do they expect the reader to automatically understand or agree with their own views, values, and definitions.

Writing with precision requires a writer to explain the specifics of the external world and never assume that readers know the facts that led to the writer's internal conclusions.

Concrete or extrinsic terms are from outside of you, and, most importantly, are described from outside of your feelings, for the reader to evaluate. This means you describe your observations, rather than your feelings or judgments.

Let's apply the basic concepts of intrinsic and extrinsic to the idea of *suspicious behavior*. You know the components of the overall circumstances that combine for you to reach the conclusion of *suspicious*. And you have your intrinsic definitions of a suspicious person. The term suspicious causes us to think *danger* and to conjure some feeling of potential threat. The appropriate initial safe response might entirely depend on extrinsic descriptions of why someone is considered suspicious. An intrinsic description likely will miss important safety considerations.

While it is possible that many intrinsic values held by you and your readers might be shared, it is also possible they are not. So to ensure precision, we concretely and exactly describe: What behaviors cause someone to be considered as suspicious?

Let's say you have been sent to investigate a suspicious person standing outside of a jewelry store. As you later write the report and your focus is on describing extrinsic details, you offer this description:

> He stood alone at the side of the front of the jewelry store for nearly forty minutes. He often paced from the side of the building to the front display windows of the store to peek inside. After visually searching the interior, he then immediately walked back to the side of the store. I watched as he repeated this behavior a minimum of five times.

> He was wearing a knee-length overcoat, despite the near ninety-degree weather outside. When another person approached the store, he quickly walked a short distance away and waited. Then he returned immediately after the person moved away from the area. He often appeared to "tug" on an object concealed under the closed overcoat.

Would this qualify to label a suspicious person in almost anyone's mind? Can you see how the extrinsic and concrete detail is more precise and valuable than writing, "He was acting suspiciously"? Does the extrinsic description offer a more precise understanding than the intrinsic label of suspicion?

The above example examines the suspicious person in order to precisely describe their actual behaviors, rather than simply offering the writer's intrinsic conclusion that he was behaving suspiciously. It eliminates the perilous assumption that the reader holds the same definition of suspicious as the writer does.

While it is possible the reader will intrinsically evaluate a precise description of factual behavior, it is less likely. Your failure to provide concrete and extrinsic descriptions can only serve to compound any confusion and contribute to the problem.

Our society demands that when officers use force, it only be applied based on reasonable and justified circumstances. Precise, concrete, and extrinsic descriptions are critical to review and analyze circumstances and incidents after the use of force.

There are times when a law enforcement officer is placed in a position to deploy force. The authorization or justification to use such force is based on the details of the *officer's state of mind*.

This obligates the officer/writer to take the state of mind circumstance, break it down piece by piece, and be able to describe it piece by piece—so that others can analyze it piece by piece. Only then can they understand exactly what the pieces combined to mean to the officer that deployed force.

This precision process is necessary to extrinsically reproduce the state of mind of an officer who has had to deploy deadly force.

Provide Piece-by-Piece Descriptions

Realistically, the use of force circumstance is not the best time to begin to apply this piece-by-piece description process. It should be practiced and reinforced countless times in normal reporting practices long before a high-stress circumstance.

To visualize this process of describing piece by piece, think of a situation as if it were a loaf of bread. To ensure you provide the appropriate, piece-by-piece, extrinsic description and eliminate any chance the reader will not agree with your intrinsic values of the incident, you must slice the loaf into small, thin, relevant slices.

Then extrinsically describe each "slice" with such particularity that the reader can see precisely how the slices add up to the total circumstance. You must write with precision and use concrete words that descriptively reveal each slice of the whole incident.

Never can a writer assume the reader will understand any thoughts or information that isn't included in a logical, detailed, chronologically connected story. The written report oftentimes is the ONLY opportunity to exhibit all the descriptions that illustrate the entire story. It truly is your obligation to provide such information.

Don't expect your reader to be a psychic and wait for a random premonition to see what happened! Take responsibility, write with precision, and TELL them.

Use Concrete Terms

The obligation to write with precision and in concrete terms extends further, from minute behaviors to offering a complete description of all aspects of the investigative report. The writer must provide specific, concrete words and avoid abstract descriptions.

For our definition purposes, *abstract* is anything that is NOT concrete. *Concrete* is specific, detailed, and immediately illustrative. Write the descriptions with particularity, in terms that are extrinsic and sufficiently detailed. That includes particularity in the description of all objects, actions, behaviors, and persons.

Expand single-word descriptions to include more informative and detailed terms:

- Person = *an approximately 40-year-old Asian female driver*
- Object = *driving a mid-1990s blue Toyota four-door sedan at approximately forty-five miles per hour*

- Action = *swerved significantly into the westbound bike lane*
- Behaviors = *to apparently impact the rear of the bicyclist*

Now combine these statements and you see the concrete descriptions actually offer a relatively detailed story. For example:

> An approximately 40-year-old Asian female was driving westbound at approximately 45 miles per hour in a mid-1990s blue Toyota four-door sedan. She swerved significantly into the adjacent bike lane as if to <u>intentionally</u> impact a bicyclist from behind.

From the information provided, how does one assess the story's suggestion that the driver's intent was to impact?

A report writer's extrinsic and concrete treatment of the driver's behaviors to "intentionally impact" can serve to define legal intent and clarify issues such as whether the driver's behavior was criminal. A detailed examination of the driver's intentions, as evidenced by behaviors, could move this story from an unfortunate traffic accident into a serious crime with a deadly weapon.

Let's examine a few other terms that writers can clarify with concrete descriptions:

Abstract	Concrete
If you mean ...	*Then write ...*
Vehicle	Green Dodge pick-up
Store	Von's Market
Gun	Glock 9mm semi-automatic pistol
Shotgun	Mossberg 20 gauge pump action shotgun
Window	Residential wood sash window
Car	2015 BMW X4 Crossover
Speeding	75 mph in a 30 mph zone
Lazy	Routinely ignored daily work
Argument	Heated disagreement, dispute, or debate

Concrete language provides clarity. Clarity is imperative when the writer's words affect considerations of personal liberty, or in cases of employment, discipline, or retention. Should an employee have their employment affected over abstract statements like the following?

- "He was always late to work."
- "She seemed to be lazy."
- "He caused a dent in the door."

Concrete terms include other facts that are critically important to consider. An issue such as how the dent was caused or which door was dented could be clarified with a few additional words. Those additional words would serve to further illustrate holes left by the abstract statements.

How about a few more examples? Let's look first at an investigative statement on the use of force with an intrinsic and abstract description: "The suspect behaved belligerently when I put him into the temporary holding cell."

> The suspect behaved belligerently, as evidenced by his behaviors to attempt to spit on me, kick me, and hit me. He also swore at me and called me a "No good miserable pig!" For his and my safety, I immediately placed him into the holding cell.

And now a burglary investigation statement in the passive voice with a vague conclusory statement: "The hammer was used to break the window."

> I found a hammer on the ground immediately outside of the broken window, lying in broken glass. As I examined the hammer, I found small slivers of glass on the head of the hammer as if the hammer had been swung to forcibly impact the glass.

The concrete, extrinsic versions provide precise details so the readers can form conclusions.

Use the Past Tense

Precision writing means you must write the story in chronological order to allow the reader to make sense of the story. Chronological order means you tell first the things that occurred first, second things second, and install the events in your report in the order they actually occurred.

Investigative writing is almost always a story about things that previously occurred. Because the events happened in the past, the story must be written using past tense verbs.

Even if the writer witnesses an event firsthand and tells the story seconds after the event, the story is in the past tense. It would be inaccurate to tell the story as if it is happening now, this very second.

Therefore, a writer must remember to stay in the past with the written descriptions. This may be difficult to remember if we are used to using the present tense when we tell stories to friends. If a student offers his experiences during the final exam to fellow students, he might tell the story using verbs in the present tense:

> The final **is** scheduled to **begin** at 0800 am on Tuesday. I **hear** my alarm at 0630 and **get** up to shower. After the shower, I **eat** a quick breakfast sandwich, **drink** a couple gulps of coffee, then **run** to my car …

Focus on the underlined verbs in the story. The present tense verbs may put you right in the action and seem exciting, but they also clutter and confuse the story. Here's why: The present tense verbs alter the story's meaning to make it seem like a current-time narrative. It seems as if the writer is doing the actions as he simultaneously describes them, and we know that simply isn't true. Using the present tense has made the story itself *inaccurate*.

If, however, the student writes the following, the story does not risk upending the value of the communication and losing the trust of the reader:

The final **was** scheduled to begin at 0800 am on Tuesday. I **heard** my alarm at 0630 and **got** up to shower. After the shower, I **ate** a quick breakfast sandwich, **drank** a couple gulps of coffee, and then **ran** to my car …

Not only is the present tense inaccurate because it implies that the events happen right as you are writing the report, but the present tense can also be confusing for the reader. Therefore, present tense verbs do not meet the goal of writing with precision. Be precise in the usage of verb tense to avoid confusion and inaccurate reporting.

Don't Mix Verb Tenses

When the writer mixes verb tenses, moving from past tense to present tense, the written product is confusing. This is another good reason to simply stay with the past tense.

For a quick visual test to ensure past tense use, look to the verb's ending letters. If they have the *-ing* ending, that indicates present tense; if the verb ends with the letters *-ed*, you can generally assume the verb is a past tense verb. English, however, also has many irregular past tense forms, which do not end in *-ed*.

A few comparisons of verb tense:

<u>Present</u>	<u>Past</u>
Running	Ran
Hearing	Heard
Seeing	Saw
Writing	Wrote
Driving	Drove
Starts	Started

Sometimes it's easier to see errors in other's work because our focus is not on creating but solely on understanding the passage. So let's proofread the following sentences to practice our present tense and past tense understandings.

Read to determine the correct verb tense in the following sentence examples:

- Officer Jones and I {<u>saw/see</u>} the muzzle flash of a small handgun.
- In spite of the house being dark, I {<u>knock/knocked</u>} on the front door.
- Then he {<u>starts/started</u>} the car.
- The officer then {<u>finds/found</u>} the gun.
- I {<u>will investigate/investigated</u>} the incident.
- They {<u>run/ran</u>} away from the car.
- We {<u>go/went</u>} to lunch.
- He then {<u>arrests/arrested</u>} Brown.

- The car {was/is} blue.
- The house may {be/have been} recently painted.

Hit the professional investigative report target with active, subject-verb-object sentences and extrinsic, concrete, piece-by-piece, past tense descriptions. Include all relevant details. Choose your words accurately. This is called documentation precision!

Chapter Questions and Writing Scenario

Chapter Questions

1. Please explain why writing an investigative report with precision is important.
2. Provide a sentence that is in active voice, first person.
3. Provide a sentence to demonstrate first person, singular, past tense.
4. What is subject-verb-object sequence, as discussed in this chapter?
5. Please explain what I mean when I say to write in your conversational style.
6. Explain the differences one might expect when reading a description written with intrinsic description versus extrinsic description.
7. Explain the concept of "slicing the loaf of bread" as discussed in this chapter.
8. Provide two sentences that demonstrate your understanding of concrete descriptions.
9. Why is it important to practice consistent use of the past tense in report writing?

Writing Scenario 5

Please read and rewrite the following paragraphs to replace the inappropriate verb tenses with past tense verbs. Then proofread to catch any other errors and improve precision further.

My back-up and I made our way into the residence to find a bloody mess. As we step into the door, I see what seems to be a metal case commonly used to hold weapons within. There are eighteen empty bullet casings inside of the metal box, and many more spread throughout the residence.

I then see a couple of burned cigarettes, two bags containing what appears to be a green leafy substance consistent with marijuana, and a white powdery substance I believe is cocaine. I see a bloody knife and a sheath all sitting on the table on the center of the house.

On top of the table there are two wallets, with two IDs, one of the IDs belongs to Richard Little and the other belonged to Jorge Garcia. There are two containers of opened alcohol, one was sitting on the table and the other one is on the floor.

There were piles of money spread throughout the house. Next to the money I see a dead male on the floor with what appears to be multiple gunshot wounds in his chest. It appears the male had suffers four gunshots on the chest and one on the right side of the head.

Target with precision.
A precise description would help here!

But Where Is the Pig?

The following is either an example of an urban legend or of questionable decision making, but certainly an example of a focused strategy to write with precision. The names and locations have been changed to protect the innocent. (I actually don't know if it is true.)

Synopsis:

Officer observes a subject in public calling for assistance. Officer contacts the subject and attempts to help. Officer observes the subject displaying symptoms of intoxication to a level of impairment that indicates the subject cannot ensure care of himself. Officer detains the subject and conducts a routine records check, which reveals multiple warrants for the subject's arrest. Subject is arrested and transported to jail.

Evidence:

No evidence collected.

Narrative:

On 01/01/13, at approximately 0012 hours, I was traveling northbound in the 6100 block of North College Avenue, in my fully marked IMPD police vehicle and in full uniform. I had my windows rolled down. I heard a male voice calling for a pig; he was saying "Suey! Piggy, piggy!" I looked over and observed three white males and a white female walking southbound on the east curb line of North College Avenue.

One of the white males, wearing blue jeans and a light colored buttoned-up shirt, looked directly at me with red, glassy, bloodshot eyes and said, "Suey piggy, piggy!" I was concerned that the man had lost his pig and the animal might be roaming around in the Broad Ripple area, so I decided to stop and assist him. Not only because the animal could represent a traffic hazard should it be loose in a high traffic area such as North College Avenue, but also because I personally understand how devastating a loss of pet can be. I wanted to assist this citizen.

I immediately pulled to and parked beside their location and contacted the male that apparently had lost his pet. I identified the white male subject from an Indiana driver's license as Bo Joe McGrath (D.O.B. 1/22/82).

While I was speaking with Mr. McGrath about his possible lost pig, I smelled a strong odor commonly associated with alcoholic beverages on his breath and person. His speech was also slightly disconnected and slurred, his gait was erratic, and his personal balance was apparently unstable.

Based on the objective symptoms McGrath exhibited, I was concerned that his level of intoxication might create an impaired situation representing a danger to himself or others. I continued my investigation to establish McGrath's level of impairment, and asked questions regarding McGrath's ability to appropriately care for himself.

During this basic investigation, I conducted a routine records check of Mr. McGrath and received

Image Credits

Photo 5.1: StartupStockPhotos, "Man Writing on Pad of Paper," https://pixabay.com/en/office-startup-business-home-office-594132/. Copyright in the Public Domain.
Photo 5.2: Copyright © Depositphotos/teptong.
Photo 5.3: Copyright © Depositphotos/maclschauer.

indication Mr. McGrath had several outstanding warrants for his arrest for unpaid parking citations.

Based on my investigation, I placed Mr. McGrath under arrest for being drunk in public, and for his several warrants. He was subsequently transported to the APC by Marion County jail wagon Unit 516.

I searched the entire Broad Ripple area for approximately thirty minutes and unfortunately was unable to locate any lost pigs and was unable to locate any persons in the area who had direct knowledge of any lost pigs.

End of Report.

Design your report to be on target and write with precision!

6
Review for Credibility

Chapter Summary

Few things are as damaging to professionalism as an investigative report that contains preventable errors. Accurate work is the ultimate responsibility of the writer, but also falls directly under the responsibilities of the supervisor or reviewer overseeing the process to ensure an accurate, succinct document.

While both the writer and reviewer are the primary critical players in the documentation and review process, there are other organizational systems in play. Components of these systems include resources such as report writing manuals that clearly establish known organizational targets for participants, with the aim of insuring the creation of consistent, professional work.

The actual accuracy validation process is typically a two-step process. The first step is to edit, evaluating the overall document to ensure issues such as chronological order, paragraph length, and wider perspective objectives are satisfied. The second step is to proofread, reviewing the document close up to ensure correct smaller construction elements, such as spelling, verb tense, and so on, are correct.

Ultimately, the collective goal must be a routine focus on both individual and organizational accountability to develop and utilize quality communication habits, and ensure the production of mistake-free work that reflects the true professional philosophies, goals, and objectives of the writer, the employer, and the profession overall.

Consider the opportunity for review a gift of accuracy to your report, yourself, your employer, and your profession.

Chapter Learning Objectives

Discuss how accurate written communication instills credibility into the reputation of the author, the organization, and the profession at large.

Illustrate the need for written communication evaluation, for both author and organizational representative.

Explain the value and practicality in the use of a report review anchor form.

Explain the value and practicality in the use of an organizational report writing manual.

Describe the benefits of reading aloud when editing or proofreading.

Discuss the purpose and focus of the editing process.

Illustrate common key indicators to focus on during the editing process.

Discuss the purpose and focus of proofreading.

Illustrate key indicators to focus on during the proofreading process.

Discuss the ethics of mistakes, intentional or unintentional, and gift of proofreading.

Throughout this text, as, likely, throughout your career, you have gained an appreciation for the need for accuracy. This responsibility to ensure accurate communication should be a main fiber of the thread that makes up the fabric of your obligation to the public or entity you serve.

The accurate report writer who satisfies the goals of the profession always applies ethical concerns to their work, focuses to match the philosophical objectives of the employer, and builds a reputation that is worthy of the risks the writer assumes on the job.

Like many other personal and professional skill sets, effective and valuable report writing is achieved only with practice, honest self-evaluation, and a conscious effort to improve.

Building a Credible Product

After the author investigates to gather all the objective and relevant information, the next challenge is to construct the information into a communication we refer to as the *investigative report*.

The information is developed into a chronologically correct and complete fact pattern, divided and displayed into bite-size pieces of information called sentences and paragraphs, and strategically organized to satisfy a variety of audience needs and agendas.

This is a challenge, and to succeed oftentimes requires more than one attempt. It is necessary to develop good editing and proofreading habits to underwrite accuracy, which in turn ensures credibility.

Many knowledgeable proofreading proponents recommend the review process to be divided into two basic functions: editing and proofreading. Editing is considered an inclusive review that focuses on broader issues, such as the chronological order of the story, or a uniform first-person perspective, or consistent past-tense verb usage.

In contrast, proofreading aligns the reviewer's perspective to notice the correctness and precision of the individual words, or the quality and function of sentences and paragraphs. The proofread would focus on specific considerations, such as spelling, or excessive sentence or paragraph length.

Proofreading for credibility is a multi-layered and generally dynamic target at which to aim. While the need for accuracy and credibility might be easily and quickly declared, the actuality is a bit more complicated, and difficult to attain.

For example, accurate written communication abides by conventions of the English language, which includes considerations such as the use of correct grammar. It also includes considerations that address what is needed to complete an accurate written document, such as successful application of an organization-specific report format.

The total evaluation process often benefits from established anchors found outside of normal written English conventions. If an organization requires a specific format or information to satisfy that specific format, it is beneficial to have those expectations clarified.

Accuracy targets are especially challenging to meet if the review process is attempting to hit an inconsistent and subjective "global moving target." When work is subjected to differing levels of writing skill, or differing levels of dedication or competencies in the writer and/or the reviewer, each participant in the profession can suffer.

Once the concept of a moving target is accepted as reality, the next component to overcome is the review function challenge. Ideally, goals are established and resources are conveniently available. The first resource needed would be a reasonable amount of time to sufficiently complete, then review the documents.

When sufficient time is not available, and circumstances dictate only giving a document a once-over, the reality is that the deadline is the priority instead of the quality of the work. As might be expected, a once-over is not the recommended process, as quality work requires reasonable accommodation of time and opportunity.

The composition and review function is less challenging when the targets or anchors are clarified. The clarification offers the participants defined organizational expectations, and shares competency goals through known reference anchors that remove the need to guess.

Any investigative report author should consider the opportunity of editing and proofreading, to view the process of reviewing, evaluating and revising a document as if it were a gift.

Importance of Addressing Specific Writing Behaviors

Frequently in this text, valuable report writing is referred to as a career-long journey, which indicates the reality of different challenges faced through different places, experiences, and assignments over the course of one's career.

Reporting requirements encountered at one stage of one's career are likely to be very different from reporting needs at a later stage. Therefore, it is reasonable, as the reviewer or teacher finds shortcomings in another's documentation, to address those shortcomings with specificity.

As a teaching illustration, the untrained but well-meaning parent, when addressing a child's errant behavior, might shout at the child, "Stop that!" While the unwanted behavior is clear in the parent's mind, the lesson is only valuable if the child understands what behavior "that" actually is! Rhetorically, how can the child stop engaging in "that" behavior if the child doesn't have clarity as to what specific behavior that actually is?

It is most instructional to the author when the reviewer is specific in their description of the errant writing practice. Initially this may seem to be a labor-intensive practice for the reviewer; however, the likelihood is that, once the author understands the poor practice, the author will not repeat it.

An added reality may be that an employee's performance is based on the employee's overall professional practices, including their writing competencies. It can be highly valuable for all involved if the employee's report-writing behaviors, good and bad, are routinely documented in some sort of report review documentation.

The report review often is a standardized form that records the quality associated with an employee's written work. This historical record not only documents the value of the work throughout whatever period is appropriate, but also provides evidence in a step-by-step effort to establish the author's competencies, measure writing development, and identify issues such as common, avoidable mistakes.

The report review also offers an exact record of the fairness process that informs the employee of miscues, or above-standard practices. Report reviews reveal the level of generosity the reviewer extended in the process to address those mistakes and develop the employee.

Report review efforts maybe be significant if the organization is ever in a position to defend unlawful termination legal action over an employee's failure to meet writing standards.

Additionally, while considerations of performance review will be discussed later within this text, suffice to say it is efficient to provide the employee with specifics about their writing in such forums as an annual performance review.

This documentation process is similarly valuable in formalized training programs, as it provides data that may be significant when assessing the behaviors of the trainee, the trainer, and/or training process oversight.

The report review document can be installed into many current online records management systems. And in the case of limited technologies, is equally effective as a triplicate form, with one copy attached to the report archive, one presented to the author for action or reference, and one maintained in the employee's file.

Remember, a balanced program encourages the overall rating to cover a range of work. The rating can be "excellent" or "superior," and not restricted to only "improvement needed" ratings. Consider the following report review example:

ANYWHERE CALIFORNIA POLICE DEPARTMENT
-REPORT REVIEW-

TO: REPORTING OFFICER H. SMITH   **OFFICER I.D. #:** (1712)
VIA FTO: FIELD TRAINING OFFICER J. MENDOZA   **FTO I.D. #:** (1456)
OVERALL RATING: RETURNED FOR CORRECTION

COMMENTS: Investigation/documentation failed to address the crime elements. Robbery report failed to sufficiently address the elements of "force or fear" in the report documentation. Specifically, the report fails to detail how or by what means the suspect "forced" and/or created "fear" in the victim to accomplish the theft. (Refer to 211 PC for criminal elements.)

REVIEWING SUPERVISOR: Sgt. B. Williams **I.D. #** (1057) **DATE:** 07/24/18

REPORTS TO BE CORRECTED ARE PRIORITY ONE
AND SHALL BE RETURNED THE SAME DAY/SHIFT IT IS RECEIVED.

INSTRUCTIONS TO OFFICER: Make appropriate corrections to your report. Indicate "corrected" in the box, initial and date below. If needed, write response in the space provided. Re-submit your corrected report with this document attached. If NO CORRECTIONS are needed, explain the reason, initial, and date in the appropriate space below. Immediately return to your Supervisor.

		OFFICER'S RESPONSE, IF NEEDED
CORRECTED	☐	
SEE RESPONSE	☐	

OFFICER'S ACKNOWLEGEMENT: **OFFICER'S INITIALS**   **DATE RE-SUBMITTED**

As some final food for thought offered to the reviewer, do not make mistakes in the completion of the report review document. If the report review form includes documented examples that the report contains issues such as spelling errors, the individual highlighting the errors in the review should refrain from making similar mistakes.

Organizational Purpose and Value of Report Writing Manuals

It is often helpful for an organization to have a standardized report writing manual (RWM) to meet consistency objectives. The RWM acts as the definitive reference or "the library of expectations" for written communication utilized by the organization.

Many examples of organization-specific RWMs exist, and are most often considered living documents, in which the resource is frequently updated and will never actually be "finished."

RWMs provide clarity, and are considered necessary to the fair evaluation of the investigative report-writing process. They often act as practical rubric in the review process for the author to understand the organization's expectations, evaluation goals, and/or written product applications.

The RWM provides relevant specificity to the author's efforts to meet review expectations, and develop successful writing behaviors. It can provide a touchstone for the developing author, as well as the reviewer, to encourage consistent evaluations from author to author, and/or reviewer to reviewer.

Would you agree that fair and fundamental questions might be, "How effectively can a developing writer know what is required in a report?" "How fair is it to be held to a 'standard of proficiency' if those standards haven't been clarified?"

A clear standard and applied RWM is a nonverbal, symbolic communication that the organization has a considered and tangible goal of achieving precision.

The organization with known standards seems to appreciate the value of employees, instead of the nonverbal communication to "try, and try again to hopefully meet an undefined target, and hopefully eventually get it right."

If an organization does not have or offer a RWM as a resource, the writer can consider obtaining another agencies' resources; first as a standard to establish writing targets, and second as a perspective-widening resource.

Many organizational RWMs include perspectives from diverse sources that effectively reflect a variety of audience needs that the author should consider.

For example, the resource may include illustrative input from crime analysis, patrol operations, investigations, criminal information system management, prosecutors, public/police records specialists, and potentially others.

A review of an RWM can provide relevant audience perspectives that are informative to those who seek advancement or promotion. In addition to organizational written communication priorities, RWMs can offer perspectives on wider organizational dynamics, which support broader decision making.

Many specialty investigative functions address the specific needs of their profession by offering RWMs. The following information represents a targeted response to the specific writing needs of members of the Association of Certified Fraud Examiners:

> Being able to write a clear and thorough report is a key component of fraud examination and can greatly influence a fraud examiner's professional credibility with litigators, management, direct supervisors, and peers. The Report Writing Manual provides simple, informative explanations detailing the elements that a fraud examination report should include and how to express the results of your investigation in an eloquent and succinct manner.

The Author's Edit Step

Now the anchors are known, the first step of the review process is the author's own edit. This typically occurs during or immediately following the report completion process.

The author concentrates on an overall or macro view of what is written. The author can reference support materials such as investigative notes or outlines, outside sources such as a dictionary or thesaurus, or any number of devices to encourage accuracy and/or precision.

Simply stated, the edit step should look to evaluate the content, including structure within sentence and paragraph, and the overall structure including correct chronological order, clarity, completeness, and style.

Most often, the author possesses the personal historical experience to know the typical mistakes they tend to routinely make. Therefore, as the author begins the edit, they should reflect back to remember and concentrate on their own history of errors.

In some writer rehabilitation strategies, the author is required to keep a written journal or historical record of past routine mistakes to refer to. This journal represents a visual checklist or quick reminder of errant writing practices to look for, repair, and avoid.

Before starting the investigation or report, the author actually begins the edit by determining the purpose of the investigation. Clearly establishing the purpose will enable a documentation strategy to be followed from the beginning, such as clarifying the type of violation in order to identify the violation's elements.

For example, if the purpose is to report on a criminal investigation, then specific elements of the crime should be the focus of the investigation and addressed in extrinsic behavioral descriptions within the documentation.

If the purpose of the investigation and report is workplace-policy driven, then the focus of the investigation should be the policy violation element and related behavioral descriptions.

Reading Out Loud Is Allowed in the Edit Step

Many sources recommend the author read the narrative aloud during the editing process, methodically listening to one sentence at a time, while moving through the document.

In this technique, the author sees the words as they read, and then how they relate to each other. Each sentence combines with the last to systematically provide a step-by-step overlay to offer a more complete understanding and thus produce a more efficient audit.

The author should listen in order to understand what is being said, then focus on repairing or clarifying incomplete phrases or sentences, to verify appropriate thoughts and ideas, as well as re-work things that sound funny. Re-work those thoughts that are not clearly presented, seem awkward, or are not readable.

The Author's Overall Edit: Purpose and Focus

The edit step acts as the first step of the overall review process. Remember, the edit's purpose is to determine whether the content presented is sufficient, accurate, and offered in a professional manner that encourages the documents' efficient consumption.

The edit's focus is more on the form of the report and not so focused on details, as that is the function of proofreading.

The editing process should focus to answer questions such as the following:

- Do all the components of the investigation come across clearly?
- Does the presentation of the evidence include the who/what/when/why/how information related to each item's discovery/collection/disposition?
- Do behavioral descriptions support or highlight the violation elements?
- Does the presentation offer all the relevant information or will the audience be thrust into a position to guess missing information to fill in the gaps?

Read the report for general and basic content, which includes the elements of the crime, chronological order, and overall conformity and appearance. Consider this opportunity as a gift to eliminate all mistakes before they reach the audience.

It is often related that any author can edit to reduce the written product by about ten percent. Therefore, part of the edit step should be to seek to reduce the wordy sentence construction that adds nothing to the meaning.

Phrases like "it should be noted" should be replaced with whatever the author previously forgot to tell the audience. Often, when phrases such as this are used, the author is really announcing that information was left out of the correct chronological place, so this seems to be the haphazard place where the information was remembered and inserted.

Unnecessary "getting up to speed" words such as "I *began* to walk back to the car" should be revised to simply say "I walked to the car."

Consider redundant descriptions such as "a *verbal* argument," "a *physical* fight," or "I *quietly* listened." These are examples of fluff words that add nothing to the sentence. The redundancy likely reflects historical speaking practice and is contrary to the goal of written precision. They can simply be eliminated from the text.

The general rule is, if word or words can be eliminated from the sentence and the sentence meaning doesn't change, the word or words should be removed.

If the content is weak on details, or factually inaccurate, a properly applied edit should reveal the shortcomings quickly and enable the author to correct deficiencies easily. When read aloud and listened to, step-by-step progressions reveal gaps in the story where information is needed. The missing information can then be installed.

The edit's intent is to remove any descriptions that are subjective, such as the author's assumptions that categorize others' emotions or feelings. Instead, the author should relate the subject's opinion of their own emotions or feelings.

Phrases that include "' believe," "I think," or "I feel" indicate a nonfactual and potentially biased personal conclusion. The objective and professional investigator will focus on established facts and not feelings. These intrinsic feelings should be avoided or removed, as they have no place in professional, fact-based investigation and documentation.

The edit applies a broad perspective review to ensure routine practices have been followed, such as using conventional methods to describe people in a "head first" or "top down" fashion, or including non-abstract descriptions of vehicles or weapons (e.g., "a gun" versus "a Glock 40 caliber semi-automatic pistol").

Quick Keys to the Edit

Here are some basic edit scan and key clues to consider when reading your report aloud.

a. *Is the information presented in chronological order?* Key clue: Look for distracting use of connective words. If the report is written in chronological order, the use of words such as "then" or "next" are not needed, and, if overused, become a distraction.

b. *Is the information offered in an objective, professional fashion or is it biased?* Professional and objective investigations are not influenced by the personal prejudice, opinions, or emotions of the author. Key clue: Consider phrases such as "I think" or "In my opinion."

c. *The author should be enthusiastic in recording all facts, as there are always two sides to a story.* Key clue: Look for different styles of reference regarding defendant or victim behavior, or the volume of information collected in the respective statements.

d. *Is the information presented factually, detailing the behaviors and evidence that illustrate the elements of the violation?* Key clue: Good investigative reports have all the necessary parts, and completely explain the relationship among the who, what, when, where, why, and how. Facts are the things the officer can disprove or prove; inferences and unsubstantiated opinions do not belong in professional investigative reports.

e. *Is the information presented accurately?* Key clue: The information simply doesn't conform to logic. Investigative reports must yield facts that are reported correctly and specifically, and make logical sense.

The edit step may be the appropriate time to review the investigative notes to confirm that the information collected is in the actual report narrative. The author should compare notes from interviews to ensure the relevant information gathered from the interviews actually made it into the narrative.

Continue to compare the information within the notes against the report narrative for accuracy, including times, dates, spelling of names, addresses, phone numbers, license plates, and so on.

Proofread

Proofreading is the final component of the overall editing process, and is accomplished after all editing revisions have been made. Proofreading focuses on exacting construction details, such as spelling, grammar, and punctuation.

Proofreading is the review component where the *small substance* of the documentation is the focus. It seeks to ensure all the conventions of written English are followed. Issues such as spelling, capitalization, and sentence and paragraph structures are reviewed to ensure they are accurate and appropriate.

With experience, the process becomes easier and more efficient, if accomplished in a systematic manner and with a strategy. Once experience establishes confidence in the proofreading process, the self-taught author will naturally develop skills to apply more accurate techniques while drafting the next document.

Proofreading is a close, detailed inspection, and when possible, it may be beneficial to set the report aside and take a break in between proofread and correction attempts. This break can serve to refresh attention and concentration to enable a fresh evaluation of the work.

The proofreader may wish to closely read through the report multiple times to ensure it is complete, clear, concise, efficiently correct, and written with precision. This proofread review will look for errors such as typos and errors of grammar, and focus to eliminate confusion by applying precise language.

The proofreading process should include a quick focus on the author's use of *homonyms*. These are words that that sound alike, but have different meanings and spellings. Words such as *"to/two/too"* or *"there/their/they're"* certainly sound alike but have different meanings.

Although words of this sort will easily pass a routine spell check, they are mistakes and must be corrected. (For reference, a homonym list is provided in the Appendix of this textbook.)

The proofreader should reflect upon the always rules and the precision-driven concepts detailed in Chapters 4 and 5. The proofreader should actively consider the purpose, necessity, and width of extrinsic descriptions, and always focus on clear, complete, and concise practices offered in conversational writing styles.

The successful proofread step will ensure information is presented in the past tense, as the report always records things that happened in the past. Even if the event described actually occurred five seconds ago, the event is in the past. This means the review should focus on any action word that ends with the letters "ing."

Another successful review criterion is the "7 and 7" guideline. This rule suggests the appropriate length of a sentence to be about seven words; more than seven words might indicate another sentence is needed.

The other seven in the formula suggests that paragraphs should contain about seven sentences before the author needs to consider starting another one.

Other Common Mistakes to Focus on While Proofreading

NOTE: The following are <u>INCORRECT</u> examples of English composition.

a.   *Never list yourself first:* "<u>Me</u> and <u>Officer Jones</u> were both correct."
b.   *Never end a sentence with a preposition:* "Where is the car <u>at</u>?"
c.   *Consistently stay in the past tense:* "I was <u>seeing</u> the man as he *walked* away."

d. *Avoid subject verb disagreement:* "Padres <u>is</u> the team that represents our town."
e. *Capitalize rank and names, but not job classifications:* "The <u>officers</u> waited." "<u>Officer</u> Jones spoke to the next door neighbor." "Yes, <u>Captain</u> Turner is fifteen minutes early."
f. *Capitalize the first word of a quote:* "<u>H</u>e told me the car belonged to his wife."
g. *Be careful with connective words:* then, but, and, et cetera.
h. Always spell check and focus on the misuse of homonyms.

To Write Better, One Should Read More!

An old adage, if you want to write better, then read more, is absolutely true. No journeyman craftsman develops their skills or reputation by avoiding the practice of the art. Find a professionally produced book, on almost any subject, and read it! Read often.

The act of reading includes cognitive visualization, recitation, repetition, and perhaps both a conscious and subconscious familiarization with the practice of written communication. One can learn and assume many skills without realizing the pain of doing so!

Editing and Proofreading Resources

The Internet and commercial world offer countless written communication improvement guides and resources. While the following suggestions are not exhaustive, they may represent a respectable place to start one's search.

For those who are comfortable with the English language:

- Richard A. Lanham, *Revising Prose*, 5th ed. (New York: Longman, 2006).
- Barry Tarshis, *How to Be Your Own Best Editor: The Toolkit for Everyone Who Writes* (New York: Three Rivers Press, 1998).

Those for whom English is a second language may wish to consider the following:

- Janet Lane and Ellen Lange, *Writing Clearly: Grammar for Editing*, 3rd. ed. (Boston: Heinle ELT, 2011).
- Allen Ascher, *Think About Editing: An ESL Guide for the Harbrace Handbooks* (Boston: Wadsworth Cengage Learning, 2006).

Chapter Questions and Writing Scenario

Chapter Questions

1. Please explain why the editing and proofreading process is a critical function.
2. Why is the editing and proofreading process considered a gift?
3. Explain what the focus is and offer at least two techniques of the editing process.
4. Explain what the focus is and offer at least two techniques of the proofreading process.
5. Detail what is meant by evaluating writing by "anchors."
6. Briefly explain the stated benefits of a report writing manual.
7. Please explain the benefits of a report review form.
8. What is meant by the phrase, "to write better, one must read more"?
9. What is the perspective of the edit?
10. What is the perspective of the proofread?

Writing Scenario 6

Please review and identify *at least 20 errors* contained in the following narrative. First circle the number of mistakes found in your edit/proofread, then attempt to make revisions and make sense of this story. (*You may wish to know that this report was mostly based on a real submitted and approved police report.*)

On 9/6/17 at approximately 2244 hours, me and Officer Bailey arrived and parked our police car in the 2700 block of New Haven reference a disturbance in the street. The no-contact complainant reported there were approximately 20 subjects in the street fighting.

Me and Officer Bailey arrived and there was a limousine stopped at the nearby intersection of New Haven and Walther Drive. There were multiple individuals walking towards the limousine. One of the males was not wearing a shirt and was bloody. I smelled the strong odor of alcohol coming from the group of subjects, and one female is closing the limousine door.

It should be noted that I truck was leaving the cul-de-sac when me and Officer Bailey parked. It was two close for me too open my door and was to far from the curb to be safe.

I asked Lewis what happened to him and he said he tripped and his face hit the pavement. When I asked where, he says it is on his face and nose. I said "No, where on the street?" Lewis said he is not going to tell me what happens and that I should just go home.

The Importance of Punctuation

In a little-known place, far away from the bustle of common life, there was a large family preparing their Holiday Festive activities. As it happened, the family were cannibals and often the selection of the main course of their feast was a 'challenge' to obtain, and always unidentified.

Additionally, this family had not become 'adept' at the use of appropriate punctuation within their written and or verbal communications.

The members of the family that acquired and provided the main course for the feast did so in secrecy and simply provided it to those that held the responsibility to prepare the meal. The identities of the 'main course' were, as a tradition not shared with anyone except the 'main course' gatherers.

The day of the Feast came, and the family gathered anticipating a full festive fair. As the reserved places were occupied around the fire pit which had cooked the 'main course', every position was occupied except that of Grandma. She was obviously missing.

As the feast ramped up to begin, the Patriarch of the family loudly announced, "Come on let's eat Grandma!' Horrified, the entire family immediately stared at her vacant place beside the fire pit. The Patriarch, seemingly impatient, again loudly declared to anyone in the vicinity, "Come on let's eat Grandma!"

Suddenly, from a hut close by, Grandma's soft voice clearly rang out "I will join you in just a moment!"

Isn't it amazing how different a communication's meaning can change without proper punctuation? In this example, had the Family's Patriarch included a comma in his declaration "Come on, let's eat Grandma!", the family members would have perhaps been less anxious about the imminent main course.

Punctuation does matter, and the misuse can drastically change a sentence's meaning. Grandma would like you to learn and apply appropriate punctuation practices!

Lewis told me he was leaving with his sober friend, wrote down his contact information then got into the car that is blue.

Before the truck left barely missing my police car door, I write down the license plate information and speak with a woman sits on the curb.

She is telling me that there were four guys that attacked him and they were aged 23 to 33 years old. At one point, she said they ran into the woods and then she said that one of them an 18 year old that assaulted him and the kids 43 year old father was urging his son to hit him while the other guys were hold him down.

The other guy present says the girl was lying and can't be trusted ever to tell any truth. He wants to have him citizen's arrest her if there are any handcuffs put on anywhere, because she deserves them the most.

For further practice, please visit: http://anecdotes-for-preachers.blogspot.com/2010/01/proofreading-is-dying-art-wouldnt-you.html

Image Credits

7

The Art of Interviewing

Chapter Summary

A significant source of information for an investigative report is captured during interviews you will conduct with incident participants, witnesses, and experts. The products of these interviews are evidence that is to be handled as delicately as any physical evidence discovered in the investigation.

There are time-proven methods for preparation for the interview, collection of interview information, and presentation of the interview in the investigative report.

Chapter Learning Objectives

Discuss the benefit of conducting a good interview.

Explain the interview preparation process.

Discuss four interview preparation techniques and why they are beneficial.

Explain why it can be beneficial to script the questions before an interview.

Describe ways to motivate yourself and train yourself to listen fully to interviewees.

Briefly discuss the difference between an interview and an interrogation.

Explain the benefits and shortcomings of the four options for transcribing and presenting interview evidence.

Explain why it is important to not conform differing witness statements.

The Benefits of Interviewing

While investigators' tools for compiling information vary, one consistent method is through an interview. An interview is information freely given or precisely extracted from the words of another.

The interview is one of the most important tools available to an investigator to obtain new information, or to clarify or expand on information already gained. An interview can reveal agendas, indicate positions, clarify facts, illuminate intent, or challenge the investigator to view things from different perspectives. It can be an opportunity to lawfully explore the minds of others.

The interview can answer questions of "who, what, when, where, why, and how" in ways that other forms of evidence cannot. The interview is perhaps the only way to offer voices to those not normally a part of the investigative process who need to be heard.

It is not, however, simply asking questions and recording the responses. The truly accomplished interviewer understands it is an art that, when conducted by intellectually and ethically sound methods, often yields more than the interviewer initially considered possible.

If you decide to investigate the art of interviewing on your own, quick Internet searches offer numerous sources and information worthy of your attention. The information will come from a variety of sources with varied emphases and backgrounds. However, you will discover common procedural themes that run through them.

The art of the interview has many facets that affect the quality of the information you obtain. Because quality information directly relates to a quality investigative report, I will briefly offer some basic successful interviewing protocols (to either jog your memory or prompt you to find out more about them).

The "perfect" environment or circumstances in which to conduct a "perfect" interview rarely exist. The following circumstances are therefore a goal or target to consider as you begin your interview experience.

Prepare, Prepare, Prepare!

Whenever possible, make the investment of time to discover the facts of the case, the people involved, how they are involved, and what prompted their involvement. Determine what information you seek *before* you contact them, when feasible.

That means you should be familiar with the issue(s)! Read and take apart the exact policy or each of the legal elements of the violation you are investigating.

Develop a pre-interview strategy of how you intend to conduct the interview and which topics you need to discuss. Anticipate the responses you are likely to receive and plan which topics or details you will focus on.

Consider the best method and environment for speaking with the person. Reflect on the circumstances to determine whether face-to-face or by telephone, at their home or at your office will best encourage productive communication.

Understand that the environment may be the one single factor that overrides all others. It is highly unlikely the interview will be productive if you choose the wrong location. For example, you may not obtain the best information should you attempt an interview in the middle of busy traffic lanes on a freeway, or in plain view of the suspect of the investigation.

The proper interview environment also considers the person who is the subject of the interview. For example, if the person is accustomed to being in control, then consider conducting the interview at a neutral location or perhaps at a location that subconsciously indicates that they are not in control of your time together.

Consider eliminating obstacles such as desks or furniture the person can "hide" behind. Often these obstacles can represent power or control symbols or provide a personal safety space they can manipulate to their advantage.

When possible, determine whether the interviewee is free from other calendar obligations, such as work constraints. Obligations to calendars can be an intentional distraction technique, but at the minimum an impending calendar obligation will be a distraction.

Be flexible, when practical, regarding the responsibilities of their lives. Some interviewees may be nursing a sick child or have worked twenty hours the day of the interview. Be appropriately understanding and respectful of their time. Also, consider acceptable methods to restrict or eliminate cell phone usage, interruptions, and other distractions.

In many cases, it may be to your advantage to share the general focus of the interview with the interviewee. Revealing the focus to gain a mutual understanding may help them consider other aspects of their responses to include information you may not have considered.

Seek to Build Credibility and Rapport

In most cases, be as open and forthright as possible in such behaviors as identifying yourself, and, if practical, explain the purpose of the interview. The end product often will be more complete if the people you interview aren't suspicious of your intent or wondering about your agenda. When they are comfortable and not distrustful of your motives, you will gain greater cooperation.

Many of those you interview will likely not be familiar with investigative processes. In those circumstances, it may be beneficial to begin an interview by answering their procedural questions, should they have any. Remember to appreciate the "examination" anxiety of anyone involved in any type of interview. And be especially aware of their mental and physical states when interviewees are crime victims or family members of those who have experienced traumatic events. Realize they are likely sharing their pain; be professionally compassionate.

Most times, when a bit of genuine sensitivity is offered, the individual will feel comfortable enough to allow accurate information to flow. If an interviewee becomes emotional, reassure the person and allow him or her to regain composure. It is also common for subjects to become apprehensive when they realize their statements are being recorded. Offer a quick explanation that your goal is to produce an accurate report and, in that effort, you wish to completely capture everything they offer to ensure that accuracy.

Script the Questions

Identify exactly what you expect to get out of the interview. When you have identified the purpose of the interview, focus your thoughts to stay on that purpose. Design an overall plan, yet be flexible in the manner in which you execute it.

If you know you will be asking emotional or difficult questions, begin with smaller or softer questions. This technique encourages momentum to develop; the more controversial questions are less conspicuous and a bit more palatable because the pace and rapport has been established.

It can be very helpful to prepare a list of questions or an outline of topics you think you need to address. Although it is impossible to offer an all-inclusive list of questions from which to choose, there are some basic ways to think about good question construction.

What goals should be considered as you construct good questions for an interview? Here are a few considerations:

- Confirm the person's name and position at the beginning of the interview. People like to hear their names pronounced correctly and feel reassured that their names will be written correctly.

- Ask open-ended questions that will elicit more than "yes" or "no" answers, unless the interview has developed into an interrogation.

- Keep your questions neutral, and always present them in non-judgmental tones.

- Ask for definitions, examples, or anecdotes to obtain supplemental illustrations.

- Ask questions to obtain the information your report readers want to know.

- Keep your questions short, focused, and to the point.

- Ask one question at a time, and then wait for the complete answer!

- Anticipate and be prepared to ask follow-up questions.

- Do not begin with preconceived opinions and never make assumptions.

- Make sure you are asking a question, rather than broadcasting a commentary.

- Do not argue with the person you are interviewing.

  ○ Remember the focus you established before the interview began.

  ○ Be polite, but persistent, to elicit a response. If needed, restate the question in different terms until you receive an adequate response to your question.

As an interview concludes, many times it is beneficial to ask if there is information not asked about that the person may wish to add. Finally, it is often useful to ask for recommendations as to who the person feels should be interviewed or contacted to collect more relevant information. In some situations where punishment is a factor, you may want to ask what level of consequence is appropriate for the offender.

Although you should follow your prepared strategy or outline, don't be so rigid or stuck to your script that you lose control or obstruct the flow of the interview.

Listen to the Answers

As incredible as it might seem, studies indicate the majority of investigators who ask questions actually don't hear the answer because they are somehow distracted as they "listen"![1]

The interviewer might be thinking of the next question, or writing notes, or allowing his or her attention to drift to another thought. Discipline your attention to avoid this!

If you are not fully listening to absorb all of the answer, you may miss an important point or a subtle indication that screams for a follow-up question or clarification.

Even if the answers offered are complete fabrications, it is the responsibility of the interviewer to focus, listen, and capture all the fabricated details, as there likely is some measure of truth included in the lies.

It is best if you remember that you are having a conversation with another human being. From one perspective, you are asking for their help. Therefore, be an active and considerate listener, which means you are involved in an interchange. Put your personal assessments, assumptions, or judgments of their circumstances in the background.

Interrogation

Interrogation is not synonymous with *interview*; they are actually very different terms. Interrogation is an information-gathering technique that attempts to gain information from a subject who is not inclined to provide the information freely.

Although interrogation may be a practice you use in an investigative report-writing scenario, the issues and techniques are beyond the scope of this textbook and may be examined in an advanced investigative report-writing class. I have witnessed valuable results gained from interrogations that were handled professionally, ethically, and legally. In the hands of an experienced investigator, an interrogation is an excellent tool. For the purposes of this text, we will briefly explain the differences between interview and interrogation. The interview is generally a free-form conversation in which information is more freely offered and exchanged. The interrogation is not generally free form; it tends to be more a more directed, pressured inquiry, conducted similarly to a cross-examination in court.

For example, let's say you came home from an event well past your normal time. Your concerned loved one will often ask open-ended interview questions, such as, "Did you have a nice time?" "What did you do?" or "Who went with you?"

If your questioner determines that you perhaps are not being completely forthcoming and open with the interview answers, he or she will likely fall into interrogation mode. Now the questions are pointed and specific, perhaps asking for a single-word or a limited-word answer. The intent is generally to paint you into a corner with facts.

The questions might then be, "So then you left the movies at what time?" or "Who did you ride with?" The "free flow" of information is now constricted by fact-specific responses.

As you consider the use of interrogation in your investigation, a variety of legal issues can arise if it is not conducted professionally—for instance, concerning the application of lawful coercion or the degree of coercion used to obtain information.

---

1 Read more about this in a definitive study of investigative interviewing: R. P. Fisher and R. E. Geiselman, "The cognitive interview method of conducting police interviews: Eliciting extensive information and promoting therapeutic jurisprudence," January 2014, http://www.cti-home.com/wp-content/uploads/2014/01/Cognitive-Interview-Method-Fisher-Geiselman.pdf.

My recommendation is that you contact a knowledgeable, legal source or advisor to familiarize yourself with the relevant considerations. Additionally, you may wish to attend a credentialed training program before you routinely interrogate subjects.

Recognize the point in time when the situation moves from an interview into an interrogation. One way to define this is to say that, during the interview of a subject, at the exact point you realize that you've formed the opinion the subject is likely your criminal suspect, you need to consider the subject's rights.

Interrogations can be defined as a systematic questioning of an individual who is in custody or is likely to be deprived of freedom as a result of the collection of information about a crime. In this circumstance, you must recognize this point and take action consistent with the US Constitution.

To be clear, from the moment you form the "criminal opinion" and think that the interviewee may lose his or her freedom as a result of the information he or she provides, you must consider the interviewee's Fifth Amendment protections. These guarantee that "a subject cannot be compelled in any criminal case to be a witness against himself." These Fifth Amendment guarantees are expressed in the advisement referred to as the Miranda Rights warning.

Recording and Presenting Interview Evidence

Make no mistake, a statement is evidence, and it is the investigator's obligation to handle statements as such. The investigator must not alter, distort, or contaminate the statement evidence in the same way the investigator cannot alter or distort a crime scene fingerprint.

Therefore, I recommend you use an exacting method to record statements, be that method your written notes or a recording device. There may be legal considerations with regard to how you record, so it is best to consult knowledgeable legal sources for clarification in your geographical area.

Voice recording is generally the most accurate method for capturing information. Recording allows the evaluator to capture exact words or sentences from within the whole of a statement.

Recording generally eliminates confusion regarding any interpretation of voice inflection or mistakes found in summarized written notes. In many cities, law enforcement officers now wear body cameras to record sound and sight. As a result, many interviewees may now be more comfortable with their statements being recorded; be aware that some, however, may not be.

If the interview is recorded, the recording can be later transcribed into a format to be included in your investigation report. Depending on the length and details of the interview, the full transcribed document can be extensive; it can burden readers looking for relevant details.

Therefore, there are options for reporting statements within your report. Each method comes with advantages and disadvantages, so it is important for you to consider which statement reporting method works best for each report. You may even wish to combine one reporting method with another. We will discuss that more in the next sections.

Background information you should provide in your narrative includes the following:

- who spoke to the person
- who took the statement
- how you located the witness
- where the interview took place
- when the statement/s were taken

Question and Answer Reporting Method

This reporting method is where you provide the EXACT question you asked the subject, then provide the EXACT answer the subject gave. This reporting method has value if you wish to offer the entire examination, step by step and question by question.

It comes with the absolute obligation to be complete, accurate, and transcribe exact quotes. Here is an example:

The following interview was attended by Detective D. Jones (ID# 2345) and Mr. John Smith (DOB 12/1/78). It occurred in Interview Room #2 of Versailles PD on 2/12/15 and was recorded.

Q = Detective Jones   A = Mr. Smith

Q- "Hello Mr. Smith."

A- "Hello."

Q- "I wanted to ask you about the night of 2/2/15, at around 6pm. Do you remember that evening?"

A- "I guess so. What did you want to know?"

Q- "I wanted to know who you were with when you were at the Day Dream Day Park."

A- "I was with a work friend of mine. His name is John Wahl."

Using this reporting method, you can see the components of the interview, observe its development, and gain an understanding of the historical step-by-step events. If those are advantages for your investigative report, then this is a reporting method option to consider.

As a disadvantage, as previously mentioned, this reporting method obliges you to exactly and accurately quote each of the participants' questions and answers.

Direct Quotation Reporting Method

The direct quotation method means exactly that: You report the entire communication, word for word, spoken by the interviewee. In some cases, you may also have the obligation to include each word uttered by the interviewer.

This method requires you to install quotation marks to indicate the words that were spoken and, as with Q&A reporting, you must provide complete, accurate, and exact quotes. This reporting method has value if you wish to reveal what was uttered. For example:

> The following interview was attended by Detective D. Jones (ID# 2345) and Mr. John Smith (DOB 12/1/78). It occurred in Interview Room #2 of Versailles PD on 2/12/15 and was recorded.

> Mr. Smith told me: "On February 2nd, just after dark, I was walking around the toddler's swing area with my friend from work, John Wahl. We had been drinking a couple beers earlier, but didn't have any more. I guess the idiot clerk at the liquor store forgot to bag all the beer we bought!"

Through this reporting method, you can see the exact words and sentences offered to gain an understanding of the exact communication. If that is an advantage to your investigational report, then this is a reporting method option you can consider.

This reporting method comes with the same disadvantage as Q&A: an obligation to exactly and accurately quote the entire participants' statement(s).

Paraphrased Statement Reporting Method

This is likely the most common statement reporting method because it offers a condensed, less cumbersome statement from the interviewee. This method takes the significant and essential information and condenses it into a briefer but accurate representation of the information provided by the interviewee.
For example:

> The following interview was attended by Detective D. Jones (ID# 2345) and Mr. John Smith (DOB 12/1/78). It occurred in Interview Room #2 of Versailles PD on 2/12/15 and was recorded.

> Mr. Smith told me he and a friend from work were at Day Dream Park on 2/2/15 at approximately 1800 hours. They had been drinking beer, but had run out. While talking near the toddler's area slide and swings …

Using this reporting method, you provide only the relevant and essential elements of the statement, saving the reader the labor and distraction of inessential story elements. If that is an advantage to your investigational report, then this is a reporting method you can consider.

Consider the disadvantages, as well: This reporting method is successful only when the writer is able to recognize, ethically extract, and accurately paraphrase significant information to present it in the report narrative. The report reader must be able trust the writer to professionally offer the significant information within the report document.

Combined Statement Reporting Methods

I briefly mentioned this option earlier in this chapter: You can also choose to combine your choices of reporting methods. For example, it is most common to combine paraphrasing with direct quotation methods. In this combination, the author can use the best of two reporting options.For example:

> The following interview was attended by Detective D. Jones (ID# 2345) and Mr. John Smith (DOB 12/1/78). It occurred in Interview Room #2 of Versailles PD on 2/12/15 and was recorded.

> Mr. Smith told me he and a friend from work were at Day Dream Park on 2/2/15 at approximately 1800 hours, walking near the toddler play area. He stated that they had been drinking beer, but had run out. Mr. Smith said, "I guess the idiot clerk at the liquor store forgot to bag all the beer we bought!"

Notice that the initial portion of the statement is paraphrased; a direct quote is added for authenticity and to more effectively reveal the witness' values.

Therefore, understand that selecting the statement reporting method(s) for the construction of your investigative report is a strategic choice. Your selected method should support the overall purpose, design, and construction of your investigative report.

Conflicting Witness Statements

In this chapter, we have established that statements are evidence and are to be handled as delicately as any other form of evidence discovered during the course of an investigation.

So how does one handle evidentiary statements from two or more witnesses who observed the same event, and yet make different or even conflicting statements about it? The manner in which you handle the differences is this: You report exactly what each of the witnesses has said.

At times, the contradicting statements may reveal personal agendas and witnesses' desires to slant information toward a particular conclusion. However, as the objective, professional investigator, your primary responsibility is to gather the facts.

You do so as the facts are presented, always seeking to minimize your prejudices or interpretations of the facts, unless you are charged to provide a conclusion. Even in those circumstances, the conclusion is offered at the end of the report, after you have gathered everything for consideration. You should not analyze each piece as it is collected because this practice would not reassure your reader as to your overall objectivity.

It is also absolutely true that honest people, including witnesses, can see and hear the same exact thing differently. That often occurs when witnesses evaluate items intrinsically.

Take a look at the image below. Do you see an old woman or a young woman?

It is likely you ONLY see one image or the other. Now try to identify the other image in the picture. I admit, it can be a bit difficult! I assure you both images are in this picture, and just because you didn't notice the other image at first doesn't mean it doesn't exist.

So it can be with witness statements; two people witness the same event or image but see or hear different things. If you then seek to discount one witness or alter a statement to make it conform to the other in any fashion, you have, in effect, corrupted evidence.

The rule to not corrupt any statement also applies to the confirmed liar's statement. It may actually be particularly important for you to have an accurate record and provide details offered by a witness who intentionally seeks to deceive.

If the unaltered facts in an investigative report reveal the intent to deceive, then the liar's veracity will be clearly and decidedly discredited throughout the balance of the inquiry. The attempt to deceive is in itself revealing and discrediting to the reader, and your opinion is not necessary.

In conclusion, remember that the report writer's sole goal is to present the facts, not to persuade to a conclusion. Relate your facts in an impartial, professional manner and trust the reader to make the appropriate conclusion.

Chapter Questions and Writing Scenario

Chapter Questions

1. Why is it important to interview witnesses and collect the information from an interview?
2. Briefly explain five of the considerations of the interview preparation process.
3. Explain why it might be beneficial to script the interview questions before the interview.
4. Were you surprised to learn that many interviewers do not fully listen to the answers provided? Why or why not?
5. Please explain when you should record an interview.
6. Briefly discuss the difference between an interview and an interrogation.
7. Explain the following methods of providing interview results: Q&A, paraphrasing, and direct quotation format.
8. Why is it a mistake to conform differing witness statements?

Writing Scenario 7

Put yourself into the role of a criminal investigator who has been assigned to interview the victim of an auto theft (or other crime of your choosing).

Prepare for the interview by writing ten open-ended questions you intend to ask the victim in order to gather information for your report.

Ask those questions to a fellow classmate who is playing the role of the victim.

Write the narrative section of a report: Select a reporting method, use the method to provide the interview statements, and incorporate them into a story.

Hand in your interview questions, notes on the answers, and the narrative section as the completed assignment.

Image Credits

Miranda Warning

You have the right to remain silent.

Anything you say can and will be used against you in a court of law.

You have the right to talk to a lawyer and have him present with you while you are being questioned.

If you cannot afford to hire a lawyer, one will be appointed to represent you before any questioning if you wish.

You can decide at any time to exercise these rights and not answer any questions or make any statements.

Waiver

Do you understand each of these rights I have explained to you? Having these rights in mind, do you wish to talk to us now?

The Interview May Not Be What You Expect

At this point in your career, you likely assume that those you intend to interview will have the ability and possess the basic understanding to effectively participate in an interview exchange. Your initial thorny issues in interviewing are often concerned with the interviewee who is not being entirely truthful and how to dig out accurate information from a reluctant witness.

But consider the potential interviewee who may not have sufficient maturity or mental capacity to participate in the conversational exchange you seek. Additionally, have you given thought to the methods you would use to interview a hearing-challenged person or a subject afflicted with other types of physical challenge?

Among these many issues we must ask the question, when is a child too young to be interviewed? The best assessment for the very young is left to stage-development experts. With older children, common sense must prevail; it is likely you will need to interview a child at some point in your career.

An unfortunate truth is that very young children are most vulnerable to all kinds of abuse, which obviously requires investigation. There are no hard-and-fast rules regarding the appropriate "historical" age of a child who is asked to provide testimonial evidence.[2]

Essentially, many of the child interview instructional courses offered focus on the best interest of the child and attribute interview success and competency mostly to the person asking the questions. The manner in which the interview is conducted and the questions are asked is crucial, including "the quantity, position, pattern, style, intent and consequence of the question repetition used by the interviewers."[3]

As you develop your investigative interview skills, you should also consider your strategies for handling atypical interviews. Begin now to develop a professional skill set or have at the ready some appropriate resources and advice.

2 R. Marchant, "How young is too young? Investigative interviews with children aged two to six," June 2011, http://www.triangle.org.uk/resource/how-young-is-too-young.
3 S. Krähenbühl, "Interviewing young children: Protocol, practice and perception in police interviews," http://www.childhoodstoday.org/download.php?id=16.

8

The Follow-Up Reports

Chapter Summary

Based on the complexities and realities of an investigative report, it is reasonable to anticipate that the written product will sometimes require additional information and attention. The need for additional reports may stem from required corrections, requests for additional information, required follow-up investigations, or requests for expert opinion.

Chapter Learning Objectives

Discuss why an investigative report writer can anticipate corrections-based follow-up reports.

Explain the attitude and/or demeanor the writer should exhibit towards a corrections-based report.

Discuss the purposes for and differences among a corrections-based follow-up report, a supplemental report, a follow-up report, and an expert opinion report.

Discuss the purposes of the four different origins of a follow-up report.

What Could It Possibly Need?

Understanding the many expansive purposes of an investigative report, combined with the challenges of fully investigating and presenting the depth of all relevant issues, a writer cannot be surprised when sometimes a report just completed is returned.

In this chapter, we will discuss some of the realities that accompany such a return. Although it is best for your career aspirations to minimize returned reports, the truth is that you will certainly experience a few. So let's develop a strategy for how to accomplish the return request.

There Are a Multitude of Things to Consider

As you have likely come to appreciate, there are numerous things to consider including as you construct the investigative report. As an analogy, preparing an investigative report is akin to cooking a stew.

First, let's throw in some basic critical ingredients, such as format, straightforward sentence structure, consistent verb tenses, and active voice. Those are just a few of the key ingredients you already know are needed.

Then you must apply an appropriate amount of description, containing extrinsic, concrete, particular details. And did you cut out the intrinsic, the abstract, and the conclusory?

Now stir in the elements of the violation your investigation must address! Season the report with an appreciation of the varied readers, their diverse agendas, and their broad range of expertise!

Finally, the investigative "stew" you have assembled, thoughtfully stirred and patiently allowed to simmer, is judged through the "tastes" of the consumers (the agendas of the readers). When one considers all of these factors, it is little wonder your investigative report doesn't always meet every reader's taste.

As a result, you should expect to have reports returned to you. Don't "stew" on this reality; use the opportunity to grow as a result of it. The fact stands that you have just had your report returned, so how you view that return is the only variable you control.

Just Smile and Say, "Yes, Sir!"

In my career experiences, I was sometimes shocked and mostly disappointed when I returned reports to writers only to see their anger at having the report returned. I didn't return the report as a punitive measure; in most cases, I returned the report to the writer because it was unsatisfactory work.

For one or more reasons, their report didn't muster up to the level it should have. When the response was obviously frustration, I wondered if the writer would rather not have the opportunity to remedy the shortcoming. Would the writer prefer to send the compromised work on through the system and allow it to represent or define their professional reputation?

Sometimes, a report is returned with a request for additional details or information that stems from a sub-surface or unannounced parallel investigation of which the original writer is unaware. For example, details of one investigation sometimes naturally illuminate behaviors of another, such as a personnel investigation.

Here's one scenario: Two officers in separate cars responded to a burglary scene, where one officer damaged the structural undercarriage of his vehicle as he parked the car. Although the original reporting officer was not aware of the damage caused at the scene, details offered in the burglary report may be essential to the personnel investigation of the damaged vehicle.

In this example, the original reporting officer may not need to know the purpose of the supervisor's request for additional detail, but only that it relates to how each of the vehicles was parked. In fact, if the supervisor reveals the reason to the original reporting officer, it may be legally construed as a violation of the employment rights of the other officer involved.

Therefore, it is best to accomplish the request without comment or any visible expression of frustration or judgment. Just do it.

Be Prepared for a Learning Curve

Throughout this textbook, I have reiterated the fact that valued investigative report writing is a lifelong pursuit of excellence. Writers begin at the beginning, with a tremendous responsibility to learn to create mistake-free communication that is guided by a clear purpose and includes all relevant information in an easy-to-follow format.

The investigative report must consider and be responsive to many agendas and often be constructed to address two or more perspectives on the policy or law. The successful investigative report has many levels that challenge the new writer to critically think about what to include and the totality of relevance.

This learning process isn't easy, and therefore the new writer should anticipate that reports will be returned for additional details and for corrections. That is simply part of the learning process.

The largest number of returned reports reflects these unavoidable, important, and natural learning processes. Whichever issue is identified for you to fix, cheerfully repair the issue and don't make *that* error ever again.

Think about the error, keep it in proper perspective, learn from it, and move to the next stage of your lifelong development as an investigator and as a writer.

The "Correction Needed" Report May Take on Different Forms

The returned report may revisit you in different forms. Often, whoever is charged with the report review function of your employer may choose to simply hand your report to you, point to a specific section, and provide recommendations of how to fix the communication.

It is also common for law enforcement agencies to have a specific report review form on which the reviewer's comments are communicated. Oftentimes, the review document is attached to the original report with suggestions for how the writer can fix or improve the indicated sections. Sometimes, a report review is sent to the writer to offer feedback or thought for professional consideration even though the report has been sent on through the system.

In law enforcement, the writer's direct supervisor often completes the report review document. However, other evaluative agencies, such as the district attorney's (DA's) office, may also return the report with a version of a report review form attached.

In cases such as this, the DA's office may not issue a criminal complaint unless something is done—as in, additional information provided. Typically, the original investigator may need to interview a witness or submit evidence for specific processing. The DA's form and the additional information requested will need to be returned to the DA's office by a certain date to be reconsidered for criminal complaint issuance.

Supplemental Report

A supplemental report typically is a separate report that is completed to accompany the original investigative report. The intent is for the supplemental report to support the original investigative document.

Common examples of supplemental reports might include the following:

- Information not known to the writer at the time of the original report, which now requires additional documentation
- Written witness accounts provided by other officers
- Other investigative-based reports that originate from expert input or opinion

If you are assigned to produce a supplemental report, it will be most common that the assignment is to investigate and document an issue that was originally unknown to you.

For example, several days ago you completed a report regarding a vehicle burglary. This morning, the victim found the suspect's jacket stashed on the side of the victim's house. You would be assigned to the victim's residence to collect the jacket, investigate, and provide a supplemental report to the original report.

Another example of a supplemental report might be when there is a large number of witnesses to interview. Let's say the crime occurred in a location that had fifty witnesses. At the time of the original incident, other investigators may be assigned to collect witness statements and place the statements into a supplemental report that will be subsequently attached to the original investigative report.

Finally, an investigative report may require additional expert evaluation, investigation, or documentation. The experts' investigations are prepared in a supplemental report. They are often referred to as an expert opinion report (see more about these in the following sections).

Follow-Up Report

A follow-up report, much like a supplemental report, is a separate report that is completed to accompany the original investigative report. The intent is to document only the follow-up portion of the investigation. It will eventually be connected to the original investigative document.

A follow-up report might be called for when the original report is assigned to a detective for additional investigation. This may occur when the original investigation is significant, as in a homicide or sexual assault. The detective would be assigned in order to apply a specific expertise or in-depth methods to add or clarify significant details required for conclusion.

Expert Opinion Report

An expert opinion report is another form of a follow-up report. The expert opinion report is typically assigned to an investigator that holds the particular training, experience, and/or knowledge within a certain field to be considered a topic expert.

In criminal investigations, a detective can be legally considered an expert once the detective has successfully passed a *voir dire* process in open court. This process occurs when the detective has been questioned about his qualifications, training, and background by courtroom attorneys.

After successfully completing the voir dire process, the detective is then legally qualified to present professional opinions in court testimony. These expert opinions may be needed in cases involving an analysis of the relationship of physical evidence; cases that require expertise in ballistics, drugs, gangs, or vehicle collision interpretations; and many others.

As an investigation is compiled, often it is necessary to establish and offer assurances of foundational perspectives. A topic expert can often consider and combine relevant facts of an investigation to offer a professional opinion. That expert analysis and investigation is documented into the expert opinion report, which gets attached to the original investigation report.

Format of Any of the "Other" Reports

Depending on the job or the geographical region you are employed in, there may be specific forms or formats suggested for these other reports. Although the format might be different, I believe there are consistencies among the formats and the different employment regions that can make the other report familiar and help you start it comfortably.

In any investigative report, the reader needs to know how and why you are obligated to write the information. Start with the origin that suits the circumstances that brought you to write another report.

The following are examples of appropriate origin statements that may begin your other report.

With regard to a correction-based report:

On 10/27/15 at approximately 1700 hours, I was instructed by Sgt. Jones to review and revise ...

With regard to an assigned supplemental report:

On 10/27/15 at approximately 1700 hours, I was at the scene of a shooting within the Daisy Day Saloon. At that location, I was assigned by Sgt. Jones to collect witness statements.

With regard to a volunteer supplemental report:

On 10/27/15 at approximately 1700 hours, I was at the scene of a shooting within the Daisy Day Saloon. At that location, I collected the following five witness statements.

With regard to an expert opinion report:

On 10/27/15 at approximately 1700 hours, I was assigned to review the circumstances of an attempted homicide that occurred within the Daisy Day Saloon. I was asked to consider whether analysis of the incident could point to or support a gang allegation.

Let's revisit the first origin above to offer a final thought: Don't be ashamed or attempt to deflect your involvement if you were directed to write a correction-based report. Simply state that as the origin of your assignment.

First, do you think the reader won't be able to determine that fact from the substance of this latest written communication? If the reason that you have now written another report (to correct a mistake in the previous report) is obvious, then who will be fooled by a hazy origin statement? Actually, that vagueness or reluctance may provide non-issue relevance for those who seek to discredit you and your report.

Second, although we often don't gain respect when we make mistakes, we do often gain respect when we admit them. Mistakes remain a component of being a human, and everyone has made them. Although you might suffer during the public examination of your mistakes in open court at the insistence of a criminal defense attorney, most juries do not realistically expect humans to always be perfect. And investigative report writers are, indeed, human.

One certain method, however, that makes a mistake worse is denying or making an attempt to ignore it. By doing so, people often double the original issue: Added to the mistake is now the exhibition of their lack of credibility.

To summarize, when you complete any follow-up report, follow the same objective, thoughtful, professional investigative practices you have already learned and applied.

Chapter Questions and Writing Scenario

Chapter Questions

1. Please explain why an investigative report writer should anticipate corrections-based follow-up reports.
2. Explain the proper attitude and demeanor a writer should exhibit when he or she receives a correction-based report. Why should the writer strive for that attitude and demeanor?
3. What are the purposes and differences among the following: (a) a corrections-based follow-up report; (b) a supplemental report; (c) a follow-up report; and (d) an expert opinion report?
4. Discuss the purposes of the three different origins of a follow-up report.

Writing Scenario 8

Put yourself into the role of a criminal investigator who has been assigned an additional investigation regarding a field officer's previous vehicle burglary crime report from the night before. Your investigation will be documented in a follow-up report.

On today's date and time, your unit supervisor instructs you to meet the victim of a vehicle burglary at the victim's residence, located at 2345 Sixth Street, in your town. You are told the victim now has additional suspect information to offer.

You respond to the residence and meet with John Smith, the victim. He tells you that one of the items stolen from his 2015 Toyota sedan was an underwater camera. Smith tells you that earlier this morning, someone took the camera to Pawn Today and pawned the item.

The pawn shop is a legally functioning company that collected valid identifying information from the person who pawned the camera. Then, Robert Stevenson, a pawn shop employee, looked at the data saved on the camera and saw a picture of the victim standing in front of the victim's residence.

Familiar with the neighborhood depicted in the photo, Stevenson called the victim to ensure the camera was not stolen property and learned the camera was stolen last evening.

Please provide a follow-up investigative narrative section documenting this component of your assigned investigation, as well as your investigation at the pawn shop.

Remember to follow the appropriate format suggested in this chapter.

Remember: Even mistakes have value if you learn from them!

Image Credits

Is This Simple Graffiti or Something More?

To the untrained eye, the blue spray paint scrawled over the freeway sign might be only a visual annoyance that, while revealing criminal behavior, is not significant. But to an expert in gang graffiti or writings, the "C," the blue paint, and the six-sided star signify a criminal organization declaring their territory.

Gang symbols and behavioral signs can be subtle, and they are constantly evolving. The following excerpt offers just a few insights into gang communication:

- The Crips' dominant color is blue. On the West Coast, however, many of them no longer openly display their gang affiliation. The Grape Street Crips in Watts and New Jersey wear the color purple.
- Most Crips "represent" by tilting their hats to the right side, wearing blue-colored laces on the right shoe, and rolling up the right pants leg, and so on. But the Crips in Minnesota represent to the left.
- Crips have been known to replace the letter "B" with the letter "C" in writings.
- Crips' symbols include the six-pointed star, which represents Life, Loyalty, Love, Knowledge, Wisdom, and Understanding.[1]

With this brief explanation of the graffiti in the image below and just a few notes about the many evolving details of gang communication, does the graffiti take on a more significant and expanded meaning? Once you understand the symbolism and meaning, what questions would you now ask about the painter?

---

[1] North Carolina Gang Investigators Association, "Gang identifiers," http://www.ncgangcops.org.

Consider the many topics within one complex case, each with its own ever-changing cache of knowledge and skills needed to assess a piece of evidence or provide specialized background information. Is the value and necessity of an expert opinion report clearer?

"Be humble to see your mistakes, courageous to admit them, and wise enough to correct them."

– Amine Ayad

9

Sketches, Drawings, and Diagrams

Chapter Summary

It is often said that a picture is worth a thousand words, and that is nearly always true in investigative report writing. The investigative report writer should seek to convey an accurate description and images that reflect the relevant information discovered in the investigation.

Writers can choose from many options besides words to provide a picture to the reader, including photographs, sketches, drawings, and diagrams. In this chapter, we will discuss these options and how they can be arrayed.

Chapter Learning Objectives

Discuss why an investigative report writer should consider offering a visual illustration to support a report.

Explain the differences among a sketch, a drawing, and a diagram.

Discuss the benefits and disadvantages of a sketch, a drawing, and a diagram.

Detail the evidentiary considerations of a supporting illustration.

Explain what an illustration's legend is and what MUST be included in a legend.

Beyond Words

How beneficial would it be to have the ability to express with no ambiguity what the investigation scene (or a part of it) looked like? Just think how effective our reports would be if our carefully chosen words, placed within perfect sentences, provided the exact same visual image in each reader's mind, providing descriptive definition and depth.

If only our words, masterfully combined and presented, could stimulate a mental image as complete as in a masterpiece painting or a perfectly composed photograph.

Yeah, that is not what generally happens. Most times, our words have limitations; they are pushed toward the middle by variable meanings, reader interpretations, and practical constraints on the number of attempts a writer can make to "paint" the perfect illustration.

In our attempt to produce crystal-clear visualizations, and with our understanding of the limitations of words, we can insert images for our readers to better comprehend certain facts and their relationships to each other. Images include both photography and illustrations.

While it is true that using photographs generally offers the most accurate scene and evidence record, it comes with an obligation to be aware of legal considerations. Because of legal issues, an investigator should have formal, credentialed training to collect photographic evidence.

Legal issues surrounding material photographs, relevant photographs, and competent photographs are beyond the scope of this text and are best discussed and detailed in a forensic photography setting.

However, most people have experience with producing a drawing, as many of us started with crayons on our parents' living room walls! We already have basic experience with hand-drawn illustrations and they can be useful in both note-taking and in your final reports. So, for the purposes of this foundational report-writing text, we'll explore rough sketches, drawings, and diagrams.

Whenever you have a pencil and paper available, you have the tools at your disposal to expand on your words and further support your descriptive goals with an image. The following sections outline the basic illustrative tools available to you to add a visual dimension to your written descriptions.

Sketches

Sketch: A Definition

A sketch is typically defined as a rough outline that is not drawn to a scale and does not provide specifics, such as overall or positional measurements. It is often a bird's-eye view, or image looking down at an area. It is considered a quick representation of the interior or exterior spaces and the relationship of the items within those spaces.

The sketch is typically best completed before any evidence is moved, and after overall scene photographs are taken (if crime scene photography is planned). In most cases, both photographs and a sketch are recommended; if photographs are not to be taken, the sketch serves an even more useful illustrative function.

The sketch can act as a means to focus on the scene and consider the relevant information contained in the area. The sketch can act as a sort of methodological visual search, or visual format outline, prompting the investigator to record the scene systematically (e.g., from side to side or from top to bottom).

The sketch can be a problem-solving tool, informally offering the investigator an at-a-glance consideration of relationships within a space, and the relationships among the things within that space.

For example, glance at the sketch in the Figure 9.1. We can see the relationships between the body, the handgun, and the wound.

Figure 9.1: Rough sketch of crime scene showing spatial relationships among items.

Admittedly, the in-depth investigation process still needs to occur to establish what really happened. But a visual review of the positional relationship of the evidence can be helpful to establish an investigative theory or theories. A theory can provide a beginning, and the beginning is an important place from which to proceed. (However, I should mention that forensic philosophies tend to discourage such initial investigative theories because the forensics specialist should document the evidence first and not seek to prove a preconceived investigative theory.)

As you review the sketch in the figure above and the following drawings and diagrams, notice that all written descriptions are positioned to be read in the same direction. That is by design. It is distracting to the reader to have to turn the image at different angles in order to read the defining labels.

In the event the drawing becomes confusing or crowded when written labels are included on the image surface, the illustrator can simply insert an index number or alpha character on the appropriate location of the drawing to designate a location. Then the illustrator should begin a legend to one

Table 9.1

Legend for Drawing	
Item marked #A	Broken Lamp
Item marked #B	Revolver – Handgun
Item marked #C	Empty Wine Glass
Item marked #D	Ashtray

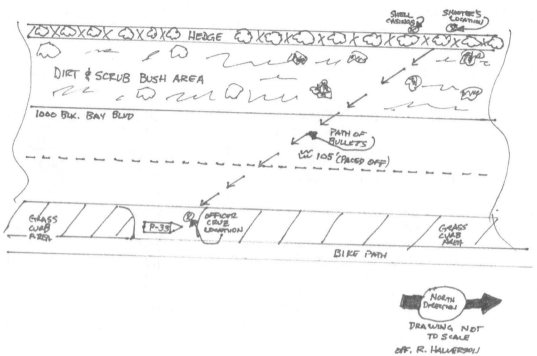

Figure 9.2: Officer's rough sketch of an exterior.

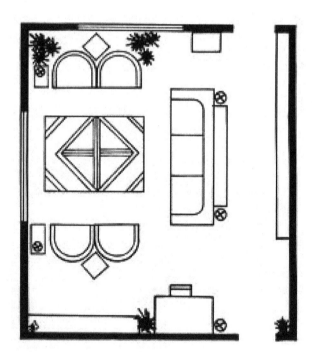

Figure 9.3: Sketch of an interior.

side of the drawing to connect the number or character to a description (see Table 9.1).

A Sketch as a Form of Notes

In many circumstances, a quick sketch can be valuable as a type of note-gathering method for the writer. The sketch in Figure 9.2 came from an on-scene officer who quickly drew the exterior location and the surrounding relationship considerations. The officer later referred to this sketch to refresh his memory as he completed his supplemental report on an investigation into the attempted murder of a police officer.

This quick sketch served as a quick representation of significant evidence locations, as well as the relationships of evidence to people, traffic lanes, sidewalks, landscape features, and other factors that deserve investigative report considerations.

In the example in Figure 9.3, you will see a more dedicated, refined sketch that has no measurements. What you see is only a visual representation of an interior living space, such as a residential family room. Even without a description, you can quickly see the overall relationships among the sofa, end tables, chairs, window locations, door openings, and so on.

We could use this visualization in an investigation report—for example, to illustrate where one person was sitting as they witnessed an event. We could indicate the witness' location with a symbol that represents that specific witness. Then the reader could look at this visual support to better understand the witness location referred to in our written narrative.

Typically, a sketch does not require sophisticated technology. A pencil, a straight edge, and a piece of paper will suffice to produce most rough sketches.

Drawings

Drawing: A Definition

A drawing is typically a refined sketch but is still presented not to scale. A drawing will often be from a bird's-eye perspective, and it may have more specific information included than a sketch would, such as parameter measurements. A drawing might contain evidence relationship measurements, such as the measured distance between a body and a weapon.

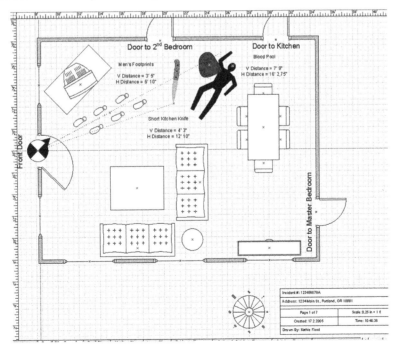

Figure 9.4: Drawing of a crime scene.

Take a look at the drawing in Figure 9.4. It is clear that this image is more formalized than a sketch; it may have been created with the assistance of a computer design program. You will notice the drawing locates evidence, including a weapon and the victim, as well as providing a representation of the relationships between items considered significant.

There is additional specified information provided, such as measurements between items of the scene that are considered significant. While measurements are provided, this drawing is not a scale diagram. In other words, though basically accurate, the reader cannot use a ruler on the drawing to measure other points of interest within the illustration.

A drawing can provide a more detailed and in-depth illustration of the relationship among items of significance to the investigator than the sketch is designed to provide. In most circumstances, the additional information aids in clarifying more complicated scenes or events.

Materials for Drawings

The materials used to complete a drawing are sometimes more sophisticated than the pencil, straight edge, and paper used to produce a sketch. Although many current investigators still use a pencil and paper, they augment their illustration tools with measuring tapes and drawing tools such as compasses, protractors, and thumbtacks. The thumbtack and a piece of string can be used as a form of benchmark post for broad circular drawings.

Other current technologies used to create drawings include GPS systems, lasers, computer-assisted drawing programs, printers, scanners, and other electronic diagramming applications. Drawing equipment investments can range from hundreds of dollars to hundreds of thousands of dollars, depending on the items.

Diagrams

Diagram: A Definition

A diagram is considered an exact drawing, and it is done in ink. It, too, typically represents a bird's-eye perspective and will illustrate significant items and their relationships to each other. Take a look at the diagram in Figure 9.5. Although it does not indicate evidentiary items, it does show a scale diagram.

In other words, once you understand that the scale indicated at the bottom of the diagram is "1 inch = 1 meter," you can use a measurement device, such as a ruler, on the diagram and determine the length across the actual window or the lounge's square footage. Being to scale is an exacting qualification of the diagram and definitely has its purpose in investigative report writing.

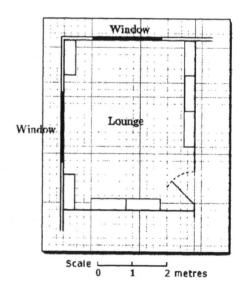

Figure 9.5: Digram of a lounge, to scale.

To create a diagram, you must be familiar with the practice of drawing to scale, as accuracy is vital.

In the diagram in Figure 9.6, it is easy to see how sophisticated an illustration can be. This illustration offers not just a to-scale, bird's-eye perspective, but also a three-dimensional illustrative component to stand up the two-dimensional image.

In order for an illustrator to be able to complete a scaled diagram, he or she has likely received specific training and has more sophisticated technology than a pencil and paper. For the purposes of this text, we'll leave further discussion of diagrams for more advanced forensic technology courses.

Admissibility of Sketches, Drawings, and Diagrams in Court

For an illustration to be admissible as evidence in a courtroom, you should consider it under the rules that govern the admissibility of any other evidence. The investigator must be prepared to testify to the veracity of the information in the illustration, the circumstances or conditions under which the illustration was created, and the process used to construct it.

Within the field, some suggest that if you begin with a sketch, and then later refine the rough sketch into a drawing or diagram, you should keep the original rough sketch in much the same way as you keep your investigative notes.

Additionally, if the investigator has someone else complete a drawing or diagram from the investigator's sketch, some legal experts suggest that the investigator witness the construction of the illustration and/or indicate his or her approval that the final drawing or diagram accurately represents the original rough sketch.

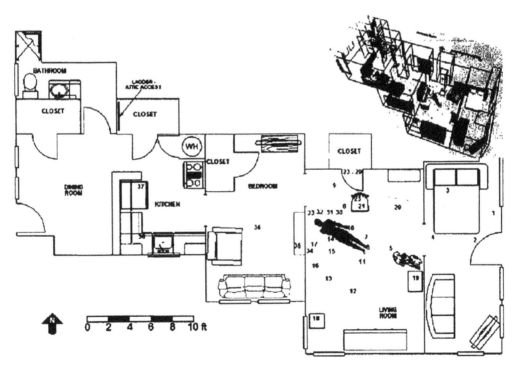

Figure 9.6: Two-dimensional and three-dimensional diagrams of a crime scene, to scale.

Information You Must Have on Your Illustration

You must include certain information on the page of any illustration! You must prepare a legend, and you MUST indicate, at a minimum, three items: the illustrator's NAME, a NORTH indication, and the illustration's SCALE, if any.

However, you may wish to also produce a legend that contains the following information:

- The case reference number
- Artist's name and identification number
- Name of the victim or complainant
- Location of the incident
- Date and time of the incident
- Investigator, the person making the sketch, and/or anyone assisting with the illustration
- Scale of the drawing or diagram, or "NOT TO SCALE"
- "NORTH" indication to orient the illustration, preferably at the top of the page

Table 9.2: Example of a completed legend.

Case # 15-23456 Crime: Vehicle Burglary Location: 555 Main Street Victim: Peter Rabbit 0930 hours, March 25, 2015	Case Agent Assigned: Det. Timothy Guava Illustration Prepared by: Det. Susan Jones Approved by: Sgt. V. Smith DRAWING NOT TO SCALE	NORTH

After your illustration is completed, I recommend you reassess the complete image to ensure the illustration accurately represents the scene, the contents, and their respective relationships. Always keep in mind that your illustration is evidence in an investigation, and it is your obligation to always represent evidence accurately.

Professionally prepared illustrations assist investigative report readers, which may include supervisors, managers, prosecutors, defense attorneys, juries, judges, and others that benefit from visualization of evidence. Make every effort to offer complete and accurate assistance to your reader.

Chapter Questions and Writing Scenario

Chapter Questions

1. When is the optimal time to accurately capture evidence in a sketch?
2. Explain the advantages of providing an illustration to support the investigative report.
3. Explain the purpose, benefits, and disadvantages of each of the following: a sketch, a drawing, and a diagram.
4. Please explain the standard evidence procedures for handling the original sketch when the illustration is refined into a drawing or diagram.
5. Explain what the practical functions of an illustration's legend are. What kinds of information should be included in the two legends suggested in this chapter?
6. List the three informational items that, at a minimum, *must* be included in a legend.
7. Why is it important to reassess the illustration before it is released to the report system?

Writing Scenario 9

Provide a rough sketch of your living room (or another space you have time to observe and sketch, such as a restaurant, a doctor's office, or a church) from a bird's-eye perspective.

Although measurements are not required for this assignment, you should include a relatively accurate representation of the furniture, the windows, the doorways, and other significant items located in that space.

On your illustration, include a legend that contains at least the three minimum informational requirements: the writer's name, a "not to scale" note, and a north directional indication.

You may use regular notebook paper or, if you prefer, graph paper. Remember to follow the appropriate format suggested in this chapter.

Image Credits

Suspect Sketches

In this chapter, we have been discussing how to supplement written descriptions with illustrations. A good police sketch of an unknown suspect is another way that words from an investigative report or from the victim can be turned into illustrations that provide a more accessible description of the offender.

Houston, Texas, has the "world's most successful" sketch artist, according to the Guinness World Records. Ms. Lois Gibson has helped solve over one thousand crimes in a career of more than thirty years.[1]

---

1 Read more of this amazing story in the July 23, 2012, Daily Mail article "Picture perfect," by Hugo Gye: http://www.dailymail.co.uk/news/article-2178040/Picture-perfect-The-amazing-police-artist-sketches-criminals-shes-seen-look-EXACTLY-like-real-suspects.html#ixzz3VXPQ1kXa.

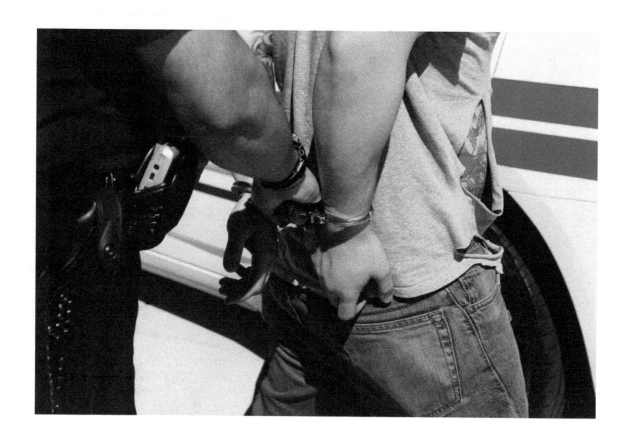

10

Probable Cause and Use of Force Statements

Chapter Summary

There may be no more significant reports than those that directly establish clear "reasonable justification" to deny a citizen's individual rights as guaranteed by the US Constitution. Although any investigative report may contain constitutional issues, in this chapter we will focus on two specific kinds of reports: the probable cause declaration and the use of force report.

These two stand out to demand complete and appropriate documentation to ensure that police powers have not been not abused and that those who apply community authority do so in keeping with the values and principles of our forefathers.

Chapter Learning Objectives

Discuss how the US Constitution authors stated that a citizen is granted their rights and why that is significant to representatives of the government.

Explain the importance of a probable cause declaration and its three typical components.

Discuss the purpose of a use of force report and the purpose of transparency, including their significance in US administration of justice practices.

Understand why writers should become accomplished at producing detailed use of force statements or reports.

Upholding the US Constitution

We live in a country that seeks to be intellectually honest and fair. The "fair play" values and goals are reaffirmed in the manner in which our government, including the legal system, operates.

Any time we act as representatives of the government, our actions are routinely measured against the principles established by the founding fathers that have been repeatedly reaffirmed within the Constitution and Bill of Rights. Several professions, including law enforcement, are literally sworn to uphold the ideals of the Constitution, and the operatives of those professions have their actions measured in constitutional terms.

The body of case decisions that, for example, relate to law enforcement's application of search and seizure is virtually innumerable and has been refined by literally thousands of considered opinions from courts at effectively all levels of government.

Issues such as when a citizen can be searched, what can be searched, and where the search is to be conducted all play vital roles in determining what is fair in the eyes of the legal evaluator.

Rights Are God Given

Before we continue our discussion, let's examine exactly where the forefathers believed that citizens' rights originate, to appreciate the value of those rights.

The beginning of the US Constitution reads as follows:

> We hold these truths to be self-evident, that all men are created equal, that they are *endowed by their Creator with certain unalienable Rights,* that among these are Life, Liberty and the pursuit of Happiness ... (Author added emphasis.)

This perspective firmly establishes the concept that, if rights are given by the Creator, then those same rights are above man's influence and cannot be infringed upon by any government or agent of the government.

Once we accept that most basic of premise, those that operate either through manipulative design or blatant ignorance to assault others' rights are clearly at odds with the design of the government.

Therefore, the key consideration for those who routinely operate in this sensitive area is to seek to balance individual rights with the need to provide enforcement services. While this balance occurs daily, it occurs with a knowledgeable effort to engage appropriate constitutional strategies. It also requires appropriate documentation to sufficiently explain these efforts.

The purpose of this chapter is not to offer legal evaluation, advice, or constitutional law analysis. Instead, we will address two significant areas of operational constitutional report writing: the probable cause declaration and the use of force report.

Probable Cause Declarations

Probable cause has been defined as being the minimum amount of information necessary to cause a reasonable person to believe that a crime has been or is being committed by a specific person.

In the United States' version of criminal law, probable cause is the standard by which persons who act under the color of authority subject their behaviors to a review of *reasonability*. Probable cause review includes consideration of the essential facts or grounds on which a crime has occurred, who is responsible for the crime, elements of potential charges that are being considered, or the grounds that justify a warrant to search and/or arrest.

The act of making an arrest is viewed as seizing a person's freedom, and that seizure of freedom from the arrestee must be reasonable. The circumstances of the arrest are based on probable cause, and the circumstances to establish reasonability of the arrest are briefly described in a probable cause declaration.

A Probable Cause Declaration Has Three Basic Components

A typical probable cause declaration should have three basic components that briefly yet appropriately address the elements of why the writer believes the actions meet the "reasonable" test of the Constitution:

- The basic yet essential story elements that reveal a crime has occurred. This part of the written Declaration should reference the arrestee's behaviors as they specifically relate to the elements of the violation.
- How the declarant "knows" or has focused on which person is responsible for the violation.
- The manner in which the suspect was individually or specifically identified.

Probable Cause Declaration Example: Part I

As an example, look at the crime description portion of a probable cause declaration that establishes a robbery/purse snatch:

> Officer Jones and I noticed a Caucasian male wearing a bright pink shirt and a black baseball-style hat. The subject was riding

"Probable cause" means recording facts that justify your actions.

What is probable cause?

Probable cause is determined by the existence of facts and circumstances that indicate a crime has been, or is being committed. That accumulation of facts leads an officer of ordinary caution to believe that the particular thing to be seized in a search is reasonably connected to the crime in question, and that it can be found at the place to be searched.

a green bicycle and traveling west on the same sidewalk as the victim, an elderly female.

The male rode his bicycle east, toward the victim. He passed her again and at approximately ten feet away, he turned his bike around and proceeded to ride his bicycle west, this time in the same direction the elderly woman was walking.

On this approach, while still riding the bicycle, the suspect grabbed her purse strap to take it off her shoulder. The victim responded by grasping the purse's strap as the suspect forcibly "yanked" the strap in his direction.

The magnitude of force used by the suspect both pulled the purse from the victim and caused her to fall to the sidewalk. The victim suffered abrasions to her hands and knees, and complained of pain to her left shoulder.

This first section of the probable cause declaration offers a description of behaviors and factors that combine to reveal that it is reasonable to determine that a crime occurred. In this case, the crime is a version of a purse snatch or street robbery where "force and/or fear" was used to accomplish the theft.

Probable Cause Declaration Example: Part II

In this component, the declarant must articulate the indications as to how or why the person arrested *was targeted* for arrest. Think of it this way: Of all the people in the vastness of the world, why was this *one person* selected as the suspect?

Let's return to our purse snatch example:

As soon as Officer Jones and I witnessed the theft occur, Officer Jones sprinted west on 'H' Street immediately after the suspect, who was riding away. Although out of my line of sight, Officer Jones ran behind the suspect and never lost sight of the suspect until Officer Jones caught up about two blocks away, where he forced the suspect and his bicycle to the ground.

Officer Jones broadcasted an update advising me he had the suspect detained in handcuffs, and he was waiting for a "curbside" line up with the victim. I contacted the victim to check her welfare. She indicated although scared and "bruised," she was OK. She told me she wanted her Coach purse back! I explained a person was being detained and asked if she was willing to ride with me to look at the detained subject. She said "yes."

When the victim viewed the detained subject, she immediately said, "That's the guy! That's the guy! What kind of guy would steal an old woman's purse?!"

With the information provided in this second section, it is clear why the person was detained and subsequently arrested. You, as reader, likely agree the detained subject is the correct theft suspect because the pursuing officer did not lose sight of him and because of the victim's immediate identification of him as the suspect.

Probable Cause Declaration Example: Part III

The third section of a typical probable cause declaration should reveal exactly how you have discovered or determined the name to attach to your suspect.

I asked the male if he was injured when he and the bicycle fell to the ground, and he said "No." I then asked him for his name and date of birth, in order to conduct a routine records check. He told me he was Michael Turner, with a DOB of 04/07/1985. Routine databanks indicated the suspect was currently on parole and had active warrants for his arrest.

During the custodial search, I also found a black leather wallet in the suspect's rear pants pocket. I located a California Driver's license bearing the same name, physical description, and a picture within the wallet. I then confirmed with Turner the information on the CDL was in fact his.

From the information provided in this third section of our example, we learn that the identification of the theft suspect was based on his admissions and the identification documents carried on his person, and were then again confirmed from routine records checks.

Varied Probable Cause Declaration Formats

As I have researched probable cause declarations, I have found examples and representations from nearly every corner and neighborhood of the United States. A probable cause declaration form and its substance may be slightly different and reflect individual characteristics based on your agency or region. However, the majority of probable cause declarations require essentially the same information as we have discussed. Figure 10.1 shows another probable cause declaration example.

When you review the figure, you will see there is probable cause to believe a trespass and/or failure to follow a lawful order crime was committed. You will also notice that, as the officer addressed the violator's behavior, a certain measure of force was used to "gain behavioral compliance" of the offender.

Use of Force Reports

Most law enforcement agencies review each individual use of force applied by their personnel. Enforcement authorities are granted authority to use force by a public that trusts law enforcement's motivations and reasonable force applications.

My belief of the foregoing statement is based upon ☒ personal knowledge ☐ information provided to me by _____, a credible person working at _____, who personally observed such offense:

On or about 11:45 June 25th, 2013 I was performing my duties of securtity in the Capitol Senate Gallery. The Gallery was full of observers watching the ongoing session. When the crowd reacted loudly to a ruling on the Senate floor the Lt. Govenor instructed to the Sgt. of Arms to restore order and clear the gallery. The Sgt. of Arms ordered the gallery cleared at which time we proceeded to ask people to leave the gallery from the east end. We were having to ask each individual to rise and had to forcibly remove some of the observers. We had systematicall cleared the sections up to where ███████████ was seated and asked her to rise and leave the gallery. After subsequent requests and final instruction to leave, she refused to comply, and was physically lifted from her seat. ████████ and I had to pull her up out of her chair. She attempted to resist by grabbing the chair, not standing, and pulling back from me. We broke her hold on the chair and got her up and as I escorted her up the gallery steps ████████ released her. I was escorting her by the arm up the steps by myself and she continued to try and pull away from me. At the top of the stairs, she spun and slapped my face with her open hand and told me to let her go. The intentional slap to the face by ████████ was offensive and I was currently wearing a State Trooper uniform identifiable by red, blue and green patch and silver Texas Department of Public Safety Senior Trooper badge. At this point I spun her around and proceeded to handcuff her for the assault. While trying to handcuff her she continued to resist by pulling her arms and attempting to twist away from me. After handcuffing ████████ she was escorted to the parking garage and placed into a patrol unit. She was advised of her Miranda Warnings at approximately 12:30am while waiting for another officer to assist with the transport. ████████ was transported to Travis County SO without further incident.

This offense was committed against the peace and dignity of The State of Texas.

Figure 10.1: Probable Cause Statement.

As a result, it is important for those in positions of authority to offer transparency as to the reasonableness of their use of force. The transparency is offered through use of force documentation.

Often, agencies will provide a type of "check the box" standard form for the officer to briefly document the circumstances of how or why that officer deployed or used force. While this brief form appropriately captures the basic statistical information to input for analysis, it does little to address potentially more complex issues.

Because of potential complexities, you are encouraged to provide a written use of force description in your investigative reports, when applicable. The ten additional minutes you invest to include a couple of additional detailed paragraphs may pay off big time.

> Many believe that whenever force is applied, mandatory and objective evaluation must quickly follow. Through critical review, thoughtful analysis of reasonableness, and statistical perspective, a rational and accurate picture can be made available for review. It is from these kinds of transparent communication that public trust is earned and maintained.

When in Doubt, Write It Out

Based on my experience, if an officer has a choice between checking a box on a form or writing out a story, he or she should write the story every single time. Many experienced in law enforcement believe that in cases of less-than-perfect use of force, an explanation of how the decision was reached can mitigate an otherwise miserable experience.

While the vast majority of force deployments are considered reasonable, some are not so quickly judged so. As others sit in judgment of the "reasonableness," they need to have available all those other things that are not included in a check-the-box format. Ultimately, it is *your obligation* to offer all the pieces that add up to illustrate why your force response was reasonable.

You can help readers "see" what you observed, felt, did, and attempted to do. In some instances, you can provide information to mentally place them into your situation and encourage them to see or hear or smell or feel the danger that prompted your reaction. Offer

great detail as to the extrinsic behaviors or movements of the suspect, including actions or words that hold silent yet threatening nuances. Give the reader the details of the surrounding lighting, landscape, and environment that worked with or against you.

You can offer all the minute details that combined to create your state of mind, how and why all of these details added up to form the "fear for your or others' safety," or fear for your very life. With a *complete* story, the reader can be provided relevant reminders that often decisions to use force may not be about what the perfect option was, but rather what option was the best choice under your circumstances.

Tailor your descriptions to provide details that address each of the various agendas of the readers. These may include policy considerations, criminality concerns, and civil litigation issues. In a serious use of force incident, there are layers upon layers of information that play into the consideration and application of force. While any use of force is obviously serious, they can be highly complex and complicated.

For proof of this issue's complexity, review standard use of force continuums illustrations that one can find on the internet. There are no definite decision paths along the lines of "If the suspect does this, then the officer should react this way." *It is your responsibility to explain your decision paths.*

Most standard use of force continuum reinforce the stark reality that each circumstance has varying degrees of force that can be used. Those degrees are based on observations that officers must often quickly analyze for relevance or significance—and then they must make an immediate decision as to the degree of an "appropriate" response.

Often, the decision-making process occurs literally in fractions of seconds, without the benefit of considered thought and objective review. The officer quickly gathers many information nuggets and analyzes them at a perhaps less-than-exhaustive analytical level. *It is your responsibility to explain those "nuggets" and what they meant to you.*

In those instances when the use of force results in greater harm or death, those cognitive processes demand explanation so they can be included and considered to render the final opinion on reasonableness.

The challenge is for the writer or incident participant to define and report each of those "slices of the incident" in sufficient detail so that any reader can identify why the response was reasonable.

The composition of a use of force report is a skill each investigative report writer needs to invest in to develop and nourish. We perform as we have practiced. Therefore, farsighted writers should seek to reinforce, improve, and practice their skills at every opportunity before a big event occurs. When the big event happens, that is not the time to start your skill development.

Many times, an officer's defense is not over right after he or she has used force to take a suspect into custody. In today's litigious society, the efforts to defend oneself often carry on for years past the original incident.

Chapter Questions and Writing Scenario

Chapter Questions

1. Based on the US Constitution, where do citizens' rights originate?
2. Understanding where citizens' rights originate, how should a representative of government authority approach citizens' rights?
3. What is a probable cause declaration?
4. What are the standard components of a probable cause declaration?
5. What is the purpose of a use of force report and who its typical audience?
6. Please explain the benefit of use of force transparency.
7. What is the test used to analyze a use of force incident?
8. Please provide a brief list of at least five use of force considerations and explain why they are important.

Writing Scenario 10

Provide both a probable cause declaration and a use of force report based on the following scenario. The final document, containing both assigned narratives, should be no more than one double-spaced, typed page.

You and your partner are in uniform and on duty. You are walking to your marked police car parked in the mall when you see a young man run from the front of a clothing store, carrying several pairs of jeans. He is being closely followed by a store employee, as identified by the store's uniform. The employee shouts, "He stole those pants!"

As the young man turns from the doorway, he makes a movement that indicates he has seen you. You immediately give foot pursuit, and from a distance of approximately fifteen feet behind the young man, you shout, "Police Officer ordering you to stop!"

About a block away, you tackle the young man and hold him on the ground as he physically resists. You use "reasonable" force to end the young man's resistance.

If your narratives need additional details, please feel free to be creative to include the necessary information.

Image Credits

Use of Force Report for the Rodney King Incident

http://law2.umkc.edu/faculty/projects/ftrials/lapd/RK262.jpg

"We often tend to look at police officers as if they are privileged, and they are because they are given the authority to use deadly force at times. But that privilege does not allow for them to use excessive force."
— David Covin

11

All Sides of the Performance Evaluation

Chapter Summary

Progressive organizations want to ensure and grow professionalism within the ranks of their organizations. Organizations often encourage employee growth, and set employee performance and behavioral anchors to guide all employees to successfully accomplish the tasks of a position. Then, organizations seek to accurately document their employees' actual behaviors to establish which are satisfactory or fall short of the goals and objectives of the organization.

As a result, performance evaluations are routine and commonly produced investigatory documentation that call for foundational thought and awareness. To be successful at any game, it is necessary for the players to be aware of the rules of the game. Both the employer and the employee benefit when there are knowns or anchors by which to measure behavior, and the assessment process is accomplished with objective intent and represents a two-way communication.

It is a statistical certainty that virtually all employees will participate in the performance evaluation process, either as one that is being evaluated or one that will be tasked with evaluating another. Because of this certainty and the significance of the final product, performance evaluation is worthy of a discussion.

Chapter Learning Objectives

Discuss why a performance evaluation is considered an investigative report.

Discuss the purpose of a performance evaluation, and its benefit to the employee and the organization.

Detail the benefit of "knowns" such as performance anchors, and their purpose.

Explain the design, need, and documentation goals that ensure a professional performance evaluation.

Illustrate how descriptions must be objective, extrinsic, and behavior based.

Discuss why is it important to encourage a two-way conversation between the parties involved in a performance evaluation.

Explain why constructive feedback is critical to the success of a performance evaluation.

Discuss the reasons why it is a mistake to forecast an employee's future in assessment documentation.

The Value of Establishing the Knowns

According to the philosopher, essayist, poet, and novelist George Santayana, those who are unaware of the past are destined to repeat it. While often quoted in the study of history, a reflective consideration of the meaning of this phrase is relevant to the concept of performance evaluations on a number of levels.

Establishing a defined theme in one's past professional behaviors is significant, as it serves as a guide to one's future behavior. It can also provide an opportunity to consider one's potential, perhaps in order to discuss a genuine plan for professional growth.

In the context of this chapter, let's open the concept of performance evaluation to include the annual performance variety, but also consider those evaluations found in daily, weekly, or monthly documentation that are so important to new employee training.

Many aspects of our lives, career growth, and skills are in a state of flex and development. Consider the process of developing competent riding skills, which likely progressed from tricycle, to bicycle with training wheels, and eventually into the skilled operation of only two wheels; it is advantageous to understand and appreciate the past, present, and future stages of gravity and mechanical balance.

Therefore, to avoid the next skinned knee, it is better to clearly establish and understand the experience of learning to balance to serve as a guiding standard to predict and adjust behavior to maintain the upright and "knees off the sidewalk" riding position.

The clearer the need to improve is to the new rider, the quicker they are able to master the two-wheel balancing challenge. Therefore, it saves skin if a performance evaluation function and valuable feedback are delivered as efficiently as possible.

The value of performance assessments lives in a direct relationship with the quality of the observations or behavioral data collected within the "investigation." They thrive under an objective and factual practice in which the actual and relevant behaviors are observed, contemplated, and extrinsically supported to be shared in the documentation.

Accomplished in the proper spirit, performance evaluation offers significant value for both the employees and the organization. The employee can gain a meaningful and appropriate view of the value of their organizational behaviors, and perhaps their place in the organizational hierarchy and an assessment of the contributions they provide.

Likewise, the organization can benefit from a form of data mining in formalized reviews. Valid assessments of employees' progress tend to measure the organization's environmental support or its development of employees.

Performance evaluations can also evaluate policy-level decision makers' global strategies to meet current and future organizational goals, and reconsider relevant employment expectations. So in a sense, the meaningful evaluation of an employee can also be seen as an evaluation of the organization.

Performance evaluation processes present multilayered challenges. The basic or foundational challenges that must be met can be generally summarized as follows:

- The employee is to *understand* what the organization behavioral expectations are.
- The organizational expectations and standards are *relevant* and reasonably obtainable.
- The evaluator or author must *objectively observe* relevant and meaningful behaviors to describe in the performance evaluation document, accurately and extrinsically.

These considerations must be met to validate and ensure confidence in the findings, recommendations, or resulting strategies. Properly accomplished, these foundational fairness issues will also tend to reduce exposure to employee/employer litigation.

Objectives of Performance Evaluations

Performance evaluation is a systematic investigation, appraisal, and documentation of the performance behaviors of employees. It often assumes the form of a standardized document used by all to evaluate and understand the abilities of a person for further growth and development.

A current trend in personnel assessment is to address the whole person—not just to address the skill sets of the current job, or even development for the next promotion, but to also prepare for leadership changes after the reviewer moves on. The organization's focus seeks to reach beyond simple skills and focuses on employee motivation, advancement, and the development of skills that support productivity and effectiveness.

The whole-person appraisal includes employee performance planning, routine coaching, and a strategy to develop the employee. It is achieved when everyone possesses an understanding of the employee's goals and the employer's objectives, observing to accurately establish, compare, and document performance; praising progress and redirecting efforts that are off base.

This concept creates a crucial advantage in employee retention and an attractive component in employee hiring, and tends to reduce tensions in the assessment process.

A whole-person review might include standard inquires such as, "Are you growing professionally?" It will then consider other aspects of the person, demonstrating interest by asking questions such as, "Are you growing personally?" This trend is seen by many professionals as empathetic and realistic, as an employer cannot only hire the professional component of a person, but employs the whole person.

As technology continues to minimize if not eliminate face-to-face contact, imaginative and interactive assessment processes create an opportunity for important interpersonal communication. It offers a realistic method by which to protect and manage the potentially evaporating valuable relational asset.

Performance appraisals are generally accomplished by systematic methods, which may include the following:

- The supervisor provides a method for the employee to contribute evaluation information, such as significant employee challenges, achievements, and a needs assessment.
- The supervisor also observes to capture, describe, and document relevant employee performance-based behaviors.
- The supervisor references organizational performance anchors to employee behaviors that establish fair job assessments and expectations.
- The supervisor references an organizationally approved rubric to rate the employee's performance.
- The supervisor considers factors in addition to work performance to provide a valid organizational perspective (i.e., resources available, training programs, etc.).
- Employers are in the position, if not obligated, to encourage and develop employees to improve their performance.

From an individual perspective, performance evaluations can satisfy many broad objectives. They provide feedback regarding employees' performance as well as document areas of strengths and areas where improvement is needed.

The employee that values honest feedback can use the information as an influential resource to reaffirm or adjust current and future work behavior strategies.

Performance appraisals also offer an organization an assessment of the global need for training and growth to develop employees. In doing so, this process can identify needed resources the employer could offer to assist employees to achieve desired overall organizational growth.

Prior to documentation, it can be wise to solicit the input of the employee to be assessed. It could be a simple questionnaire seeking the employee's input on this evaluation period's greatest accomplishment, greatest challenge, and so on. The subject's input at the onset of the evaluation can help to identify employee development needs or recognize skill-set growth.

As the evaluator or investigator prepares the performance evaluation, it is recommended that they solicit the employee's opinion by asking questions such as the following:

- What is the one thing you like most about your job?
- What is the one thing about your job you are most dissatisfied with?
- Detail one key strength you bring to the organization.
- Briefly name one thing about yourself you could improve.
- Please name something our organization accomplishes effectively.
- Please name something our organization can do to be more effective.
- What is the biggest thing I could do to better support you?

Not only does the investigator potentially gain new or reinforce existing insights or perspectives, but the entire organizational process can gain favor by incorporating important employee stakeholder validation into the process.

While an obligation may exist for the employee to participate, stakeholder cooperation is preferred in order to maximize efficient results. Cooperation encourages everyone to exchange honest reflections, and supports relevant and meaningful interactive feedback strategies.

It is often said that those closest to a challenge often understand the problem dimensions the best. Active inclusion of an employee can provide relevant and valuable information to supervisors or management.

Organizational Advantages of Performance Evaluation

It is easy to understand that employee evaluation can also reflect a mirror image of the organization itself. Organizational issues such as leadership quality or training needs become clear as one reviews employee assessments.

Effective employee performance appraisals can be seen as seen as a valuable return on investment for the organization. The objective and complete documentation provides several benefits:

- Insufficient employees can be rehabilitated or dismissed.
- Promotions or assignment selections are based on fact and not personality.
- Compensation packages, including raises or bonuses, are based on fact and not subjectivity. The focus is on merit, not on unproductive criteria such as seniority.
- Documented performance needs assist the framing of training policies and programs.
- Performance evaluations stress the importance of honest, relevant communication between all levels of an organization's strata.
- Honest communication that supports an employee's value grows relationships between supervisors and line staff, and supports cordial and congenial relationships.
- Performance evaluations tend to serve as a motivational tool. All gain a sense of satisfaction when efficient job targets are achieved. Satisfaction is gained by the employee as a result of validated achievement, and satisfaction is gained by the supervisor as a result of influence invested into the successful employee.
- Performance appraisals motivate positive efforts, and encourage important growth for all.

A potential revelation which can emerge that reflects on the organization is that common development needs may exist for a class of skill set. These needs may prompt a call for organizational recognition and response, to create programs that address employee development.

Finally, the dedicated, participatory, and valued application of employee performance appraisal processes tends to influence the working habits of all employees, as each likely realizes the evaluation process will also include them at some point.

Employee Advantages of Performance Evaluation

One goal of a performance evaluation is to provide honest and meaningful feedback to an employee regarding the quality of their work. The purpose of the documentation is to establish a record that reinforces the positive behaviors the employee is displaying, and to identify and offer resources or strategies to improve the behaviors that need adjustment.

While informal communication can serve to address correct and incorrect employee behaviors, they are often not complete and somewhat dangerous because of their informality. They often do not serve to extrinsically document behaviors for clarity, and corrupt the value to be gained by addressing the employee formally.

Additionally, informal communications offer an insufficient legal foundation for other employee-based actions, if necessary. Formal reviews which *accurately* document employee behaviors are most valuable, as they serve to transparently identify the acute cases.

Constructive and formal performance evaluations ensure employees are involved in a declared development strategy and act as a benchmark document, now and in the future.

The honest evaluation ultimately defines employee behaviors that have or have not met unit or organizational goals, expectations, and objectives. As a benchmark document, it should also define why the employee's behaviors did or didn't meet the anchors.

The employee no longer needs to guess how their work performance is assessed or how it was ultimately valued—they will know. They will know where they stood during the current evaluation period, and can measure improvement against the next evaluation period when that evaluation is presented.

The Functional Performance Evaluation

A typical performance rating scale includes five factors: outstanding, exceeds requirements, meets requirements, needs improvement, and poor.

While box-checking evaluations might be easier to accomplish, one must realize that even summarized labels and general classification words matter in performance evaluations.

Any rating factor should be highly considered, and a check mark beside an evaluation category seems inadequate. A valuable performance evaluation should be a considered task invested in by all process participants. Ultimately, it is an interactive communication that significantly impacts another's career, and there are inherent dangers in box-checking formats.

Written descriptions and comments are often required for those ratings that fall into the extreme ends of the rubric; however, progressive organizations may prefer written descriptions of employee behaviors to clarify and support all rating levels.

The descriptions must be accurate, supported by factual observations, and focused. The descriptions should focus on extrinsic detail, and fully explain those behaviors that clarify the specific dimensions of the evaluation category or anchor addressed.

The descriptions should never include subjective perspectives or any form of prejudice, whether that takes the form of hero praise or groundless disparaging commentary. The comments must be focused on actual relevant, historical behaviors; acts or actions that occurred within the evaluation period indicated.

Table 11.1. Categories of Performance Evaluation

Position Knowledge	Cooperation
Assumes responsibilities outlined in job description Follows/implements policies/procedures Creates/implements new ideas/standards Demonstrates high skill level in position function Demonstrates willingness for position growth Attends trainings as planned	Demonstrates willingness to achieve common goals Accepts suggestions gracefully Readily adapts to change Takes instruction promptly/accurately Willingly assists with other departments Accepts new tasks/responsibilities positively
Communication	**Initiative**
Communicates effectively with civilians Communicates regularly/effectively with co-workers Communicates regularly/effectively with supervisor Contributes positively at staff meetings/training Discusses ideas/information in a positive/constructive manner Expresses caring, helpful, and positive demeanor	Analyzes situations and makes reasonable conclusions Takes appropriate action without waiting for direction Proactively seeks information and support when needed Exerts leadership Encourages positive decision making Introduces new and innovative ideas Completes work and attains goals as planned
Professionalism	**Dependability and Quality**
Exemplifies professional demeanor Displays loyalty to the Organization and its mission Promotes appropriate behavior in the workplace Handles staff conflict appropriately	Demonstrates effective planning for timely task completion Results of work are orderly, accurate, and thorough Supports overall department standards Punctual, begins tasks promptly, and is focused on duties Follows through on tasks and job responsibilities Attends all required meetings/training Gives adequate notice of absence
Management: Planning and Development	**Management: Hiring and Evaluation**
Develops/adheres to established timelines for projects Involves staff in the planning and implementation process Organizes/schedules regular staff meetings and training Remains within monthly budget Projects and prepares for future needs Sets and attains clear, measurable, and feasible department goals	Actively recruits high-quality staff Is involved in the interview process Provides constructive criticism and feedback Challenges staff to improve in areas of weakness Utilizes staff strengths to enhance department quality Ensures and monitors proper behavior and job performance Documents staff actions appropriately and in a timely manner Produces accurate, detailed, and well-written evaluations
Management: Supervision and Training	
Establishes/maintains clear expectations Observes staff behavior and performance; provides ongoing coaching Closely monitors staff hours, punctuality, and workload Leads regular staff meetings Encourages staff to attend training and deepen knowledge of position Makes well-thought-out, fair, and appropriate decisions Manages staff conflict promptly and appropriately Produces well-trained and high-quality employees Maintains a highly motivated staff team	

Source: Adapted from: http://www.co.pierce.wa.us/documentcenter/view/40773

Evaluations Must Be Restricted to a Period of Time

Most performance evaluations document an employee's behaviors over the course of one year. In the case of documenting the training of a new employee, the evaluation period could be for a single day, a week, or a month.

The substance or forms of evaluation are similar to annual reviews in nature, but the behaviors cover a shorter span of time. While the evaluation period is less, the documentation intentions and purposes are ultimately the same; to provide an objective and accurate snapshot of employee performance.

The following annual performance evaluation example requires an anchor assessment of the level of the employee's contribution. In this instance, the choices are contributor, extraordinary contributor, and below contributor.

The form then requests written employee perspectives and behavioral input regarding positive factors as well as areas for improvement that support the assessment.

A Sample Self-Assessment
Annual Performance Evaluation Form
Non-Probationary, Classified Employees

Employee Name: Jane Smith	PeopleSoft ID#: 100012345	Position #: 00044
Department: English Department	Date prepared: August 5, 2008	

Core Responsibilities, Special Assignments & Departmental Values

Core Responsibility	Evaluation	
1	☒ Contributor ☐ Extraordinary Contributor ☐ Below Contributor	Overall Rating
	Positive Factors / **Areas For Improvement**	Described Behavioral Example
	In my supervision of Kate, the Office Services Assistant, I have observed that she has learned her position very quickly. She has told me often that she feels encouraged in her job and our working relationship. All performance management deadlines have been or are being met. / I need to help Kate more on the technical aspect of her job and how it fits into the big picture.	
	Additional Comments	
	I'd like to update Kate's position description to include student/department scheduling. I think it would challenge her a bit more and help her learn a new program.	
2	☒ Contributor ☐ Extraordinary Contributor ☐ Below Contributor	
	Positive Factors / **Areas For Improvement**	Described Area or Plan for Improvement
	I think I have done a good job maintaining the Director's schedule and making her appointments. I always make sure needed repairs are made quickly. / I'd like to work on sending out correspondence and e-mails that are error free. Even though I proof-read them before I send them, I still seem to make mistakes. I feel like I need to show more attention to detail in my role as building coordinator.	
	Additional Comments	
	I would like help with correspondence and e-mails before I send them out. I feel embarrassed occasionally with my grammatical errors.	
3	☐ Contributor ☐ Extraordinary Contributor ☒ Below Contributor	
	Positive Factors / **Areas For Improvement**	
	Student records are accurate and well-managed. / There are times when the office is full of students and I find myself disorganized when that happens. I feel like I can't control the flow of students during certain hours.	
	Additional Comments	

Figure 11.1: Sample Self-Assessment

The potential benefit of this practice is to document and hear the employee's view of areas where they can improve. It provides a venue for two-way communication, and most importantly offers the employee a stakeholder investment in their future.

Resources outside observed behavioral documentation are meaningful and relevant to an evaluation, and at some level should be included. Examples of these might include customer or citizen's letters of commendation, letters of reprimand, and unofficial documentation such as counseling session memorandums.

Often a performance evaluation will offer specific categories or anchors of defined employee behaviors for the evaluator to consider, apply as standard criteria, and/or address. While evaluation categories and subcategories of anchor dimensions might differ among various organizations and entities, it is likely that basic evaluation criteria will be essentially consistent.

"Your evaluation is based on the next 30 seconds. Go!"

We Need Clear Specifics to Respond To

Adults are believed to learn best when they are provided an example they can specifically relate to their life. Performance evaluation writing techniques are best when they offer the employee relevant behavioral examples to support their understanding of the evaluator's opinion of their performance.

Below is an example of a daily performance evaluation statement in which the trainee's behavior generally fits a listed category. Notice that the evaluator offers a specific behavior description that supports their opinion.

> Officer Doug continuously exceeds Field Training Officer expectations in the role of a trainee. He effectively adapts to change, and routinely makes adjustments in response to a variety of circumstances encountered in calls for service. He maintains a positive attitude, and utilizes this attitude in his customer service–based interactions and responses. Officer Doug is an active listener, and involves the citizen's participation to identify and implement suggestions from those he contacts.
>
> For example, on Monday April 27, we were dispatched to a reported barking dog call where Officer Doug spoke to the reporting party. During that contact he …

In this example, the author offered a generalized assessment then provided a specific description of Officer Doug's behavior that specifically supported the general assessment of "exceeds FTO expectations."

It is much easier to highlight an employee's successful behaviors, but it is at least equally important to identify employee behaviors that need improvement. Always provide written commentary that is clear, fair, and specifically targeted.

Refer to the following performance assessment of a high-ranking staff official documented a year before the December 1941 attack on Pearl Harbor:

"Colonel Phillips was recognized by the staff as without force and far too weak for a position of such importance."[1]

It is difficult to understand what behaviors prompted the assessment, as perhaps they were known only to the author. Later, this evaluation was endlessly evaluated and examined to establish behavioral context during the subsequent post-attack hearings of 1942. No known record exists, but one wonders what the stated "weak" conclusion meant to Col. Phillips when the evaluation was originally presented in 1940. Did he understand what behaviors contributed to that conclusion, or how the weakness label began? Or how it grew to manifest into behaviors others interpreted to be weak, so he could develop a strategy to correct his behaviors to change the staff's perceptions?

Without example, did the generalized weak assessment approach the level of concern for a superior to rehabilitate or even replace Col. Phillips with a stronger leader? Those questions were asked countless times during and after the Pearl Harbor incident examination. This "description" of Col. Phillips also called general leadership into question.

While not offered to Col. Phillips in 1940, consider the value added by further defining the conclusions "without force" and "far too weak" by including a supporting extrinsic behavioral example, such as the following:

> Colonel Phillips is reluctant to address or correct procedural errors of staff members, such as their routine failure to submit completed documents on time. There is no record or documentation these subordinate routine mistakes were addressed by the Colonel.

Providing the information that the colonel failed to address or missed routine deadlines of his employees offers objective context to the statements "without force" and "far too weak." It provides perspective and clarification, and removes the appearance of unsupported conclusions communicated through unsupported evaluation and missing extrinsic descriptions.

Additionally, an extrinsic description provides a foundation for an employee to understand needed improvement or rehabilitation:

> As a Community Relations Specialist, during this evaluation period Bob was successful in offering monthly Neighborhood Watch meetings at 27 locations, exceeding the minimum goal by 11 meetings.

> However, he did not satisfy performance goals and expectations to review, assess, respond to, and input the data from seven citizen group surveys into the CRS system. Bob indicated he is unfamiliar with the necessary technology to accomplish this task. This will be specific area that Bob needs to improve. To assist Bob in his application of technology, on 6/16/18 he is scheduled to attend ...

When the specific description to support the generalized assessment is provided, the employee is likely clear and able to quickly determine the reason for the conclusion. Their rehabilitation strategies are clearly justified as necessary and coherent.

The employee should appreciate and embrace this opportunity to capture an optimal understanding of the basis of their employer's opinion and expectations. With this clarity, the employee can understand what needs correction, why, and ultimately how to develop into the employee his organization expects.

---

1 Prange, Gordon W.; '_At Dawn We Slept_', McGraw Hill Publishing, 1981. Page 61.

If employees are an organization's most valuable asset, such clarity offers the employee information to assist them to change if they wish, and perhaps understand the reason their career mobility has stagnated.

And if the employee doesn't agree with the supported conclusions, at least the employee has foundational clarity to understand the strategy that was used.

Always Provide Constructive Feedback

Most times, the employee truly seeks advice for their future. They can greatly benefit as much if not more from a discussion about growing their strengths as they can from rehabilitating their shortcomings. The theory behind this focus is to encourage the employee to do more of something they already do well. Here is an example:

> Linda will need to focus on her mentoring and developmental skills to share her knowledge and experience with her team members. Linda has demonstrated she can lead a team very well, and it would be beneficial to the organization and the team members to learn Linda's skills.

And it is valuable to outline basic expectations or strategies for the next year:

> Additionally, delegation is an important skill of leadership, so over the next year Linda will identify sections of her leadership responsibility and assign or delegate it to individual team members to accomplish.

By highlighting Linda's mentoring and developmental skills, her awareness and or growth needs are clearly and specifically addressed. This could be a meaningful technique to encourage Linda to develop into a better leader. And it was communicated within a positive and rewarding frame of reference.

Forecasting the Future

One very common mistake is for the performance evaluation author to forecast the employee's future performance behaviors or future achievements, with comments such as, "if this employee continues her present efforts, she will be the number one employee in the history of employees."

Statements such as these, while perhaps considered accurate for a future estimation, represent simple conjecture offered by an evaluator of questionable objectivity. Just as in other forms of investigative documentation, it is important to stay in a past-tense perspective.

Offering an opinion on the employee's future represents a clear bias, indicating how the supervisor subjectively feels about the employee, and those feelings have no foundational value in an objective appraisal of an employee's behaviors.

Forecasts are difficult to intellectually support or prove, and are nearly impossible to defend; especially in litigation circumstances. They tend to offer no real value, draw attention to the author's feelings about the employee's skills outside of a defendable behavioral context, and simply act to dilute the evaluation's objectivity.

While they might be a useful tool for encouragement, forecast evaluation declarations have no practical place in a valued performance evaluation.

Chapter Questions and Writing Scenario

Chapter Questions

1. Please explain the benefits an employee can receive from a properly accomplished performance evaluation.
2. Please explain the benefits an employer can receive from a properly accomplished performance evaluation.
3. Why is it important for an organization to establish and offer knowns, such as performance anchors, for those involved in the employee evaluation process?
4. Why is it important to extrinsically describe specific examples of employee behavior to assess performance?
5. Please detail the benefit of two-way communication in a performance evaluation process.
6. How is two-way communication achieved in a performance evaluation process?
7. Please describe and offer an example of constructive feedback.
8. What is employee forecasting in employee evaluations? Provide at least two reasons that justify the practice's discouragement.

Writing Scenario 11

Please review the following descriptions found in actual performance evaluations as they addressed quality of work anchors. The first set can be a model for the positive exchange of information. The second set needs your thoughtful improvement.[2]

1. Positive appraisal phrases on quality of work
   a. "John is a detailed-oriented and thoughtful person. Therefore, his work is always completed on time and with high quality."
   b. "John always maintains accuracy in his work."
   c. "John does not neglect any detail of any task given to him."
   d. "John commonly produces error-free products."
   e. "John's work performance is very focused. He does not ignore any detail at work."
   f. "We can rely on John, as his performance is of consistent, exceptional quality and accuracy."
2. Negative appraisal phrases on quality of work

This section is for you to revise; please try to improve the descriptions.
   a. "We cannot rely on John. He rarely gives us products of the quality we expect."
   b. "Products made by John contain many errors. They rarely pass any inspection phase."
   c. "John doesn't focus on the details of his tasks. As a result, his products contain many errors."
   d. "John doesn't understand the key requirements of his job."

---

[2] "Appraisal Phrases on Quality of Work," Performance Review Phrases. Copyright © by Performance Review Phrases. Reprinted with permission.

A Humorous Look at Misquotes Describing Performance Goals

Words always matter, and precision is a goal of all investigative report authors. But that goal isn't always perfectly accomplished.[3]

A magazine recently ran a "Dilbert quotes" contest. They were looking for people to submit quotes from their real-life Dilbert-type managers. Here are some of the submissions.

1. "As of tomorrow, employees will only be able to access the building using individual security cards. Pictures will be taken next Wednesday and employees will receive their cards in two weeks."
2. "What I need is a list of specific unknown problems we will encounter."
3. "E-mail is not to be used to pass on information or data. It should be used only for company business."
4. "This project is so important, we can't let things that are more important interfere with it."
5. "Doing it right is no excuse for not meeting the schedule. No one will believe you solved this problem in one day! We've been working on it for months. Now, go act busy for a few weeks and I'll let you know when it's time to tell them."
6. "My boss spent the entire weekend retyping a 25-page proposal that only needed corrections. She claims the disk

---

[3] "Appraisal Phrases on Teamwork," Performance Review Phrases. Copyright © by Performance Review Phrases. Reprinted with permission.

e. "John is unreliable for the creation of a quality product."

f. "He spends little time revising his performance before handing over."

3. Positive appraisal phrases on teamwork

a. "John displays a spirited commitment to teamwork. He readily cooperates with his team members to get the job done."

b. "John is very good at encouraging other members to do the job by supporting their best effort."

c. "John respects every team member."

d. "John appreciates the new ideas and communication of his team members."

e. "John is very active in asking for the opinion of his team members before making a decision."

f. "John is reliable when working with his team members and expects the same from them."

4. Negative appraisal phrases on teamwork

This section is for you to revise; please try to improve the descriptions.

a. "John doesn't have a good relationship with his team members. He sometimes refuses to accept their opinion."

b. "John may be a person of independence. He is not suitable to teamwork tasks."

c. "John doesn't want to share his information with others in relation to the job."

d. "John is inactive when required to cooperate with others."

Image Credits

I gave her was damaged and she couldn't edit it. The disk I gave her was write-protected."

7. "Teamwork is a lot of people doing what 'I' say."

8. "My sister passed away and her funeral was scheduled for Monday. When I told my boss, he said she died so that I would have to miss work on the busiest day of the year. He then asked if we could change her burial to Friday. He said, 'That would be better for me.'"

9. "We know that communication is a problem, but the company is not going to discuss it with the employees."

10. "We recently received a memo from senior management saying, 'This is to inform you that a memo will be issued today regarding the subject mentioned above.'"

11. "One day my boss asked me to submit a status report to him concerning a project I was working on. I asked him if tomorrow would be soon enough. He said 'If I wanted it tomorrow, I would have waited

until tomorrow to ask for it!'"

12. "(Company name) is endeavorily (sic) determined to promote constant attention on current procedures of transacting business focusing emphasis on innovative ways to better, if not supersede, the expectations of quality!"

12

Other Written Communication

Chapter Summary

It is likely that even the most basic complete investigative report may require additional types of written communication and documentation. A basic knowledge of other types of written communication may be required by the new report writer to accomplish communication tasks outside the investigative report.

This chapter will briefly discuss the basics of routine written business communication often required outside of the investigative report itself. This includes the standard business format letter, the memorandum, routine email communication, and the employee's communication through social media.

Chapter Learning Objectives

Discuss why additional written communication mediums may be required in a business environment.

Explain the design, need, and purpose of the business letter, memorandum, and email, and considerations regarding participation in social media.

Discuss the general target markets—similarities and differences among the business letter, memorandum, and email, and beneficial and nonbeneficial uses of social media.

Communication Can Reinforce

Up to this point, we've focused our discussions on building the foundations for investigative report writing. While investigative report writing is a critically important skill to master, it is not the only written communication function for the new investigator to develop.

It is important to acknowledge that other forms of written communication can have effects upon a new employee's reputation and career. We will briefly discuss them in this chapter.

In both law enforcement agencies and private businesses, routine communications serving routine operational functions are frequent and necessary. In order to accomplish operational functions, there is a critical need for people to share information with each other.

The goal is to accomplish routine business communication in a professional and efficient fashion. When this is done, the communicators can both enhance the business of running a business and contribute positively to their own reputations.

Overall Goals of Written Correspondence

The various business communication styles and mediums are all relatively similar, and therefore relatively easy to identify and practice. Additionally, many of the optimal report-writing techniques that we previously discussed and practiced are effective for other business communication. For example, techniques for being clear and concise, such as writing in short, active voice, subject-verb-object sentences, are preferred by the business communication audience. Audience for both investigative report writing and written business communication prefer simple, accurate, and succinct thought development and professional, error-free presentation.

Focus to ensure that no part of your correspondence will be misunderstood. This goal helps keep the language you use simple and easily understood. Include the relevant information, yet remain brief; get to the point as soon as possible.

As in investigative report writing, business communication should always be considered a legal document. Although perhaps intended for only one recipient, a business document can at any time can be subject to various forms of public review. Other potential audiences that can access any form of written communication you produce may include supervisors, administrators, management, and even the general public.

In all types of written communication, the writer carries a significant responsibility to construct the communication in a fashion that supports the value and intent of the message, and does not detract from it.

Therefore, consider each and every communication as if your job depends on the value of what you have written. Consider each word and sentence to ensure they represent you, your company, and your profession in the best possible light.

Attempt to identify your audience, when possible. By doing so, you can direct the correspondence's contents to fit the needs and agendas of your readers. For example, if your audience has not been routinely exposed to technical terms, then explain them or avoid using them in the first place.

If your written communication is designed to be an internal document, respect the command structure and remember to demonstrate respect for those who hold a rank higher than yours. Consider an appropriate balance as you address them—not too formal and *definitely* not too informal. In most paramilitary organizations, it is best if you refer to them by their rank and allow them to suggest a more informal reference.

One concrete rule in any professional writing is the *absolute requirement* to be accurate. Therefore, write, read, revise, proofread, revise, and proofread again. Anything said or written can affect your professional reputation; mistakes are not often overlooked or forgiven.

When you need to go beyond the four types of writing we cover in this chapter, use the Internet to search for written communication examples. A quick search will reveal multiple examples of pre-written correspondence that work as templates. Examples range from pre-employment cover letters to customer complaint responses. Search for solid, well-written examples when you need to compose new types of correspondence.

Business Letters

In spite of technological advances, the old-fashioned business letter still has a place in both business and society.

In fact, some industry sources believe there is not only a need to continue to use "snail mail" communication options, they propose that a postal letter holds more value and more impact today than other, easier forms of electronic communications.

Your written business letter needs to have a dedicated opening; a middle in which you convey the main portion of the message; and an end, which is often a call to action.

Beginning

The opening of the letter will set the tone for your communication. Be friendly yet professional and get to the point of the letter. For example, it might be appropriate for you to clearly state, "I am writing in regards to …"

Middle

Tell your reader exactly what you wish to say. Explain your intent in as few words as possible. If you are seeking a particular response, action, or result, say so. Be conversational, but not too familiar.

The End

The end of the letter is your chance to summarize the key points made in the middle and restate the planned course of action or the action you expect from the reader. Encourage the reader to contact you for additional information or to present concerns. It is generally appropriate to thank them for their time and attention.

Business Memorandum

While the business letter is generally targeted toward a single person or entity, a memorandum (memo) is typically offered to a larger number of employees or members of an organization. The memo is often used to offer a timely communication broadcast to a wide audience—most commonly internal.

Used for a variety of purposes, memos may communicate promotions, personnel changes, policy changes, or a project update. They can be designed to address a variety of workplace challenges, such as employee vehicle parking issues, or they can request input from a group for a particular program or project.

Additionally, the memorandum is often used as a cover letter for an internal investigation or internal review; it functions to summarize a detailed investigation. In these cases, the intended audience can be highly restricted and specifically targeted.

The writing techniques to construct a memorandum generally parallel the business letter, and both have many similarities: a formal style, a preference for clear and direct statements, and the unquestioned need for professional accuracy.

Know your intended memo audience and target your message to that specific readership. As in the business letter, the tone of a memorandum must be professional, concise, and focused. Your wording should be in active voice and devoid of slang or department-specific codes and terms.

Memorandum Heading

The memorandum begins with a heading. This section identifies the recipients, the sender, the date the memo was sent, and the subject of the memo. Make sure you have complete recipient lists, ensuring that names, ranks, and titles are spelled correctly and that all who need to receive a copy are included. (Figure 12.1 shows a basic memo heading.)

Opening

The opening paragraph simply states the purpose of the memo. Keep it brief—only a few sentences. Save the details for the body of the memorandum; don't repeat them. Memorandums do not begin with a salutation.

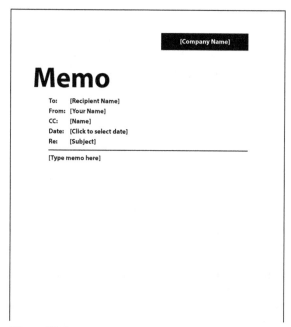

Figure 12.1

Body

The body of the memo is where the information the audience needs to know is organized. It is generally recommended that the most important information should be offered first, followed by less critical details or less important information.

Generally speaking, memorandums are to be kept brief, typically no longer than one page, and should not include attachments. If you do have an attachment, include it at the end of the memorandum.

If the memorandum is more than one page, consider including headings to keep readers on track and help them locate and quickly review its topics. Additionally, the writer can repeat on each page the heading information, such as the subject line, and sequentially number each following page.

Closing

The closing is your opportunity to reinforce the action you propose to your reader. Convey a positive attitude as you summarize your recommendations, findings, or conclusions. Include only enough information to clearly convey your request or conclusions; avoid restating the detailed information presented in the memo's body.

Traditionally, memorandums do not have signature lines at their conclusion, although they may be personalized with hand-scripted initials beside the sender names listed in the heading.

Email Communication

Email is now the most common form of routine written communication. While email is generally considered to be a more informal and targeted message than a memo, there are accepted conventions, standards, and etiquettes that should be followed.

Generally, the messages should always include a clear, specific subject listed in the email's heading. This information quickly conveys the intention and purpose of the communication and can prevent the communication from falling into those messages routinely ignored—or the spam or junk folder.

Because most email messages are aimed at busy, professional people, the subject should be a concise description of the topic. The subject quickly allows the recipient to prioritize their time investment and allows them to decide to read now, later, or never.

Although most emails expect a response within twenty-four hours, you can indicate other expectations in particular situations. If your email is time sensitive, you can indicate that by marking it of high importance and/or indicating a critical time frame in the subject line.

Write in an active voice. Avoid writing in capital letters as many consider the practice rude. Avoid large fonts and, as a general rule, avoid the use of colors. In most cases, the text of the message should not be excessively informal. It's always best to maintain a professional business demeanor in your communication.

Avoid lengthy messages and lengthy attachments. Be sure to recheck email addresses and ensure the attachments are correct for each message before sending. And always *proofread* to avoid annoying grammar and punctuation mistakes and bigger, career-busting errors.

If you know your recipient well, it may be acceptable to open the correspondence with their first name along with a cordial greeting. In other cases, appropriate salutations refer to the recipient by their rank, or Mr., Mrs., Ms., or Miss.

If you are not sure of the gender of the recipient, "Dear Sir or Madam" or even "To Whom It May Concern" will most often be an appropriate salutation.

Make every attempt to keep the message brief and focused, with a specific purpose and language. Never write as if you are texting and attempting to save data charges. Write in complete and punctuated sentences, avoiding pseudo-words such as "GR8."

This point deserves reinforcement: *Always remain mindful that all of your messages may be available to the public for general exposition and review, with or without your knowledge or approval! Never write anything that could be construed to be unprofessional, cause embarrassment, or invite civil litigation!*

Social Media

The utilization of social media platforms has exploded to influence most facets of daily communication, including the workplace. Cell phones, email, computers, and the Internet are now practically indispensable tools of social interaction that offer communication capabilities and message opportunities twenty-four hours a day.

Studies show the corporate use of social media and networking has blossomed as an effective tool to communicate with customers, employees, and other entities. According to an article in the *Harvard Business Review*, "Fifty-eight percent of companies are currently engaged in social networks like Facebook, microblogs like Twitter, and sharing multimedia on platforms such as YouTube."[1]

The article goes on to predict that seventy-nine percent of companies already have or will have social media in place in the next few years.

Social media has significantly changed the way people communicate, including opportunities to offer commentary. The instant messaging abilities of social media allow us to disseminate and skim value through messages related to management, marketing, and human resources.

A Successful Social Media Formula

There are basic considerations for successful communication between an entity such as a corporation and their clients. A partial summary of this formula is as follows:

Know the Audience

Just as precision language has been key throughout this text, it is imperative here to clearly identify exactly who the audience is, in order to communicate with them directly.

By clearly understanding the target market, you can more efficiently design the message to resonate with that group. It is considered most effective to engage with a smaller group rather than to attempt to communicate with a large following.

---

1   A Report by Harvard Business Review Analytic Services "The New Conversation: Taking Social Media from Talk to Action," *Harvard Business Review*, April 20, 2016.

Set Goals and Establish Expectations

Experience has clearly indicated that social media involvement without a clear goal and established expectations is a recipe for an ineffective use of resources, and likely to be highly frustrating.

Goals might include gaining a certain number of new fans per day or per week, and can be facilitated by posting a link to Facebook on the company's website. By setting goals first, a plan can be tailored to meet reasonable expectations, and measurable success.

Meet the Challenge to Remain Connected to the Target Audience

Once the effort and investment are made to connect with the target audience, that effort must continue in order to remain connected over time. This means that routine review and response are required to maintain lines of communication with clients; otherwise the clients will simply fade away.

Understand the Advantages and Disadvantages of Social Media

One of many concerns as people attempt to clarify the blurred definitions of social media use is exactly what messages are appropriate, and what harm communication or comments can cause the sender. It should be particularly concerning to the candidates who seek employment and find themselves subjected to a pre-employment background investigation.

Accept as fact that what you post on personal social media sites CAN and often does affect your employment status and chances of being hired! While the extent or frequency of the effects are still subject to analysis, the initial studies are clear: There are absolute effects that originate from social media posts, and some are not positive.

A May 2015 survey conducted by Harris Poll and released by *CareerBuilder*[2] indicated that more than half (52%) of two thousand employers contacted during the survey admitted they actively considered social media content in the evaluation of a candidate's skills and qualifications. And this figure has risen significantly compared to previous similar studies, creating the reasonable expectation that this trend will continue to rise in the future.

Employers, either with permission from the candidate, or through a covert friend request from a manager, follow applicants to evaluate their social media presence. While this can suggest they are truly interested in the prospective or current employee as a person, it calls into question how one navigates successfully through the murky waters of social media in the job application process.

Make no mistake, the evaluator's intention is to learn information, such as the candidate's interests, hobbies, and extracurricular involvements or activities. They may be

---

2   http://www.careerbuilder.ca/share/aboutus/pressreleasesdetail.aspx?sd=5%2f14%2f2015&siteid=cbpr&sc_cmp1=cb_pr893_&id=pr893&ed=12%2f31%2f2015

interested in gaining a sense of how a candidate may fit within organizational environment or culture, or anticipate a potential collision with corporate standards.

Some questions that are restricted from human resource inquiry are easily discernable by reviewing a candidate's social media account. For example, questions revolving marital or relationship status and religious affiliation are often openly revealed in social media sites through personal accounts.

Studies also indicate that after researching the candidate online, the percentage of employers who do not go on to hire the applicant has significantly increased. In light of this realization, while seemingly a contradiction, over thirty-three percent of employers admit they do not hire candidates who have no social media presence.

According to the 2015 Harris Poll survey[3], employers screen out candidates after they review the candidates' social networks simply due to their dissatisfaction with the colorization of the posts themselves. For example, those employers contacted indicated they had passed on candidates for one or more of the following reasons:

- shared inappropriate photographs or information (46%)
- posted photos of themselves drinking or using drugs (41%)
- posted negative comments about their previous employer or coworkers (36%)
- demonstrated poor communication skills (32%)
- posted discriminatory comments related to race, religion, gender, etc. (28%)

Conversely, proper use of social media can be beneficial in the hiring processes. When a candidate displays proper and/or professionally attractive messages, the candidate may increase their employment desirability. Based on the study, some of the identified positive messages included one or more of the following considerations:

- The applicant's personality fits with the company culture (46%).
- Background information supported their professional qualifications for the job (45%).
- The candidate showed a professional image (43%).
- The candidate is well-rounded (40%).
- The candidate demonstrated great communication skills (40%).

Friends

Another point to consider are posts from family and friends that may also appear on a candidate's site. Their communications, through words or images, can directly translate or reflect a negative association to the candidate. More often than not, this reality is not always considered and supports the strategy of selecting one's friends and followers carefully.

Final Thought Regarding Social Media

The way in which they manage their online persona can speak volumes about current or potential employees. Accept the fact that employers are, in increasing numbers, seeking to use social media to gain information before or after they hire someone.

---

3   http://www.careerbuilder.com/share/aboutus/pressreleasesdetail.aspx?sd=5%2F14%2F2015&id=pr893&ed=12%2F31%2F2015

It is almost a relative certainty that each person has an online presence, and that presence can easily be found by simply typing a name into Google and reviewing the results. The question that could be asked is, "Would an employer hire that person?" If the answer is not an immediate "Yes," then perhaps consider editing.

And always, be deliberate and consider what you are posting!

Chapter Questions and Writing Scenario

Chapter Questions

1. Under which circumstances can an investigative report writer anticipate that other written correspondence will be necessary?
2. Explain the specific purpose and target reader for each of the following types of correspondence: (a) business letter; (b) memorandum; (c) email; (d) performance evaluation.
3. Why is it a necessary and critical function for the writer to proofread any written correspondence before sending it?
4. Explain the types of risks one takes when they actively post and participate in social media.
5. Do you agree with employers' routine practice of considering a candidate's use of social media in hiring practices? Explain why or why not.

Writing Scenario 12

Construct an employment application cover letter that contains the following information.

You are interested in a posted and open law enforcement position at Blue Lakes Police Department.

You have completed the application and required initial background history information and wish to attach those documents with the cover letter. Be sure to mention your interest in the position.

The letter is to be addressed to Captain Robert Eugene, Blue Lakes Police Department, located at 2345 Soft Water Drive, Blue Lakes, California 98764. It is to mostly fill one page, be written in the standard business letter format, and have both your signature and contact information.

Image Credits

Five Tips for Writing an Effective Email[4]

To get your email read, you need to first get it noticed. Using these tips will help you grab the attention of the receiver and keep them engaged so that he or she will read the entire contents of the email.

1. Identify the purpose of the email: It is very important for you to identify the purpose of the email prior to writing it, and then to make that purpose clear in the subject and beginning of your email. All too often people simply click on the compose button and start typing without taking the time to actually consider in full why they are contacting a person and what they want to say. Knowing the purpose of your email is important because if you, as the sender of the email, haven't identified why you are contacting someone, then the receiver will likely be just as unsure about the point.

4 "Five Tips to Writing an Effective Email," http://grammar.yourdictionary.com/grammar-rules-and-tips/five-tips-to-writing-an-effective-email.html. Copyright © by LoveToKnow Corporation. Reprinted with permission.

2. Use the subject line wisely: The subject line is one of the most important parts of an email. In many cases it will determine whether or not the receiver will even open the email. Take the time to select a meaningful, straightforward subject line that succinctly identifies the reason for the email.

3. Make sure you are identifiable: There are many cases where emails are ignored or bypassed because the receiver isn't familiar with the sender of the email. Take the time to make sure that your full name is placed as the sender so that the receiver will know who you are. Avoid using initials or nicknames, as many people tend to ignore emails that are not sent with whole names that they recognize.

4. Get to the point: Make sure your emails are concise. People want to know what the email is about as soon as they open it. After a brief greeting followed by a comma, make sure the next few lines are related specifically to the subject of the email. If this is a reply to another email, reply immediately to any questions posed in the original email. When composing the email, do not use unnecessary words. Short sentences and paragraphs are better than long ones. Use an active voice, such as "We are sending your order today," instead of, "Your order will be sent by us today."

5. Make sure your email is readable: There is nothing more annoying than an email that cannot be read for various reasons. Whether it's because of poor grammar or spelling, or the use of inappropriate fonts and abbreviations, or even worse, an email written in bright colors or all capital letters, it is always best to use the proper format when sending an email. Proofread your email before sending it, and keep the formatting simple. Put a blank line between paragraphs. Remember: An email is a form of communication; it is not a piece of artwork.

A-1

Investigative Report Format

INVESTIGATIVE REPORT FORMAT

ORIGIN:

....

....

....

....

INVESTIGATION:

....

....

....

....

STATEMENTS:

....

....

....

....

INJURIES:

....

....

....

....

PROPERTY DAMAGE:

....

....

....

....

FOLLOW UP:

....

....

....

....

PROPERTY TAG: C6507017	**CHULA VISTA POLICE DEPARTMENT LABORATORY REPORT**	CASE NUMBER: **10-0509030**
CODE SECTION: **11-44**	CRIME: **Coroner's Case**	DATE OF OCCURRENCE: **04/19/10**
VICTIM: **Smith, Ernest J.**	LOCATION: **513 Plum Streets**	
REQUESTED BY: **Agent S. White #625**	DATE OF REQUEST: **04/09/10**	

CRIME LABORATORY NOTIFICATION:

On 04/09/10, at approximately 1041 hours, Chula Vista Police Department Crimes of Violence Agent S. White (ID #625), notified me that the Crime Laboratory's assistance was requested to process the scene of coroner's case at 513 Plum Street, in Chula Vista. I first proceeded to the Chula Vista Police Department arriving at approximately 1030 hours, Chula Vista Police Department Crime Laboratory Volunteer C. Steele (ID #V99) and I proceeded to 513 Plum Street, arriving at approximately 1122 hours. Upon arrival, we met with Agent S. White (ID #625) who briefed me on the sequence of events.

DOCUMENTATION & EVIDENCE COLLECTION RESPONSIBILITIES:

Forensic Specialist B. Vance (#1044)
Photographs of Crime Scene
Evidence Collection
Sketch of Crime Scene

CRIME SCENE PROCESSING:

On 04-09-10, at approximately 1132 hours I started photographing the exterior and interior of 513 Sequoia Street. The photographs were completed at approximately 1354 hours. The photographs were uploaded to the Chula Vista Police Department secure digital imaging management system. A copy of the photographs were burned onto one (1) photo disc **(Item #25)** and submitted to the Chula Vista Police Department Evidence Control Unit on 04/13/10.

On 04/09/10, starting at approximately 1225 hours, a non-scaled sketch was prepared showing the living, dining and kitchen areas of 513 Plum Street, Chula Vista. The sketches were completed at approximately 1240 hours. A final computer generated version of the sketch will be completed upon request.

On 04/09/10, at approximately 1242 hours, a presumptive test for blood was performed on a dried brown stain located on a wooden ramp leading from the family room to the garage. The test was negative for the presence of blood. At approximately 1241 hours, a presumptive test for blood was performed on a dried brown stain on the garage floor. The test was negative for the presence of blood.

On 04/09/10, starting at approximately 1248 hours, **nineteen (19)** items of evidence were collected from 513 Plum Street. The evidence collection was completed at approximately 1355 hours. The following table lists the item number, item description, location collected and time collected.

Item #	Description	Location Collected	Time Collected
1	Trash Can	Kitchen	1331 hrs
2	Swab Set	Kitchen Floor	1248 hrs
3	Swab Sets	Kitchen Floor	1251 &1252 hrs
3	Paper Shredder	Family Room	1317 hrs
5	Swab Sets	Family Room North Wall	1257 & 1258 hrs
6	Swab Sets	Kitchen Floor	1259 & 1300 hrs
7	Swab Sets	Hutch in Kitchen	1355 & 1356 hrs
8	Swab Sets	Living Room Carpet	1304 & 1305 hrs
9	Swab Sets	Living Room Carpet	1307 & 1307 hrs
10	Swab Sets	Living Room Carpet	1309 & 1310 hrs
11	Swab Sets	Living Room Carpet	1312 & 1313 hrs
12	Swab Sets	Living Room Carpet	1313 & 1314 hrs
13	Swab Sets	Cabinet in Living Room	1316 & 1317 hrs
14	Wallet	Dinning Area Table	1325 hrs
15	Wallet	Dining Area Table	1326 hrs
16	Adress Book	Dining Area Table	1326 hrs
17	Envelope	On Kitchen Wall Above Phone	1326 hrs
18	Miscellaneous Papers	Dining Area Table	1326 hrs

WITNESS PROCESSING:

On 04/09/10, starting at approximately 1400 hours, **one (1)** item of evidence was collected from **Maria Smith (04/16/1931)**. Officer A. Jones (ID #658) was present during the processing of **Johnson.** The processing of **Smith** occurred at 513 Plum Street. The evidence collection was completed at approximately 1400 hours. The following table lists the item number, item description and time collected.

Item #	Description	Time Collected
19	Reference mouth swab from **N. Smith**	1400 hrs

EVIDENCE DISPOSITION:

The above listed recovered items of evidence **(Items #1–20)** were sealed in separate packaging and submitted to the Chula Vista Police Department Evidence Control Unit on 04/13/10 and will be retained until final disposition of this case.

CRIME SCENE SECURED:

On 04/09/11, at approximately 1405 hours, I notified Agent S. White (ID #625) that I had completed processing 513 Plum Street. Chula Vista Police Department Crime Laboratory Volunteer C. Steele (ID #V99) and I proceeded to the Chula Vista Police Department arriving at approximately 1400 hours. On 04/09/10, at approximately 1430 hours, recovered items of evidence **(Items #1–#19)** were secured in the Chula Vista Police Department Crime Laboratory Exam Room #2.

AUTOPSY:

On 04/12/10, I proceeded to 5570 Overland Drive, San Diego, (San Diego County Medical Examiner's Office), arriving at approximately 0920 hours.

At approximately 0926 hours, I started photographing the autopsy of **Ernest Joseph Smith (03/27/1925).** The autopsy photographs were completed at approximately 1150 hours. Agent J. Green (ID #651) was present during the autopsy of **SMITH.** The photographs were uploaded onto the Chula Vista Police Department secure digital management system, recorded onto a photo disc **(Item #25)** and submitted to the Chula Vista Police Department Evidence Control Unit on 03/13/10.

On 04/12/10, starting at approximately 0955 hours, **five (5)** items of evidence were collected from the victim, **Smith.** The evidence collection was completed at approximately 1202 hours. The following table lists the item number, item description, location collected and time collected.

Item #	Description	Location Collected	Time Collected
20	Reference mouth swabs	From **Ernest J. Smith**	1013 hrs
21	Left hand nail scrapings	From **Ernest J. Smith**	1018 hrs
22	Right hand nail scrapings	From **Ernest J. Smith**	1014 hrs
23	Vial of blood	Received from medical examiner	1202 hrs

<u>EVIDENCE DISPOSITION:</u>

The above listed recovered items of evidence **(Items #20–24)** were sealed in separate evidence packaging and submitted to the Chula Vista Police Department Evidence Control Unit on 04/13/10. The evidence will be retained until final disposition of the case.

On 04/12/10 at approximately 1212 hours, I notified Agent J. Green (ID #651) that I had completed processing the victim, **Ernest J. Smith (06/27/1925)** at the autopsy. I proceeded to the Chula Vista Police Department, arriving at approximately 1240 hours. The recovered items of evidence **(Items #20–23)** were secured in the crime laboratory exam room #2, at approximately 1245 hours.

END OF REPORT.

Tara B. Vance #1044:	**Date**
Technical Review:	**Date**
Administrative Review:	**Date**

AGENCY	CAD INCIDENT NUMBER		MISCELLANEOUS INCIDENT ONLY	AGENCY CASE NUMBER		
	L123			11-123456		

RELATED CASE NUMBER (KEY CASE)		MISCELLANEOUS INCIDENT ONLY	FROM DAY	DATE	TIME
NONE		☐	SATURDAY	5/26/2011	1836

CODE SECTION AND DESCRIPTION (ONE INCIDENT ONLY) OR TYPE OF MISCELLANEOUS INCIDENT	THROUGH DAY	DATE	TIME
243(e)(1) PC - Domestic Battery	SATURDAY	5/26/2011	1905

LOCATION OF INCIDENT	CITY	BEAT	DISTRICT
222 Tree Street #E	Your City	11	

REPORTING OFFICER	ID NUMBER	DIVISION	DATE OF REPORT	TIME
Adams, John	112	PATROL	5/26/2011	1910

PRIMARY VICTIM'S NAME	PRIMARY SUSPECT'S NAME	SUSPECT'S DOB	AGE RNG
Smith, Larry	Jones, Shirley		55

SYNOPSIS:

Suspect and victim have been in a dating relationship for approximately six months, and cohabitating for a majority of that time. During an argument, the suspect sat on top of the victim, and struck him several times in the head. As the victim fled the residence, the suspect tackled him and took away his cell phone as he attempted to call police for help. The suspect was arrested, and the victim desires prosecution.

EVIDENCE:

None

NARRATIVE:

On 05-26-11 at approximately 1836 hours, I was dispatched to 222 Tree Street #E, reference a report of domestic violence. At the scene, I was greeted by the victim, later identified by his California driver's license as Larry Smith, who was locked out of his residence. I asked him who locked him out of his residence. Smith told me his live in girlfriend, later identified by previous booking photographs as Shirley Jones, had locked him out of his residence. He also told me Jones had punched him in the face with closed fists several times. I did not see any visible injuries on Smith. I made several attempts to get Smith to answer the door, but she never responded. Smith gave me consent to force entry into his apartment. I was able to pull the security door open without damaging in. Again, I knocked on the apartment door, and told Jones to open the door. As I was about to force entry past the second door, Jones opened the apartment door. I detained Jones.

Jones appeared to be under the influence of alcohol. She had slurred speech, an unsteady gate, and the odor associated with an alcoholic beverage on her exhaled breath. I informed Smith of why she was being detained, and the allegations of battery being made by her boyfriend. Jones did not deny the allegations, but became very agitated and screamed at Smith, "Is this what you want, you fucker?" Jones also made

REPORTING OFFICER	ID#	DIVISION	REVIEWED BY	DATE REVIEWED	TIME REVIEWED
Adams, John	112	PATROL			

CODE SECTION:	243(e)(1) PC - Domestic Battery	CASE NUMBER:	**11-123456**
		REPORT DATE:	5/26/2011

several claims Smith, a convicted ex-felon, had a pistol under the carpet in his apartment. I allowed Jones to show me where the pistol was supposed to be hidden. I did not find the pistol, or any such hiding place. I had Smith sign the arrest form, and based on his statements, I arrested Jones. I had Officer Lincoln (1113) transport Jones back to the PD, while I took a more detailed statement from Smith.

Smith told me he was in his apartment with Jones and she was "drunk". According to Smith, Jones becomes violent when she is drunk. He asked her to lie down on the couch, and Jones said, "you bitch, you asshole, what are you going to do?" Smith explained to me he has many physical disabilities, and Jones knows he cannot defend himself. When Smith sat down in the chair, Jones jumped on top of him, straddling him. It was at this time, Jones hit Smith in the face and head approximately five times. I asked Smith on a scale of 1 to 10, how hard did Jones strike him? He answered "10". Eventually Jones got off of Smith and he took the opportunity to flee the residence. According to Smith, Jones tackled him outside the residence, and took his cell phone from him. I asked Smith what he was planning to do with the phone? He told me he was going to dial 911 for help. Jones was able to use a neighbor's telephone to call police. I provided Smith with the required domestic violence information. He declined an immediate response by DVRT, but requested a later contact.

At the PD, I read Jones her Miranda warning from my department issued notebook. She answered "Yes" to understanding her rights as I had read them to her. In response to wishing to make a statement to me about her being arrested, Jones only said, "It's a lie". She made no further statements, and I did not question her further. I later transported Smith to County Jail.

END OF REPORT.

REPORTING OFFICER	ID#	DIVISION	REVIEWED BY	DATE REVIEWED	TIME REVIEWED
Adams, John	112	PATROL			

AGENCY	CAD INCIDENT NUMBER		AGENCY CASE NUMBER		
	L002	MISCELLANEOUS INCIDENT ONLY	**11-123457**		
RELATED CASE NUMBER (KEY CASE)			FROM DAY	DATE	TIME
NONE		☐	SUNDAY	1/2/2011	2353
CODE SECTION AND DESCRIPTION (ONE INCIDENT ONLY) OR TYPE OF MISCELLANEOUS INCIDENT			THROUGH DAY	DATE	TIME
23152(b) VC D.U.I					
LOCATION OF INCIDENT			CITY	BEAT	DISTRICT
Mesa Lakes Road and Rogers Ave			Your City	11	
REPORTING OFFICER	ID NUMBER	DIVISION		DATE OF REPORT	TIME
Dean Martin	502	PATROL		1/3/2011	0110
PRIMARY VICTIM'S NAME		PRIMARY SUSPECT'S NAME		SUSPECT'S DOB	AGE RNG
State of California		Sandwich, Ruben		10/24/1984	27

NARRATIVE:

On 01/02/11 at approximately 2328 hours, I was in the #2 left hand turn lane southbound on Mesa Lakes Road at Telephone Canyon Road at a red light. Directly in front of me was a silver Nissan 350Z CA plate's 1ABC234. When the light turned green the vehicle chirped its tires and turned eastbound onto Mesa Lakes Road. The vehicle turned wide going into the bike lane and chirped its tires a second time as it turned. The vehicle quickly accelerated up to 60 mph. I activated my overhead lights and conducted a traffic stop on the vehicle at Mesa Lakes Road and Rogers Avenue. Officer Fiddle #108 was behind as I conducted the traffic stop.

I contacted the driver and asked for his driver's license, insurance and registration. He handed me his California driver's license identifying him as Ruben Sandwich. While talking with Sandwich, I noticed his eyes were red watery and bloodshot, he had a strong odor of an alcoholic beverage emitting from his person and he had slurred speech. Sandwich said he had 1–2 beers at his friend's house.

I had Sandwich step out of the vehicle. I questioned Sandwich about his drinking, eating and sleeping. Other questions I asked of Sandwich included any medical history and physical problems. For his complete answers refer to the attached supplemental.

I told Sandwich I was about to conduct voluntary Field Sobriety Tests on him. Part of the test was to listen to the directions completely before doing the test. Once given, I gave Sandwich the opportunity to ask any questions about the test. Once Sandwich said he understood, I asked him to do the test. The HGN and one-leg stand tests were performed on the sidewalk, which appeared to be flat, level and smooth. The walk and turn test was performed on the paved street which appeared to be flat, level and smooth. The following is an overview of Sandwich's Field Sobriety Test:

Gaze Nystagmus: Using the tip of my pen about twelve to fourteen inches away from Sandwich's face, I had him track my pen without moving his head. Sandwich was unable to smoothly follow my movement,

REPORTING OFFICER	ID#	DIVISION	REVIEWED BY	DATE REVIEWED	TIME REVIEWED
Dean Martin	502	PATROL			

CODE SECTION:	23152(b) VC D.U.I		CASE NUMBER:	**11-123457**
			REPORT DATE:	1/3/2011

and he displayed distinct Nystagmus at the extremes and prior to 45 degrees. Sandwich was swaying from side to side and front to back approximately 3–4 inches during the test. I had to remind him to keep his head still during the test.

One Let Stand Test: Sandwich lifted his right leg during the test. He swayed while balancing, used his arms to balance and he did not look at his foot while counting.

Walk and Turn Test: Sandwich was instructed to put his left foot on a straight roadway line and put his right foot in front of his left heel to toe, this was the start position. Sandwich fell out of the start position four times and I had to remind him to stay in the start position. During the test he missed heel/toe three times, stepped off the line three times and stopped walking once but then continued. He miss counted his steps going back down the line and walked ten steps instead of nine.

Preliminary Alcohol Screen Test (PAS): I explained to Sandwich that the PAS was voluntary and he did not have to take it. Sandwich blew into the PAS with results of .179 and .172 BAC.

Before I gave Sandwich the PAS test I told him I knew he had more than two beers and asked him how many beers he really had. He said he had four beers.

Based on Sandwich's answers and test performance I placed Sandwich under arrest for DUI at approximately 2353 hours.

I advised Sandwich of the Implied Consent Law, and placed him in the back of my patrol unit. I drove him to the PD for further processing. Sandwich's vehicle was impounded by Dixons Towing.

At PD, Sandwich blew into the Intox machine at 0021 and 022 hours with both results being .16 BAC. Sandwich was later released on his written promise to appear in court.

END OF REPORT.

REPORTING OFFICER	ID#	DIVISION	REVIEWED BY	DATE REVIEWED	TIME REVIEWED
Dean Martin	502	PATROL			

AGENCY	CAD INCIDENT NUMBER			AGENCY CASE NUMBER **11-123457**		

RELATED CASE NUMBER (KEY CASE)	OFFICER'S REPORT ONLY ☐	FROM DAY SATURDAY	DATE 5/26/2011	TIME 2139

CODE SECTION AND DESCRIPTION (ONE INCIDENT ONLY) 594(b)(1) PC Vandalism more than $400.00	THROUGH DAY SATURDAY	DATE 5/26/2011	TIME 2315

LOCATION OF INCIDENT 222 Boston Boulevard	CITY	BEAT 13	DISTRICT

REPORTING OFFICER Jefferson	ID NUMBER 234	DIVISION PAT/T1	DATE OF REPORT 5/27/2011	TIME 0135

PRIMARY VICTIM'S NAME Boston Apartments	PRIMARY SUSPECT'S NAME Arnold, Benedict	SUSPECT'S DOB	AGE RNG 24

SYNOPSIS:

A known suspect used blue paint to graffiti property at the apartment courtyard, and various vehicles parked on the street adjacent to the apartment property. The suspect was unable to be located. The cost of the damage is approximately $500.00.

EVIDENCE:

Item #	Description	Location Found	Found by	Tag # or Disposition
1	@6 oz. Bottle of blue paint	Grass in front of complex.	Off. Delmont	C#12345
2	4 photographs of vandalism	Various locations	Off. Delmont	C#12455

NARRATIVE

On 05/26/11 at approximately 2315 hours, I responded to the above address for a call of vandalism. When I arrived I immediately noticed a green Ford SUV with blue graffiti spread over the roof, hood and windshield areas of the vehicle. I also saw a white glass bottle with blue paint lying in the grass area in front of the apartment complex, near the Ford SUV.

The reporting party/manager of the complex identified herself with her CDL as being Roxanne Redlight and was waiting to speak with me near the Ford SUV. Redlight told me that she was informed by one of the tenants, Lawrence Turnsignal, that somebody had "tagged some of the cars" on the street. She said when she came out of her apartment, she noticed several areas in the complex courtyard that had had been vandalized with blue paint. She then walked from the courtyard to the street to find the Ford covered in 'dumped' blue paint.

Redlight contacted the owner of the Ford SUV (apt #74) as well as the complex owner. The owner asked her to call the police and file a criminal report. Redlight explained this wasn't the first time this sort of incident had occurred. Because of the similar vandalism incidents and the methods used, including the

REPORTING OFFICER Jefferson	ID# 234	DIVISION PAT/T1	REVIEWED BY	DATE REVIEWED	TIME REVIEWED

| CODE SECTION: | 594(b)(1) PC Vandalism more than $400.00 | CASE NUMBER: | **11-123457** |
| | | REPORT DATE: | 5/27/2011 |

color of the paint, Redlight suggested that I speak with the tenants of apartment number 187. Redlight was confident the residents that lived there might know the suspect.

Redlight explained that when she completed her last night security 'rounds' through the complex, she noticed a grey Honda sedan parked along the west curb line. She explained the Honda was parked 'immediately beside' where the bottle of paint was discovered. She told me the Honda had been vandalized with the same 'exact' color of paint a few months ago, and that the vehicle owner had sought criminal prosecution of the suspect in that case. Redlight thought although the car was not parked here currently, the Honda may again had been vandalized in tonight's incident.

I made contact at apartment 187 and, with the assistance of Officer Yellowlight, a qualified Spanish language translator, spoke with Paris Cancun, the owner of the Honda. Cancun said the suspect was her ex-boyfriend, Berlin Acapulco (DOB 01/02/1988). He came to her residence tonight to 'argue' over money he feels she owes him. She followed him out of the apartment and into the courtyard. As he left the property, she witnessed him "write" on the vehicles and the courtyard. Cancun said that he had done this before and, "It's not a big deal since he didn't write anything bad."

I asked Cancun for contact information for Acapulco. She provided a cell phone number but didn't know his address, or any other way for me to contact him other than his cell phone. She told me she thought he lived somewhere in Chula Vista near 'L' Street but was not able to provide specific information. She said he does not own a vehicle, and gets around by borrowing other people's cars.

I asked Cancun what type of vehicle she owned and she said "None." I asked if a grey Honda sedan was connected in any way with her or the people connected with her apartment. She seemed reluctant when she responded "No, I don't know anything about a grey Honda." and denied that any such vehicle has been ever connected to her or her apartment.

I made routine records checks of data systems to determine if Acapulco had a vehicle registered in his name, which revealed no such records.

After speaking with Cancun, I made contact with the owner of the Ford SUV. She did not want to press charges and would not provide her contact information for the report. She explained she had just moved into the complex, and did not want any problems; "maybe if you find him he could just wash my car and hopefully the paint will wash off."

While I was conducting the investigation, Agent Delmont arrived and documented the damage with 4 digitial photographs that were later logged into Property. Additionally, Agt. Delmont collected the blue paint and also submitted it into Property under the corresponding Tag number.

END OF REPORT.

REPORTING OFFICER	ID#	DIVISION	REVIEWED BY	DATE REVIEWED	TIME REVIEWED
Jefferson	234	PAT/T1			

AGENCY	CAD INCIDENT NUMBER			AGENCY CASE NUMBER		

RELATED CASE NUMBER (KEY CASE)	MISCELLANEOUS INCIDENT ONLY	FROM DAY SUNDAY	DATE 1/17/2011	TIME

CODE SECTION AND DESCRIPTION (ONE INCIDENT ONLY) OR TYPE OF MISCELLANEOUS INCIDENT	THROUGH DAY	DATE	TIME
422 PC Criminal Threats	SUNDAY	1/17/2011	

LOCATION OF INCIDENT	CITY	BEAT	DISTRICT
444 Lux Luther Haven			

REPORTING OFFICER	ID NUMBER	DIVISION	DATE OF REPORT	TIME
Waxfetler	234	INV.	1/19/2011	1025

PRIMARY VICTIM'S NAME	PRIMARY SUSPECT'S NAME	SUSPECT'S DOB	AGE RNG
Blanco, Pony	Skunk, Anthony	2/2/1988	

I provided Redlight with the criminal case reference number and asked how much she thought the damage would cost to repair. She said she was not certain, but estimated "It will be at least $500.00 to clean the paint out of the stucco walls."

After I cleared the scene, I called Acapulco in an attempt to gain his statement but found that his phone was apparently shut off. I did not leave a message for his return call.

This in an investigative follow up report to original crime reports dated 1/17/2011.

Suspect not in custody: Anthony Anody SKUNK (DOB 02/02/1989)

ONE:

Victim Blanca has a valid & served TRO against the Suspect SKUNK.

The suspect and victim went to lunch with each other. During lunch, the victim went to her car to look in a bag the suspect had been carrying. She found a handgun inside the bag. The victim confronted the suspect about the gun. He threatened her, verbally.

TWO:

Evidence collected by me and logged into CVPD property on 04/15/11, under tag # C123456.

1-   Micro cassette tape of my phone conversation with Blanco 01/18/11.

2-   Micro cassette tape of my phone conversation with Blanco 01/18/11.

REPORTING OFFICER	ID#	DIVISION	REVIEWED BY	DATE REVIEWED	TIME REVIEWED
Waxfetler	234	INV.			

NARRATIVE

CODE SECTION:	422 PC Criminal Threats	CASE NUMBER:	
		REPORT DATE:	1/19/2011

THREE:

On 01/17/11 at approximately 08:00, I checked my voicemail and heard a message left from Blanco after I missed her original telephone call. I am familiar with Blanco because I spoke to her, last week, regarding a prior investigation which was documented in an original crime report dated 01/13/11, case # 11-01234567.

In that investigation, she reported her ex-boyfriend, Anthony Skunk, verbally threatened her and vandalized her vehicle. After investigating that matter, Blanco said there wasn't damage to her vehicle and she wasn't concerned about what he said to her during that incident. She didn't want to prosecute or pursue the matter in court because she and Anthony were again getting along well. She didn't want to have anything disrupt their relationship because they have children together.

I returned Blanco's call. I recorded our conversation and later logged the micro cassette #1 into evidence under tag # C123456. The following is a synopsis of her statement. For exact details, refer to a soon to be transcribed written account of the actual tape itself. (Additionally, I spoke to Blanco in a least two other phone conversations that were not recorded. Those statements are included in this report as well.)

Blanco said she say Skunk on Saturday 01/17/11. She and their children picked Skunk up from his friend's house, located on the southeast corner of Ketchup Avenue and Mustard Street, in Chula Vista. (She believes the actual address is 234 Ketchup Avenue.) Blanco said Skunk has been staying with his friend Lawrence Raccoon at that residence.

Their plan was to go to Skunk's father's house so their children could open the Christmas gifts their paternal grandfather had for them. They didn't go there though, because the grandfather cancelled the visit. Instead, they decided to go to the Chili's restaurant (Eastlake location) to have lunch. I asked Blanco if she remembered who the server was at the restaurant so I could contact to obtain his/her statement. She didn't remember who served them and never had possession of the meal receipt.

When Skunk got into Blanco's vehicle, he was carrying a black "Raiders" bag, which was about the size of a medium purse. He kept it with him in the front seat. When they got out of the car at the restaurant, he put the bag in the trunk of her vehicle. The way he seemed to keep the bag near him, and the way he was keeping an eye on it, piqued Blanco's interest.

During lunch, she excused herself, saying she had to get something out of the car for one of the children. She went to the vehicle, opened the bag and looked inside. She saw the bag contained various papers, CD's, some cologne, and a handgun, which she thought was a revolver. She saw the gun but didn't touch it.

I asked her if she could describe the gun. She thought the top was a silver colored metal, and the grip was dark brown in color. She doesn't know much about guns and didn't touch this one to examine it further.

REPORTING OFFICER	ID#	DIVISION	REVIEWED BY	DATE REVIEWED	TIME REVIEWED
Waxfetler	234	INV.			

CODE SECTION:	422 PC Criminal Threats	CASE NUMBER:
		REPORT DATE: **1/19/2011**

She went back into the restaurant and asked Skunk about the gun. He was very angry with her because she had no permission and shouldn't have gone through his bag.

Skunk told Blanco he had the gun for 'protection'. I asked Blanco what she thought he was referring to by saying that. She had no specific explanation, offering that he is a LOCOS DUCK gang member, so she assumes he's carrying the gun to protect himself from other gang members.

Skunk told her that if she said anything to anyone about the gun, "She'd be considered a rat and that would put her and her family's lives in danger." I asked her what she felt he meant by that statement. She felt it was a threat.

Blanco told me she definitely felt it was a threat. I asked her if she felt he was capable of following through with the threat. She didn't know if he would, personally, hurt her or her family, but she was afraid he would have one of his friends hurt her or her family if he knew she went to the police about the gun.

I asked her what happened after she asked Skunk about the gun. She said the, pretty much, ended their lunch and she took him back to the Raccoon residence. Blanco said she hasn't talked to Skunk since then.

Later, I made arrangements for Blanco to come to CVPD, after she got off work so I could interview her in person and video tape the interview.

From my prior contacts with Blanco, she told me she and Skunk dated and lived together for two years. They ended their relationship in February 2010 when Blanco discovered that Skunk was taking her jewelry and pawning it.

She describe two prior incidents of domestic violence (10-045678 and 10-167890), which were minor in nature. I researched those cases and discovered Skunk was arrested in both incidents, but the DA's Office rejected prosecution in those cases.

I used the computer system to verify the status of the TRO (#98765). The records check indicated it is a valid TRO. It was served on 11/26/10 and expires on 11/26/14.

On 01/18/11 at approximately 0900, I contacted Detective D. Whitewall assigned to CVPD's Gang Unit to advise him of the suspect, the incident and the possession of the firearm. He said he would look into it and make the appropriate officer safety notices.

On 01/18/11 at approximately 1030, I contacted Alcie, a case worker assigned to DVRT. I asked her to contact Blanco to offer support services to her. I spoke with Alcie about an hour later. She said she phoned Blanco at work, and Blanco told Alcie that she couldn't talk during work hours and agreed to call Alcie back, later on.

REPORTING OFFICER	ID#	DIVISION	REVIEWED BY	DATE REVIEWED	TIME REVIEWED
Waxfetler	234	INV.			

NARRATIVE

CODE SECTION:	422 PC Criminal Threats	CASE NUMBER:	
		REPORT DATE:	1/19/2011

On 01/18/11, at about 1600, Blanco called me. I recorded the conversation and logged the micro cassette tape into evidence as item #2.

Blanco said she was afraid and refused to come to the station to talk to me. She said, if this situation ever goes to court, she doesn't want Skunk to know she talked to or cooperated with the police.

I asked her if she felt what Skunk said to her was a warning or a threat. She felt it was both. She feels her life would be in danger if he knew she told the police, but if he didn't know she told the police, she didn't' have to worry about being hurt. Right now, with her assumption that he doesn't know she went to the police, she doesn't feel her life is in danger. If he was arrested, or he otherwise found out she went to the police, she feels strongly her life would be in danger.

I asked her what his demeanor was when he said it to her. She said he was angry. He was angry that she went through his belongings. He talked to her in a normal tone of voice. He didn't want to make a scene at the restaurant. As he talked to her, he leaned forward, but the table was between the, so he "didn't get in my face." He tone of voice was angry and his facial expressions were that of being angry.

I asked her what his demeanor was when she dropped him off at his friend's house. She said he had calmed down. They hadn't spoken since.

I asked her if they argued in the restaurant. She said they didn't. He voiced his anger that she went through his belongings, but she didn't say anything back to him.

Their children were present when this occurred, but they are only one and two years old, so they didn't understand what was going on. Because of their young age I didn't interview them.Additionally, I spoke to Blanco during another phone call to clarify some issues. She verified she didn't know if the gun was loaded or not. She did not touch it or inspect it. She believed it was a real gun.

Skunk did not, and has never threatened her with a gun or threatened to use a gun against her. Blanco is concerned about the threat because she knows the TRO directly denies Skunk's ability to possess a firearm.

As far as she knows, there were no other witnesses to Skunk possessing the handgun. She didn't tell anyone about what happened until 01/21/11, when she told her parents. She didn't tell them sooner because she knew they would be upset that she met up with Skunk and spent time with him.

I advised Blanco that the TRO was in place to prohibit Skunk form being around her. She said she understood that purpose and would not have any further contact with him.

END OF REPORT.

REPORTING OFFICER	ID#	DIVISION	REVIEWED BY	DATE REVIEWED	TIME REVIEWED
Waxfetler	234	INV.			

AGENCY	CAD INCIDENT NUMBER			AGENCY CASE NUMBER **11-123457**		
RELATED CASE NUMBER (KEY CASE)		OFFICER'S REPORT ONLY ☐		FROM DAY SATURDAY	DATE 6/10/2011	TIME 1924
CODE SECTION AND DESCRIPTION (ONE INCIDENT ONLY) 11377 (a) H&S Possession of a Controlled Substance				THROUGH DAY SATURDAY	DATE 6/10/2011	TIME
LOCATION OF INCIDENT 1927 Agua Caliente			CITY		BEAT 23	DISTRICT
REPORTING OFFICER F. Corsair	ID NUMBER 234	DIVISION PAT/T1		DATE OF REPORT 6/10/2011		TIME 2354
PRIMARY VICTIM'S NAME State of California		PRIMARY SUSPECT'S NAME Gong, Ding Dong		SUSPECT'S DOB 2/2/1961		AGE RNG

Additional Charges: 11350- H&S Possession of Narcotics
11364- H&S Possession of Narcotics Paraphernalia
3056 PC- Parole Violation

SYNOPSIS:

Known suspect currently on parole was consensually contacted. Upon consensual Fourth Waiver search, suspect was found to be in possession of a controlled substance, a narcotic substance and narcotics paraphernalia. The suspect was also found to have violated conditions of his parole when in possession of these illegal items. The suspect was arrested, processed and a parole hold issued.

EVIDENCE:

The following list of evidence was discovered by Officer Corsair (ID# 234). All items were subsequently weighted, tested and logged into Evidence by Officer Delmont (#345) under property tag# C12345.

Item #	Description	Location Found	Found by	Tag # or Disposition
1	Gong's paperwork from glove box	Vehicle's glove box	Off. Delmont	C#12345
2	Black plastic flashlight, with photo and female undergarment	Gong's person	Off. Delmont	C#12455
3	1 vinyl Velcro pouch	Vehicle's glove box	Off. Delmont	C#12345
4	2 glass narcotics smoking pipes	Vehicle's glove box	Off. Delmont	C#12455
5	1.8 grams of an off white powdery substance, believed to be methamphetamine.	Vehicle's glove box	Off. Delmont	C#12345
6	5 assorted non-scheduled prescription tablet	Vehicle's glove box	Off. Delmont	C#12455
7	1 Oxycontin tablet.	Vehicle's glove box	Off. Delmont	C#12345
8	1 cassette recording tape	Recorded on scene	Off. Delmont	C#12455

REPORTING OFFICER F. Corsair	ID# 234	DIVISION PAT/T1	REVIEWED BY	DATE REVIEWED	TIME REVIEWED

NARRATIVE

CODE SECTION:	11377 (a) H&S Possession of a Controlled Substance	CASE NUMBER:	**11-123457**
		REPORT DATE:	6/10/2011

NARRATIVE:

On June 10th, 2011 at approximately 1924 hours, I was driving northbound in the 1900 block of Agua Caliente when I noticed a vehicle parked directly in front of 1927 Agua Calente. The vehicle was an older green Ford pick-up truck (Ca. 7K4563). I know this address from prior narcotics related contacts, arrests and a documented history to be that of an address of high narcotics related activity. I have personally made more than 5 arrests directly in front of this address of subjects in possession of controlled substances that were either standing or in vehicles parked in front of this address.

I drove closer to the parked vehicle, I saw a male subject, later identified as Ding Dong Gong (02/02/61), who was leaning into the opened passenger side door of the vehicle, and appeared to be sorting items in or around the glove box area of the truck. I parked my marked patrol vehicle without activating overhead lights or police equipment, and exited it approximately 6 feet behind Gong's truck.

As I crossed between the front of vehicle and the rear of Gong's, I stepped up onto the sidewalk and approached Gong. As I along the side of the truck, Gong looked up and saw me and said "Hello Officer." He leaned from inside the vehicle and stood straight up outside the opened passenger door. As did so, he simultaneously quickly shut the glove box door, locked it and removed the keys.

I asked him if he had a few minutes to speak with me and he agreed. I asked Gong if he was living in the area, to which Gong replied that he didn't. He then asked me why I was interested where he lived, to which I replied that I simply had an interest. I told him I was curious as to who he was and why he might be hanging out in front of this particular address if he did not live in the area. Gong again said he did not live at the address and again wondered why I might want to talk to him. Again, I explained I was interested in the reason he was parked in front of this specific house.

As I explained to Gong the motivation for our consensual contact, I could see his hands were obviously shaking. I could see his breathing to be rapid and short, as indicated by the quick rise and fall chest movements. His lips and mouth seemed to be unusually dry, as evidenced by his continual licking of his lips with his tongue and small white accumulations in each of the corners of his mouth. I recognize these outward symptoms as being consistent with someone under the influence of a CNS stimulate, such as cocaine or methamphetamine.

I asked Gong for his identification and he produced his California Driver's License (CDL# E6789012). As he offered his ID, he volunteered that he was currently on California Parole. I asked for what violations and he said "only drugs". I then explained to Gong because he was on parole, I wanted him to sit down on the curb near the rear of the pickup truck so I could conduct a records check on him to make sure he was in compliance with the conditions of his parole.

REPORTING OFFICER	ID#	DIVISION	REVIEWED BY	DATE REVIEWED	TIME REVIEWED
F. Corsair	234	PAT/T1			

NARRATIVE

CODE SECTION:	11377 (a) H&S Possession of a Controlled Substance	CASE NUMBER:	**11-123457**
		REPORT DATE:	6/10/2011

As I explained myself to Gong, he became very confrontational and slightly aggressive. He stated he was not going to have a seat on the ground. I reminded Gong that he was on parole, he was parked and standing in front of a known narcotics related house, and I was going to insure that he was in total compliance of his parole conditions. Gong would not allow me to complete the explanation, and continued to be loud and verbally confrontational. At this point, I activated my Department issued cassette voice recorder which is fastened to my service belt. It recorded the sounds of the following exchange of events.

Based on my initial observations of Gong exhibiting symptoms consistent with under the influence of a CNS stimulant, the fact he was a self admitted parolee for previous drug violations, the fact he had no ties or explanations for being in the neighborhood, and was literally parked and standing in front of a known narcotics house, I believed I had reasonable suspicion to detain him for my safety and to insure he was not involved in any criminal activity.

At this point, I clearly stated I was not asking Gong to sit down, I was ordering him to sit down on the curb or the only other choice he had was sit in the back seat of my patrol car. Gong continued to resist my lawful order and again declined shouting "Just because I'm on parole doesn't mean I don't have rights!"

As Gong refused to comply with my lawful orders, I removed my taser from its holster and activated the power switch which lit up the laser aim light. I shined the laser aim light at Gong's chest and again instructed him to sit on the curb. This time he complied, immediately sitting down in front of me. I instructed him to place his hands behind his back because I was going to apply handcuffs. Again he complied. As I applied the handcuffs I explained that Gong was only being detained and absent of illegal contraband or a parole hold in the system, we would be parting ways in about 15 minutes.

I then holstered my taser. Gong again attempted to stand up and I pushed him back onto the ground in the sitting position. I again removed my taser, activated the power switch which again activated the laser aiming light and directed it toward his feet. I was clear yet again that he needed to sit calmly and no additional use of force would be applied. Although he initially physically complied, he continued to be confrontational and very verbal.

I requested additional cover units for my protection as Gong fell to his back, then began to roll side to side. During one of these extreme rolling movements, I saw him reach around his torso and pull a black plastic flashlight from his front pants waist band. In his extreme body movements, I saw him 'toss' the flashlight onto the roadway under the rear bed of his pickup truck. I made a visual note of where the flashlight rested as I monitored Gong's now extreme and violent body roll movements. During this time he was loudly shouting for anyone to come and help him; that the 'cop was beating him' and he had done nothing wrong.

Other units arrived to help me calm Gong down. I explained to Gong that he was still under a formal detention, and moved from the ground and onto the front fender of my vehicle.

REPORTING OFFICER	ID#	DIVISION	REVIEWED BY	DATE REVIEWED	TIME REVIEWED
F. Corsair	234	PAT/T1			

NARRATIVE

CODE SECTION:	11377 (a) H&S Possession of a Controlled Substance	CASE NUMBER:	**11-123457**
		REPORT DATE:	6/10/2011

A records check of Gong's information indicated that he was both on parole as a result of narcotics related offenses, and was a narcotics registrant.

I asked Gong if he had any illegal items on his person or within his vehicle. He stated he did not, and although of the compliance requirements, I asked Gong for permission to search both his person and his vehicle. He granted me permission to search both.

The search of Gong's person revealed no illegal contraband. As I began the search of the vehicle, I explained to Gong I needed to collect the keys to the vehicle to open the glove box I had seen him lock. Gong immediately attempted to decline his permission, and stated the vehicle did not belong to him. Whether or not the vehicle actually was owned by Gong was not relevant, as it was obviously under his 'dominion and control' as evidenced by his behaviors when I originally approached him. And because he is on parole, he voluntarily relinquished his Fourth Amendment rights as a condition of parole. He acknowledged this fact.

During the search of the vehicle, nothing of evidentiary value was discovered or collected from the passenger compartment area. I did open the locked glove box with the keys I had collected from Gong's pocket, and found the same key fit the door lock as well as the ignition lock.

Upon opening the glove box, I located a wallet. I opened the wallet to find a California Narcotics Registrant card in the name of Ding Dong Gong. I also located recent DMV vehicle receipts and registration paperwork bearing Gong's name and the truck's identifying information. Additionally, two of the DMV documents bore a signature that appears to be that of Ding Dong Gong. Based on the collection of paperwork from the wallet, It appeared that Gong was somewhere in the process of registering the pickup truck into his name.

I asked Gong if the wallet was his and he stated "No." I asked if the paperwork inside the wallet was his, and he said "No." I asked him if he could explain the incredible coincidence of the paperwork, a Narcotics Registration Card, signatures and receipts all bearing the same name as his. He did not respond to the question, instead he told me to "Go to hell."

I returned to the vehicle's glove box and found a black plastic Velcro cell phone type bag which contained 2 approximate 4 inch glass smoking pipes, with residue in the bulb portion. Both of the pipes were burned and blackened at the bulb end and coated inside the bulb end with an off white cloudy residue. Presumptative test conducted later of the residue scraped from these pipes indicated the residue to be methamphetamine.

Further search of this Velcro bag revealed two purple plastic gloves, with the finger tips of each glove removed. The balance of the glove had been tied up in a knot and served as a container for something held within the knot. I untied the first of the gloves and recovered 5 loose assorted pills, all of which were identified by the California Poison Control Center (CPCC) as prescription substance, but not controlled

REPORTING OFFICER	ID#	DIVISION	REVIEWED BY	DATE REVIEWED	TIME REVIEWED
F. Corsair	234	PAT/T1			

substance. In the other glove was a single pill, which was identified by the CPCC as Oxycontin, a Schedule II requiring a prescription to possess. No further evidentiary items were recovered from the vehicle.

I then recovered the flashlight I had earlier witnessed Gong toss under the truck. I removed the light bulb end of the device and found a picture of an undressed youthful appearing Asian female. Also contained in the device was an apparently unclean pair of female undergarments stuffed within the battery section of the flashlight. The dried 'residue' could have indicated the potential evidence of a sexual assault. This item was impounded and logged under item #3 in the event it would hold any possible relevant future significance, Detective Sergeant Dan Durable was notified at approximately 2120 hours via voice mail message of these items in the event they prove to be relevant.

Gong decided that he rather leave his truck parked and locked in front of this addressed instead of having the vehicle impounded. Gong was transported to the PD for processing.

At approximately 2030 I brought Gong to Interview room #3. Gong made a spontaneous statement that "That truck isn't mine!! And I don't know what was in Carlos' truck glove box!" I interrupted Gong to read to his Miranda rights per my PD issued card. He indicated he understood his rights and did not wish to make a statement outside of his attorney's presence. No interview was therefore conducted.

A routine records check revealed the truck to be registered to Javier Jimenez Gallager in a residence in Valley Center. The registration check also showed there was a Release of Liability to Walter Polo in Tijuana, Mexico. The paperwork within the vehicle indicated that in April of 2011, Gong had purchased the vehicle from Polo for $75 dollars and started the registration process with DMV. There were no other names listed as applying for DMV registration for the vehicle.

At the conclusion of the Booking process, Gong was transported to S.D. County Jail.

END OF REPORT.

CHULA VISTA POLICE DEPARTMENT
DECLARATION AND DETERMINATION
(PROBABLE CAUSE FOR WARRANTLESS ARREST)

ARRESTEE:		
DOB: 04/29/56	**DL/SSN/ID#:**	**BOOKING#** 09-01180
VIOLATION DESCRIPTION: 243(e)(1) PC-DV Battery		
DATE/TIME/PLACE of ARREST: 01/17/09 1905 Hrs.		
ARRESTING OFFICER / ID#:		

FACTS ESTABLISHING ELEMENTS OF CRIME AND IDENTIFICATION

On the above date and time I contacted the suspect (arrestee) for the following reason:

Officers received a radio call to _____ reference domestic violence; a male reporting his live-in girlfriend had struck him in the face.

Suspect was identified by the following: (curbside line-up, photo I.D., etc.)

Suspect was identified by previous booking photographs.

Suspect and Victim are involved in the following relationship:

☐ SPOUSE ☐ FORMER SPOUSE ☒ DATING/ENGAGED (Past or Present)

☒ COHABITANT ☐ FORMER COHABITANT ☐ CHILD in COMMON

☒ Suspect and Victim were involved in an argument/fight. During the dispute, the suspect battered the victim causing:

☐ VISIBLE INJURY   ☒ NO VISIBLE INJURY

☐ Suspect violated Restraining order #   which is valid and has been served. Protected Person is Victim.

Victim / Witness told the Officer the following:

The suspect _____ and the victim _____ are cohabitating together; they get into an argument. During the argument, _____ cross the face with an open hand approximately five times. As _____ exited the residence, _____ tackled him to the ground, and took away his cell phone as he attempted to dial 911 for help. Zaragoza used a neighbor's telephone for assistance.

Officer observed:

The victim, _____ was sitting outside of his residence upset and complaining about the strikes to his face.

Suspect later transported to COUNTY JAIL / LOS COLINAS.

☐ SEE ATTACHED REPORTS, INCORPORATED HEREIN BY REFERENCE
I DECLARE UNDER PENALTY OF PERJURY THAT THE FOREGOING IS TRUE AND CORRECT TO THE BEST OF MY INFORMATION AND BELIEF. EXECUTED ON ___1-17-09___ IN THE COUNTY OF SAN DIEGO, STATE OF CALIFORNIA. BY: _____   (SIGNATURE)   APPROVED BY:
ON THE BASIS OF _____ THE FOREGOING DECLARATION _____ AND ATTACHED REPORTS, I HEREBY DETERMINE THAT THERE: _____ IS _____ IS NOT PROBABLE CAUSE TO BELIEVE THIS ARRESTEE HAS COMMITTED A CRIME _____   _____ (DATE)   (TIME)   (MAGISTRATE'S SIGNATURE) BY _____ (FOR TELEPHONIC APPROVALS)

FORCE USED YES NO ☐ ☐	**CHULA VISTA POLICE DEPARTMENT** **USE OF FORCE REPORT**				CASE NUMBER	

CODE SECTION AND DESCRIPTION (MOST SERIOUS INCIDENT)	MONTH	DAY	YEAR	DAY OF WEEK	TIME

LOCATION OF INCIDENT	SUSPECT'S NAME (LAST, FIRST, MIDDLE)	RACE	SEX	AGE

VIDEO OR AUDIO RECORDING: YES ☐ NO ☐ DISPOSITION: ☐ LOGGED, TAG # _____ ☐ OTHER: _____	SUSPECT ARRESTED YES NO ☐ ☐ IF NO ARREST WAS MADE, EXPLAIN WHY

SUSPECT LEVELS OF RESISTANCE
(CHECK ALL THAT APPLY AND EXPLAIN)

☐	**PSYCHOLOGICAL INTIMIDATION** (PROFANE LANGUAGE, CLENCHING FIST)	
☐	**VERBAL NON-COMPLIANCE** (NON-COMPLIANCE TO OFFICER'S DIRECTION)	
☐	**PASSIVE RESISTANCE** (GOING LIMP, DEAD WEIGHT)	
☐	**DEFENSIVE RESISTANCE** (AVOIDING CONTROL, PUSHING, PULLING, RUNNING AWAY)	
☐	**ACTIVE AGGRESSION** (PHYSICAL ASSAULT ON OFFICER OR OTHERS)	
☐	**DEADLY FORCE ASSAULTS** (ASSAULTS WITH WEAPONS)	

OFFICER LEVELS OF CONTROL
(CHECK ALL THAT APPLY AND EXPLAIN)

☐	**VERBAL DIRECTION** (DESRIBE COMMANDS AND IF WEAPON POINTED AT SUSPECT)				
☐	**SOFT EMPTY-HAND TECHNIQUES** (MUSCLING, JOINT LOCKS AND PRESSURE POINTS)				
☐	**HARD EMPTY-HAND TECHNIQUES** (HAND, LEG AND FOOT STRIKES, NECK RESTRAINT)				
☐	**INTERMEDIATE WEAPONS** (TASER, SIMS, OC, BATON, FLASHLIGHT)				
	☐ TASER APPLIED: ☐ TURNED OVER TO W/C ☐ TASER LASER, ARC, OR THREAT ONLY	SUSPECT UNDER INFLUENCE OF DRUGS ☐ ALCOHOL ☐	# OF APPLICATIONS	SERIAL NUMBER	TASER EFFECTIVE YES ☐ NO ☐
☐	**DEADLY FORCE**	**REFER TO CASE REPORT**			

ADDITIONAL DETAILS
DESCRIBE ADDITIONAL RELEVANT INFORMATION, WHICH MAY INCLUDE THE EFFECT OF CONTROL(S) USED, OR THE EXTENT OF SUSPECT/OFFICER INJURIES.
MORE DETAILED DESCRIPTIONS AND INFORMATION SHALL BE WRITTEN IN CASE REPORT.

☐ **NO ADDITIONAL RELEVANT INFORMATION. REFER TO CASE REPORT FOR DETAILS.**

☐ SUSPECT(S) INJURED ☐ TREATED	HOSPITAL OR TREATING FACILITY	PHYSICIAN	☐ INJURIES PHOTOGRAPHED ☐ MEDICAL RELEASE SIGNED AND ATTACHED
☐ OFFICER(S) INJURED ☐ TREATED	HOSPITAL OR TREATING FACILITY	PHYSICIAN	☐ INJURIES PHOTOGRAPHED ☐ IOD PACKET DELIVERED TO SUPERVISOR

WITNESS/OFFICER PRESENT	I.D.#	WITNESS/OFFICER PRESENT		I.D.#	WITNESS/OFFICER PRESENT			I.D.#
SUPERVISOR NOTIFIED	I.D.#	DATE NOTIFIED	TIME	WATCH COMMANDER SIGNATURE		I.D.#	DATE	TIME
REPORTING OFFICER	I.D.#					DATE OF REPORT		TIME

PROPERTY TAG: D91919	CHULA VISTA POLICE DEPARTMENT LABORATORY REPORT	CASE NUMBER: 10-19191
CODE SECTION: 209 PC	CRIME: Kidnapping for Ransom	DATE OF OCCURRENCE: 01/10/11
VICTIM: Duck, Daffy	LOCATION: 474 Disney Way	SUSPECT: Bunny, Bugs
REQUESTED BY: Agent W. Coyote (ID #911)	DATE ASSIGNED: 01/10/11	

DESCRIPTION OF WORK REQUESTED:

Examine and process the below listed item for latent prints and swab for DNA material.

EVIDENCE RECEIVED:

On 1/11/11, I received the following item of evidence from the Chula Vista Police Department Evidence Control Unit.

#9 – Broken Ceramic Pieces– One (1) sealed brown paper bag containing ten (10) multicolored broken, ceramic pieces from an unknown figurine.

RESULTS AND CONCLUSIONS:

On 1/11/11, in the Chula Vista Police Department Crime Laboratory, the above listed item of evidence was processed for latent prints. Prior to latent print processing, the following items of evidence were each given an individual identifying letter designation.

Item #	Description	Letter Designation
9	2 ½" x 2 ¼" x 1/8" piece	A
9	3 ½" x 1 ¾" x 1/8" piece	B
9	2 ¼" x 1 ½" x 1/8" piece	C
9	4 ½" x 2 ¾" x 1/8" piece	D
9	2" x 1 ¼" x 1/8" piece	E
9	2 ½" x 1 ¼" x 1/8" piece	F
9	6 ¼" x 3 ¼" x 1/8" piece	G
9	3" x 2 ¼" x 1/8" piece	H
9	2" x ¼" x 1/8" piece	I
9	5 1/8" x 5 1/8" x ¾" piece	J

The following table lists the item number, processing method, results and latent print item numbers.

Item #	Processing Method	Results	Item Number
9A	CAE Fume; Black Powder	No latent prints were developed	—
9B	CAE Fume; Black Powder	No latent prints were developed	—
9C	CAE Fume; Black Powder	No latent prints were developed	—
9D	CAE Fume; Black Powder	No latent prints were developed	—
9E	CAE Fume; Black Powder	No latent prints were developed	—
9F	CAE Fume; Black Powder	No latent prints were developed	—
9G	CAE Fume; Black Powder	No latent prints were developed	—
9H	CAE Fume; Black Powder	No latent prints were developed	—
9I	CAE Fume; Black Powder	No latent prints were developed	—
9J	CAE Fume; Black Powder	No latent prints were developed	—

On 01/11/11, at approximately 1235 hours, one (1) swab set for DNA material **(Item #9.01)** was collected from the surfaces of pieces **#9D, #9G** and **#9J**.

DISPOSITION OF EVIDENCE:

The swab set **(Item #9.01)** was sealed in evidence packaging and submitted to the Chula Vista Police Department Evidence Control Unit on 1/12/11. All received evidence **(Item #9)** was sealed in evidence packaging and returned to the Chula Vista Police Department Evidence Control Unit on 01/12/11 and will be retained until final disposition of this case.

END OF REPORT.

_____   _____

R. Runner #1044:   **Date**

_____   _____

Technical Review: **Date**

_____   _____

Administrative Review: **Date**

PROPERTY TAG: C98765	CHULA VISTA POLICE DEPARTMENT LABORATORY REPORT	CASE NUMBER: 11-12345
CODE SECTION: 11-44/11-45	CRIME: Medical Examiner's Case/ Suicide	DATE OF OCCURRENCE: 01/01/11
VICTIM: Jones, George John	LOCATION: 61 East Elm Street	
REQUESTED BY: Agent J. Smith #651	DATE OF REQUEST: 01/01/11	

CRIME LABORATORY NOTIFICATION:

On 01/01/11, at approximately 1402 hours, Forensic Specialist D. Brown (ID #123) notified me of a request for the Crime Laboratory's assistance to process a possible suicide scene at 61 East Elm Street in Chula Vista. I proceeded to the Crime of Violence Unit arriving at approximately 1412 hours and met with Agent S. Green (ID #321). Agent Green requested I proceed to 61 East Elm and process the scene. Crime Laboratory Volunteer C. White (ID #V103) and I proceeded to 61 East Elm, arriving at approximately 1438 hours.

Upon arrival, I met with Crimes of Violence Agent O. Black (ID #717), Crimes of Violence Agent J. Smith (ID #651) and members of the Chula Vista Police Department Patrol Unit and was briefed on the sequence of events.

DOCUMENTATION & EVIDENCE COLLECTION RESPONSIBILITIES:

Forensic Specialist T. Gray (#1044)
Crime Scene Processing
Autopsy

CRIME SCENE PROCESSING:

On 01/01/11 at approximately 1450 hours, I started photographing the exterior and interior of 61 East Elm Street. The photographs were completed at approximately 1742 hours. The following photo log lists the photograph number and a description of the photograph.

Scene Folder Photo #	Description
1	Establishing view of the cross street signs for Poplar Ave and East Elm St
2–6	Establishing views of the front yard and drive way (south side) at 61 East Elm
7	Establishing view of the front door (south side) at 61 East Elm
8	Establishing view of the interior front entry way at 61 East Elm
9	Establishing view of the hallway leading to the bedroom at 61 East Elm
10–13	Establishing views of the hallway full bathroom at 61 East Elm
14–25	Establishing views of the southwest (master) bedroom at 61 East Elm
26–29	Establishing views of the southwest (master) bathroom at 61 East Elm

30–42	Establishing views of the west and northwest rooms at 61 East Elm
43–55	Establishing views of the north (office) room at 61 East Elm
56–61	Establishing views of the kitchen at 61 East Elm
62–73	Establishing views of the dining area at 61 East Elm
74–87	Establishing views of the garage at 61 East Elm
88–92	Establishing views of the ½ bath/storage room at 61 East Elm
93	Establishing view of the rear door (north side) leading to the backyard at 61 East Elm
94–107	Establishing views of the family room at 61 East Elm
108–125	Establishing views of the backyard (north side) at 61 East Elm
126–129	Establishing views of **George John Jones** located in the grassy area in the backyard at 61 East Elm
130–131	Medium views of the left side of **Jones**
132–133	Medium views of the soles of the left and right shoes on **Jones**
134–137	Close up views of dried red stains on the sole of **Jones'** left shoe
138–140	Close up views of dried red stains on the sole of **Jones'** right shoe
141–142	Medium views of dried red stains on the top of **Jones'** right shoe
143	Medium view of dried red stains near the shoe hemline of **Jones'** right pant leg
144–148	Close up views of dried red stains on **Jones'** right pant leg with and without a scale
149–150	Medium views of dried red stains on the thigh area of **Jones'** right pant leg
151	Medium view of dried red stains on the right side and back panel of **Jones'** t-shirt
152–153	Close up views of dried red stains on the back panel of **Jones'** t-shirt with and without a scale
154–155	Medium views of dried red stains on the right side of **Jones'** t-shirt
156–157	Close up views of dried red stains on the right side under the arm area of **Jones'** t- shirt with and without a scale
158	Medium view of the top of **Jones'** head
159–161	Medium views of **Jones'** right arm and hand
162	Medium view of **Jones'** left arm and hand
163	Medium view of dried red stains on the left side of **Jones'** face
164	Close up view of **Jones'** left hand
165	Medium view of dried red stains on the back panel near the neckline of **Jones'** t- shirt
166–167	Close up views of dried red stains on the back panel near the neckline of **Jones'** t- shirt with and without a scale
168–172	Medium views of the left side of **Jones**
173–174	Close up views of dried red stains on the left side of **Jones'** pants with and without a scale
175–177	Medium views of dried red stains on the rear panel of **Jones'** left pant leg
178	Medium view of red stains on the top of **Jones'** left shoe

179–180	Close up views of dried red stains on the rear panel of **Jones'** left pant leg
181	Medium view of brown colored debris on **Jones'** left rear pant pocket
182–183	Close up views of brown colored debris on **Jones'** left rear pant pocket with and without a scale
184	Medium view of a razor type tool located on the grass in the backyard at 61 East Elm
185–186	Close up views of the razor type tool with and without a scale
187–188	Medium views of an area of dried red stains on the cement patio with and without a scale
189	Medium view of a blue colored jacket on the cement patio
190–194	Close up views of dried red stains located around the jacket with and without a scale
195–196	Close up views of the razor blade portion of the razor type tool with and without a scale
197–198	Close up views of the handle portion of the razor type tool with and without a scale
199	Medium view of an area of dried red stains on the cement patio
200–204	Close up views of the area of dried red stains on the cement patio with and without a scale
205	Medium view of medication bottles located on a dresser in the southwest (master) bedroom at 61 East Elm
206–208	Close up views of medication bottles located on a dresser in the southwest (master) bedroom at 61 East Elm
209–212	Medium views of the blue colored jacket **(Item #1)**, location of a swab set of dried red stains **(Item #2)** and the razor type tool **(Item #3)** located in the backyard at 61 East Elm
213–216	Medium views of the front side of **Jones**
217	Medium view of dried and wet red stains on the grass area under where **Jones'** head and arms were located
218–219	Medium views of an injury to the left side of **Jones'** neck
220	Medium view of dried red stains on the right front panel of **Jones'** pants
221–222	Close up views of dried red stains on the right front panel of **Jones'** pants with and without a scale
223–224	Medium views of dried red stains on **Jones'** right front pant leg near the shoe hemline with and without a scale
225–227	Medium views of dried red stains on **Jones'** right front pant leg with and without a scale
228–229	Close up views of miscellaneous items removed from **Jones'** pants pockets
230	Medium view of an injury to the left side of **Jones'** neck
231–232	Medium views of the palm side of **Jones'** left and right hands
233	Medium view of **Jones'** teeth and inner lips
234–235	Medium views of the grassy area after removal of **Jones**
236	Close up view of the integrity tag on the sealed body bag
237	Close up view of two (2) identification cards with the name "**George John Jones**"

On 01/01/11, starting at approximately 1545 hours, a not to scale sketch was prepared showing the grassy area, body position and location of evidence recovered from the backyard of 61 East Elm Street. The sketch was completed at approximately 1600 hours. A computer generated version will be completed upon request.

On 01/01/11, starting at approximately 1711 hours, **three (3)** items of evidence was collected from the back yard at 61 East Elm Street. The evidence collection was completed at approximately 1714 hours. The following table lists the item number, item description and time collected.

Item #	Description	Location	Time Collected
1	Blue colored jacket	Cement patio	1711 hrs
2	Swab set of dried red stains	Cement patio	1714 hrs
3	Razor type tool	Grass area	1711 hrs

On 01/01/11, starting at approximately 1733 hours, **three (3)** items of evidence was received from Medical Examiner Investigator D. Maple (ID #24). The evidence collection was completed at approximately 1733 hours. The following table lists the item number, item description and time collected.

Item #	Description	Time Collected
4	Blue jeans	1733 hrs
5	Brown colored, loafer type, left shoe	1733 hrs
6	Brown colored, loafer type, right shoe	1733 hrs

SCENE SECURED:

On 01/01/11, at approximately 1755 hours, I notified Agent Smith (ID #651) that I had completed processing the scene at 61 East Elm. At that time, Crime Laboratory Volunteer C. White (ID #V103) and I proceeded to the Chula Vista Police Department arriving at approximately 1809 hours. At approximately 1814 hours, I secured the recovered items of evidence **(Items #1–6)** in the Crime Laboratory Exam Room #2.

CRIME LABORATORY NOTIFICATION:

On 01/02/11, at approximately 0855 hours, Crimes of Violence Agent O. Black (ID #717) notified me that the autopsy was scheduled on 01/02/11 at 0930 hours. Crime Laboratory Volunteers C. Steel (ID #V99), M. Wood (ID #V102), C, White (ID #V103) and I proceeded to the San Diego County Medical Examiner's Office arriving at approximately 0925 hours.

AUTOPSY:

On 01/02/11, at approximately 0943 hours I started photographing the autopsy of **George John Jones (01/12/1957)**. The photographs were completed at approximately 1021 hours. The following photo log lists the photograph number and a description of the photograph.

Autopsy Folder Photo #	Description
1–12	Establishing photographs of **Jones** clothed and in the unzipped body bag
13	Identification view of **Jones'** face
14	Close up view of the body bag seal which had been cut prior to the start of documentation
15–17	Establishing views of the back side of **Jones** prior to washing
18–23	Close up views of **Jones'** left and right hands prior to washing
24–26	Close up views of an injury to the left side of **Jones'** neck prior to washing with and without a scale
27–30	Establishing views of **Jones** after washing
31	Identification view of **Jones'** face after washing
32–33	Establishing views of **Jones** after washing
34–35	Close up views of the injury to the left side of **Jones'** neck after washing with and without a scale
36–37	Close up views of a section of missing skin on **Jones'** right forearm after washing with and without a scale
38–41	Close up views of **Jones'** left and right hands after washing
42–44	Establishing views of the back side of **Jones** after washing
45	Medium view of the injury to the left side of **Jones'** neck
46–48	Close up views of the injury to the left side of **Jones'** neck with and without a scale

On 01/02/11, starting at approximately 0948 hours, **five (5)** items of evidence were received from the pathologist during the autopsy of **George John Jones (01/12/1957)**. The evidence collection was completed at approximately 1128 hours. The following table lists the item number, item description, location collected and time collected.

Item #	Description	Time Collected
7	Blood Vial	1128 hrs
8	Inked set of fingerprints	1102 hrs
9	Rib section	1121 hrs
10	Watch	0948 hrs
11	Tan colored t-shirt	0950 hrs

<u>SCENE SECURED:</u>

On 01/02/11, at approximately 1134 hours, I notified Agent O. Black (ID #717) that I had completed documenting the autopsy of **George John Jones**. Crime Laboratory Volunteers C. Steel (ID #V99), M. Wood (ID #V102), C. White (ID #V103) and I proceeded to the Chula Vista Police Department arriving at approximately 1201 hours. At approximately 1210 hours, I secured the recovered items of evidence (**Items #7–11**) in the Crime Laboratory Exam Room #2.

<u>EVIDENCE DOCUMENTATION:</u>

On 01/03/11, starting at approximately 0950 hours, I began documenting and packaging **Items #1–11**. The documentation and packaging of **Items #1–11** was completed at approximately 1025 hours.

<u>EVIDENCE DISPOSITION:</u>

Recovered items of evidence (**Items #1–#11**) were sealed in separate evidence packaging and submitted to the Chula Vista Police Department Evidence Control Unit on 01/10/11.

The photographs of the scene and autopsy were uploaded to the Chula Vista Police Department's secure digital imaging management system. A copy of the photographs were recorded onto one (1) photo disc (**Item #12**) and submitted to the Chula Vista Police Department Evidence Control Unit on 01/10/11.

All evidence will be retained until final disposition of the case.

END OF REPORT.

_____   _____
T. Gray #1044:   **Date**

_____   _____
Technical Review: **Date**

_____   _____
Administrative Review: **Date**

PROBATION OFFICER'S REPORT

THE PEOPLE OF THE STATE OF CALIFORNIA

V.

RN:

CN:

AKA:

COURT NO.:	**DEPT. & JUDGE:**	
DA FILE NO.:	**ATTORNEY:** PD	
HEARING DATE/TIME:	**PROB. CASE NO.:**	
PROBATION OFFICER:	**PO TELEPHONE:**	

ADDRESS:		**TELEPHONE NO.:**	**BIRTHPLACE/CITIZENSHIP:** Citizen

BIRTH DATE:	**AGE:** 20	**RACE:** WHITE	**SEX:** M	**HT:** 600	**WT:** 190	**EYES:** BLUE	**HAIR:** BROWN

DRIVER'S LIC. NO.:	**INS NO.:**	**OTHER ID DATA:** (Obsolete)Unmapped–NONE NOTED–(Obsolete) Default

DATE OFFENSE COMMITTED: 07/12/2007	**DATE CONVICTED:** 08/03/2007	**HOW:** PLEA	**CUSTODY STATUS:** In Custody ──────── EM B

INVESTIGATING ARRESTING AGENCY:	**DATE COMPLAINT FILED:** 07/19/2007	_____ **NO:**

CII NO.:	**FBI NO.:**	**ARREST REPORT NO.:**	**BOOKING NO.:**

CONVICTED OF:

Count 1 VC 10851(a) Unlawful Take and Drive a Vehicle
Count 4 VC 2800.1(A) Evading Peace Officer, a misdemeanor

PRE PLEA AGREEMENT:

"Dismiss Balance; stip 365 c/c w/probation cases _____

RECOMMENDATION: Formal Probation

RELATED COURT DATA:

Pursuant to the plea bargain, the PC 666.5(a) prior auto theft enhancement on Count 1, Count 2, PC 496d, Buy/Receive/Conceal/Sell/Withhold Stolen Vehicle, Count 3, PC 23152(a), Driving Under the influence of Alcohol/Drugs, Count 5, VC 12500(a), Unlicensed Driver, and the PC 1203(e)(4) presumptive ineligible for probation allegation was dismissed with Harvey, Blakely, and Arbuckle Waivers.

The defendant is also appearing before the Court for Sentencing After Revocation in _____

PC296 STATUS:

THE OFFENSE:

SOURCES OF INFORMATION for this section

CVPD report _____ dated 7/12/07; DA file

On 7/12/07 at approximately 5:50am, a _____ officer was parked in the 400 block of __ Street when he observed an older white pick up pass him at approximately 60 mph traveling northbound on ____ Ave. in a 35 mph zone. The officer followed the vehicle to conduct a traffic stop. When the truck arrived at the intersection of ____ Ave and __ Street, it stopped for the red signal. When the driver of the truck, later identified as the defendant, saw the officer, he made a left turn west onto __ Street in violation of the red signal light and sped away fast. The officer activated his overhead lights and followed the defendant. The defendant was traveling between 60 to 70 mph in a 35 mph zone. At the next signal light, the defendant turned right and went in the westbound lanes of Park Way at about 50 to 60 mph in a 35 mph zone. The officer activated his siren, but the defendant continued to evade the officer (Count 4). When the defendant arrived at ____ Ave, he turned south running the stop sign at the intersection. He then immediately turned west on __ Street at approximately 60 mph. He stopped and yielded to the officer at ___ Ave.

The defendant was contacted and displayed symptoms of being under the influence of alcohol, (dismissed Count 3). He consented to a PAS test and it revealed his BAL .115%. Field Sobriety Tests were not conducted due to officer safety and he was transported to the _____ station. At the station a blood draw was taken.

The defendant was admonished and agreed to make a statement. He stated he had been with his younger brother, _____ that evening hanging out with various friends and drinking. He consumed 7 or 8 beers between 2030 and midnight on 7/11/07. Someone gave him the keys to the truck at about 0230 while he was at a house on _____ in _____. He was not sure if the owner of the truck knew he had it, but the person who gave him the keys knew the owner of the truck owed ____ money. The owner of the truck is named, _____ He drove the truck around with his brother for awhile and about 0400 he picked up his ex-girlfriend and she rode around with them. He planned to drop her off at her home, but it was too early to wake up the family. He drove around Chula Vista and saw the officer coming up behind him. He sped away and his passengers both yelled at him to stop and pull over for the officer. He finally did so.

At the scene when he stopped, an officer asked the defendant about the vehicle. He said it was an unreported stolen vehicle (Count 1 and dismissed Count 2). He had taken it from a guy who owed him money for drugs. He was "taxing" the owner until he paid the money that he owed him. He doubted the owner would actually call the police to report it stolen due to the nature of the situation.

The defendant's passengers were not arrested. He was booked into jail. A record check revealed he never had a California driver's license (dismissed Count 5).

VICTIMS:

RESTITUTION: $648.95

VICTIM NOTIFIED OF P&S HEARING: X Yes _No: INTENDS TO APPEAR: X Yes _No

---

SOURCES OF INFORMATION for this section
Telephone conversation with victim on 8/15/07

(address withheld)

A letter of notification of the defendant's sentencing was sent to the victim on 8/15/07. On this date, the undersigned spoke to the victim. He stated his vehicle was not insured at the time because it was not being used and was "parked." It sustained damages as well as items were missing from inside the vehicle and it had to be gotten out of impound. He will submit a detailed list to the undersigned for inclusion with this report or at the defendant's sentencing hearing.

_____ stated he would like the Court to "throw the book at him." The defendant had received the key to the vehicle from an ex-friend of the victim, _____ . Since receiving his vehicle back, he has had it re-keyed. He plans on attending the defendant's sentencing hearing.

On 8/20/07, the victim submitted a list of his of his losses and is requested restitution in the amount of $648.95. The undersigned has attached the victim's information to this report for the Court's information.

DEFENDANT'S STATEMENT:

SOURCES OF INFORMATION for this section

Interview with the defendant at the _____ Detention Facility on 8/18/07

The defendant did not submit a written statement on the probation questionnaire.

The defendant stated he and his younger brother were drinking at his friend _____ house in imperial Beach. The defendant asked _____ if he could borrow his truck. He told him, "no." The defendant kept asking him and convinced him to let him borrow the truck. He told _____ he would return in an hour. He and his brother left in the truck and went to pick up the defendant's ex-girlfriend in _____. They returned to ____ house and consumed some more beer. The defendant, his brother, and his ex-girlfriend then left the house and drove the truck in _____ and into _____. The defendant made a turn on a red light and a police officer stopped him and he was arrested.

He admitted he had consumed 12 beers and did not have a driver's license. The truck belonged to ___ and when the defendant was arrested the truck had not been reported stolen. He did not find out the vehicle was stolen until two days later as _____ did not want to pay for the impound fees and reported it stolen.

When asked about him residing in _____a, he admitted he left the local area in June and did not have permission of his probation officer.

He feels betrayed by _____ and is not going to talk to him anymore.

In regards to sentencing, he would like the Court to grant him probation and honor the plea agreement for 365 days custody. He wants to return to _____ where he will be residing with _____ and working for him. He wants to continue to get an education.

CRIMINAL HISTORY:

SOURCES OF INFORMATION for this section

JUVENILE RECORD:

DATE	AGENCY	CHARGE	DISPOSITION
4/16/02	SDSO	PC 242, Battery	

The minor's stepmother stated the minor assaulted her after they were involved in an argument over a skateboard and homework. They engaged in a physical altercation after she attempted to take away his skateboard. The minor pushed her to the ground. He was arrested after officers determined he may have caused injury to his stepmother. _____ refused medical treatment, but did request the minor be charged.

| 10/16/03 | SDSO | Ct. 1, HS 11357(e), Possession of Marijuana on School Grounds, misd |

The assistant principal at _____ High School contacted the minor regarding a behavior issue, When he passed a chewing gum wrapper to the co-participant, _____ another student. The assistant principal took the gum wrapper from _____ and determined there was a marijuana cigarette inside. He then checked _____ back pack and found a folding knife and two lighters. _____ had tried to conceal a marijuana smoking pipe by dropping it. The pipe was retrieved by the assistant principal and the Sheriff's Department was called.

<u>Adult Record:</u>

| 12/1/04 | SDSO | Ct. 1, VC 10851(a), Unlawful Take/Drive a Vehicle Ct. 2, VC 10851(a), Unlawful Take/Drive a Vehicle; Ct. 3, PC 484, Petty Theft; Ct. 4, VC 20002(a), Hit and Run |

The defendant stole two vehicles from his parent's home. One was eventually returned and the other one was involved in a roll over accident as the defendant was driving it under the influence.

| 12/25/04 | SDSO | Ct. 1, VC 10851(a), Unlawful Take/Drive a Vehicle; PC 12022.1(b), Committing felony while out on bail/OR Ct. 2, PC 496d, Receiving Stolen Property PC 12022.1(b), Committing felony while out on bail/OR |

The victim's vehicle was stolen from the driveway of his home in _____. He had started the car to warm it up and had left the vehicle unlocked and idling in the driveway. He went into the house and when he came out it was gone. The car was equipped with LoJack and it was activated. The vehicle was located parked on _____ Street in _____ with the defendant behind the wheel. The defendant committed this offense while out on OR status in _____

7/12/07	CVPD	Ct. 1, VC 10851(a), Unlawful Take/Drive a Vehicle; PC 666.5(a) Prior auto theft conviction; Ct. 2, 496d, Receiving Stolen Vehicle; Ct. 3, VC 23152(a), DUI, misd; Ct. 4, VC 2800.1(a), Evading Officer, misd; Ct. 5, VC 12500(a), Unlicensed Driver, misd PC 1203(e)(4), Prob denial priors

PROBATION AND PAROLE:

SOURCES OF INFORMATION for this section

Juvenile and Adult Probation files

Juvenile Probation Adjustment:

The defendant was adjudged a ward of the Court on 5/20/02 after sustaining a true finding for PC 242, Battery. As conditions of probation, in part, he was ordered to abide by a 7:00pm curfew, abide by the rules at home and of his parents, participate in counseling, not use or possess any controlled substance or alcohol and submit to testing, complete 20 hours of community service and pay a $25 restitution fine.

On 3/5/03, the defendant was found in violation of probation for two positive drug tests for marijuana. He was continued a ward and committed to Juvenile Hall for 3 days (1 consecutive weekend).

At a review hearing on 5/20/03, the defendant had tested positive for marijuana on 1/28/03, but subsequent tests had been negative. He successfully completed the CHOICE Program. He was employed and had completed all of his conditions of probation except for the community service work.

On 7/16/03 a Juvenile Detention Order was issued as the defendant had left his home on 7/3/03.

On 8/19/03, the defendant appeared in Court and the JDO was recalled. He admitted violating probation by failing to attend school and failing to complete community service work. He was continued a ward and committed to Juvenile Hall for 3 days, to serve 1 consecutive weekend.

On 10/16/03, the defendant was arrested for HS 11357(e), Possession of Marijuana on School Grounds. On 10/21/03, the defendant appeared in Court and admitted to the offense. He was continued a ward on 11/4/03 and committed to the _____ Program not to exceed 90 days and ordered to successfully complete the _____ Day Center Program.

On 1/23/04, the defendant appeared in Court and admitted to violating probation by failing to follow the rules of the person with whom he was placed, failing to abide by the Court ordered curfew, and testing positive for marijuana. He was continued a ward and committed to Juvenile Hall for 9 days and ordered to successfully completed the _____ Day Center Program.

On 2/23/04, a JDO was issued as the defendant was AWOL from home.

On 3/16/04, the defendant appeared in Court. The JDO was vacated and the defendant was continued a ward and a psychological evaluation was ordered. He appeared in Court on 4/20/04, and he was continued a ward and placed on home supervision. He was also ordered to take his medication as prescribed, and to take the first bed available at the _____ and complete the program.

On 9/20/04, Jurisdiction was terminated.

Overall, his adjustment to juvenile probation was marginal at best.

Adult Probation Adjustment:

On 2/7/05, the defendant was granted 3 years formal probation in _____ after pleading guilty to auto theft charges. As conditions of probation, in part, he was ordered not to use or possess any controlled substance or alcohol and to submit to testing, attend substance abuse and psychiatric counseling if directed by the Probation Officer, take psychotropic meds as prescribed by doctor, report to P.O. as directed, report any change of address or employment to PO within 72 hours, and obtain consent of the P.O. before leaving the county.

The defendant was scheduled for an orientation appointment with probation on 6/1/05. He failed to appear for this appointment, but called probation and stated he had moved to an address in _____. His appointment was rescheduled for 7/8/05.

On 7/8/05, the defendant arrived late for his scheduled orientation appointment. The appointment was rescheduled for 7/11/05. He appeared on that date and his conditions of probation were explained and he received copies of all necessary information. He was subsequently scheduled for a compliance appointment on 11/14/05.

On 11/14/05, the defendant failed to appear for his compliance appointment. On 11/16/05, Probation called the defendant and advised him he had failed to appear to his appointment. He stated he was not in treatment and not employed. He was directed to enroll in an outpatient treatment program within 10 days or get on the waiting list, attend 2 NA/AA meetings per week until he entered a treatment program, and have proof of his income and monthly payments to R&R by his next appointment. He was also informed mail sent to his address in _____ had been returned and he was told if he moved he was to notify probation within 72 hours. Additionally, the defendant had tested positive for methamphetamine on 7/12/05. He was scheduled for a compliance appointment on 3/20/06. Subsequently, his appointment was rescheduled to 5/11/06.

On 4/24/06, Probation received a telephone call from the defendant's mother. She stated he had missed his appointment in March because he was ill. He is dual diagnosed and not taking any medication. She was informed of the defendant's appointment in May. The defendant got on the telephone and he was told he had to be in a treatment program and attending NA/AA meetings twice per week. He began swearing and passed the telephone to his mother. She was told to contact _____ for assistance.

On 5/10/06, the defendant's mother contacted Probation. She stated the defendant was sent to _____ Hospital and would remain in the facility for two weeks. However, it appeared he would only be in the facility for a few days and then transition to a crisis house. He had not been taking his medication.

The defendant was not available for his appointment on 5/11/06 and it was rescheduled for 7/20/06.

On 6/23/06, the defendant contacted Probation and stated he was not enrolled in a treatment program. His family needed him due to their illnesses. He stated he was bi-polar and couldn't sustain employment. He indicated probation was making his life hard. He was directed to enter a treatment program.

On 7/20/06, the defendant appeared for his appointment. He failed to provide proof of compliance on any of his conditions and had excuses. He failed to produce a urine sample for drug testing. He was directed to report on 7/21/06 for testing. On that date he appeared for testing and the results were subsequently positive for marijuana.

On 6/25/07, an appointment notice was sent to the defendant for a compliance appointment on 7/11/07.

On 7/2/07, he appeared at the _____ Probation Officer and requested to reschedule his appointment on 7/11/07. He did not have any verification of employment, enrollment in treatment, NA/AA meeting attendance, psychotropic medications, or payments. He was told he had to keep his scheduled appointment.

On 7/11/07, the defendant reported as directed. He stated he had been living in _____ for the past few months and wanted courtesy supervision. However, he was told he was not in compliance. He stated he was attending college in _____ and his life had improved dramatically. He was employed in construction. He was scheduled for another compliance appointment on 8/1/07 and told he needed to provide verification of his previously ordered conditions as well as enrollment in college. He was given permission to return to _____ pending his next appointment.

The defendant was arrested on new charges on the instant matter.

Overall, the defendant's performance on probation has been non existent and a dismal failure.

PERSONAL DATA:

The following information was offered by the defendant. Unless noted otherwise it has not been verified.

Birth Place and Areas of Residence:

The defendant was born in _____ and has resided in the local area all of his life.

Current Living Situation:

The defendant was residing with his father in _____ at the time of the instant offense. Just prior to that living situation, he had relocated to _____ when he had resided for a couple of months. He plans on returning to _____ upon his release from custody.

Family Relationships:

The defendant is the oldest child born from his parent's union. His parent's marriage ended in divorce 15 or 16 years ago. Both of his parents had remarried. He has a younger brother and sister from his parent's union. He has an older step brother and an older step sister from his step mother. He has an older half sister from his father. His mother passed away on 6/24/06. His father continues to reside in _____. He described his childhood as good and reported no abuse. His relationship with his family is "awesome."

Marital Status and Dependents:

The defendant is single and has no children.

Family Criminal History:

The defendant's younger brother has been arrested as a juvenile for assault and battery. His father was arrested on unknown charges years ago.

Acquaintances:

The defendant associates with "good people" who have goals in life.

Pro-Social Activities:

The defendant enjoys surfing, bowling, playing video games, and playing pool.

Education:

The defendant completed the 11th grade before he was expelled from _____ High School. He was expelled for smoking marijuana on campus, locking the teacher's gate to the parking lot, and truancy. He stated he was attending a GED program in Stockton.

Military Service:

The defendant has not served in the armed forces.

Employment History:

The defendant was first employed during the summer at age 15 for a construction company. He worked at this job during the following summer when he was 16. At age 17, during the summer, he was employed for _____ as a stocker/cashier. At age 18, he began working full time for a construction company and was in their employ from September to December, until he was arrested as an adult. At age 19, he worked doing odd jobs and plastering. In June 2007, he moved to _____ to work for a stucco company. He was referred to this job by a friend who had gotten out of prison. This friend knew the owner of the company and knew he needed people to work for him. The defendant plans on returning to this job upon his release.

Financial Information:

The defendant describes his financial condition as "horrible." He believes he owes a hospital bill from April 2007 when he had surgery on his hand. He does not have any assets.

Psychological and Medical Problems:

The defendant stated he did not have any medical or psychological problems. When asked about any diagnosis he may have received, he then stated at age 11 or 12 he was diagnosed as being bipolar. He had been taking prescription medication for this mental illness, but has not taken any for several years. He believes he can control it. He is not taking any medication while in custody.

Substance Abuse and Treatment History:

The defendant first consumed alcohol at age 15 or 16. He began consuming it more frequently by age 18, usually on the weekends. He consumes beer to the point of getting a "buzz." He last consumed beer on the day of the instant offense. He does not believe he has a problem with alcohol.

In regards to drugs, he began smoking marijuana at age 12. At age 15, he tried methamphetamine and cocaine. He was living in a motel in downtown _____ as he had moved out of his father's home. At age 17, he tried mushrooms. Between age 16 and 18 he was using methamphetamine on a daily basis, about 1 ½ grams per day. He began decreasing his use and tried to quit. About two years ago, he was using methamphetamine one time per week. When his mother became ill, he tried to quit using it. He last used methamphetamine in July 2005. At age 19 he used Ecstasy once. He denies the use or experimentation with any other drugs or abuse of prescription drugs.

Gang Affiliation:

The defendant denied any association or membership in any gang.

Immigration Status:

The defendant is a U.S. citizen.

Future Plans:

The defendant plans to get his GED, go to college, and work in _____.

COLLATERAL INFORMATION:

SOURCES OF INFORMATION for this section

Telephone conversation with _____ on 8/18/07

On 8/18/07, the undersigned contacted _____ in _____. He stated the defendant was welcomed to reside with his family. The defendant would be required to attend school and not use alcohol or drugs.

SENTENCING DATA:

As to Count 1:

Possible Circumstances in Mitigation:

Rule 4.423(b)(3): The defendant voluntarily acknowledged wrongdoing at an early stage of the criminal process.

Possible Circumstances in Aggravation:

Rule 4.421(a)(7): The defendant was convicted of other crimes for which consecutive sentences could have been imposed but for which concurrent sentences are being imposed.

Rule 4.421(b)(2): The defendant's prior convictions as an adult are numerous.

Rule 4.421(b)(4): The defendant was on probation when the crime was committed.

Rule 4.421(b)(5): The defendant's prior performance on juvenile probation was unsatisfactory.

Rule 4.408(a): Pursuant to the plea bargain, the PC 666.5(a) prior auto theft enhancement, Count 3, VC 23152(a), and Count 5, VC 12500(a) were dismissed which could have had additional consequences.

Prison Term Analysis:

The circumstances in aggravation outweigh any mitigant and warrant the upper term. The possible prison terms for VC 10851(a) are 16 months, 2 years, or 3 years.

Consecutive sentencing of _____ to the instant matter could be justified pursuant to Rule 4.425(a)(1) in that the crimes and their objectives were predominantly independent of each other and Rule 4.425(a)(3) in that the crimes were committed at different times or separate places, rather than being committed so closely in time and place as to indicate a single period of aberrant behavior. However, in the interest of justice, concurrent sentencing is recommended.

Count 4, VC 2800.1(a) is a misdemeanor and punishable by no more than 1 year in custody.

Suggested Prison Term:

Crime	Suggested Base Term	Recommended Term	Recommended	Stay
Ct. 1, VC 10851(a)	Upper 3 years	3 years	0	

VC 10851(a), SCS190050	Middle 2 years (concurrent)	0	0
VC 10851(a), SCS190257	Middle 2 years (concurrent)	0	0
	Total Term:	3 years	

EVALUATION:

As to Count 1:

Probation Eligibility:

Rule 4.413(a): Pursuant to PC 1203(e)(4), the defendant is presumptively ineligible for probation except in the unusual case. The undersigned has reviewed Judicial Council Rule 4.413 and its subsections and is aware to the authority pursuant to Rule 4.408(a) to find any other relevant criteria that would support the finding of the unusual case. The undersigned finds Rule 4.408(a) applies in that in the interest of justice a grant of probation with local custody is warranted.

Circumstances Supporting a Grant of Probation:

Rule 4.414(b)(3): The defendant appears willing to comply with the terms of probation.

Rule 4.414(b)(4): The defendant has the ability to comply with reasonable terms of probation as indicated by the defendant's age, education, health, mental faculties, and family background and ties.

Circumstances Supporting a Denial of Probation:

Rule 4.414(b)(1): The defendant has a significant prior record of criminal conduct.

Rule 4.414(b)(2): The defendant's prior performance on probation was unsatisfactory and he was on two felony grants of probation when he committed the instant offense.

Rule 4.414(b)(7): The defendant appears to be without remorse.

Discussion:

The 20 year old defendant is appearing before the Court today for sentencing on the guilty plea to VC 10851(a), Unlawful Take/Drive a Vehicle, a felony and VC 2800.1(a), Evading a Peace Officer, a misdemeanor.

He is also appearing before the Court for Sentencing After Revocation in _____ and _____

The defendant was observed by a _____ Police Officer on patrol traveling 60 mph in a 35 mph zone. The officer followed him in an effort to initiate a traffic stop. The defendant stopped at an intersection for a red light, but when he saw the officer, he made a turn in violation of the red signal light and sped away fast. The officer activated his overhead lights and followed the defendant. The defendant traveled between 60 to 70 mph in a 35 mph zone and at the next signal light, he turned at about 50 to 60 mph. After the officer activated his siren, the defendant continued to evade the officer. He subsequently ran a stop sign and made another turn at approximately 60 mph. He eventually yielded to the officer and displayed symptoms of being under the influence of alcohol. His BAL was .115%. His brother and girlfriend were in the vehicle with him and were released.

When stopped at the scene, the defendant told the officer the vehicle was an unreported stolen and he had taken it because the owner had owed him money for drugs. The defendant did not possess a driver's license.

The victim stated the vehicle was not insured at the time because it was "parked." It sustained damages as well as items were missing from the vehicle. He had to have it taken out of impound. He would like restitution and will submit a detailed list of his losses to the undersigned or at the defendant's sentencing hearing. He intends on appearing at the hearing.

In regards to sentencing, he believes the Court should "throw the book at him." He said he did not know the defendant and he (defendant) had received the key to the vehicle from the victim's ex friend, _____ .

The defendant stated he was drinking beer at the victim's house and convinced him to allow him to drive his truck. He took it and picked up his ex-girlfriend and returned to the victim's house. He later took the vehicle again and had his younger brother and his ex-girlfriend in the vehicle with him. He went into _____ from _____ and was stopped and arrested when he made an illegal turn.

He admitted he had consumed 12 beers and did not have a driver's license. He does not believe he was drunk. He also stated the vehicle was not stolen and it wasn't until two days later that he was told it was stolen. The owner of the vehicle did not want to pay the impound fees and reported it stolen.

He feels betrayed by the victim and is not going to speak to him anymore. He would like the Court to grant him probation and abide by the plea agreement for 365 days custody. He desires to return to _____ where he intends on attending school and seeking employment.

The defendant has a prior record dating from 2002 as a juvenile. He did not perform well on juvenile probation and had several probation violations stemming from leaving his placement to testing positive for drugs. Jurisdiction was ultimately terminated in 2004. Within three months of termination of juvenile wardship, he committed his first adult offense, auto theft. He was out of custody on OR awaiting adjudication when he committed another auto theft 24 days after his first offense. He subsequently was convicted on both matters and granted formal probation. His performance on formal probation has been a dismal failure. He has failed to enroll and complete a substance abuse program, gain employment, report to probation as directed, pay on his court ordered fines, and recently had left the county without permission when he admitted he was residing in Stockton. He appeared for a scheduled appointment with his Probation Officer on 7/11/07 and was subsequently arrested on the instant matter the following day.

The defendant has a history of alcohol and substance abuse, scattered employment and has lacked a stable living environment. The undersigned is concerned that the defendant continues to fail to realize he should not be driving a vehicle without a license or even consuming alcohol. He placed his passengers at risk of serious injury or even death as well as himself and any unsuspecting motorist or pedestrians when he committed the instant offense. His brazen actions in this offense are further indications of his blatant disregard for the laws set by society, to directives of probation and the orders of the Court. He still does not appear to have accepted responsibility for his behavior and will most likely continue to commit law violations. It is highly likely he will end up in state prison on a probation violation or for his next offense. It is hoped this lengthy time in custody will have a sobering effect on him and he will make a conscious decision to change his behavior upon his release.

Therefore, after taking all factors into consideration, the undersigned recommends a grant of formal probation with 365 days custody.

CUSTODY DATA:

Date Confined	Date Released	Place	Custody Days
07/13/2007	08/30/2007 (In custody)	CJ	49
		PC 4019 credits	24
		TOTAL CTS	73

RECOMMENDATION:

Formal Probation (See Probation Order Attached)

Respectfully submitted,

CHIEF PROBATION OFFICER
BY: _____

Approved: _____

I have read and considered the foregoing report.

_____
JUDGE OF THE SUPERIOR COURT

END OF REPORT.

PROBATION OFFICER'S REPORT

THE PEOPLE OF THE STATE OF CALIFORNIA	COURT NO	DEPT. & JUDGE _____ DEPT. ___
V. RN: CN: AKA:	DA FILE NO.	ATTORNEY Appointed
	HEARING DATE/TIME 11/03/94 08: 30AM	PROB CASE NO.
	PROBATION OFFICER	PO TEL. NO.
ADDRESS	TEL. NO.	BIRTHPLACE/ CITIZENSHIP

BIRTH DATE	AGE 30	RACE BLACK	SEX MALE	HT 5'08"	WT 175	EYES BROWN	HAIR BLACK
SOC. SEC. NO.		DRIVER'S LIC. NO	INS. NO.		OTHER ID DATA		
DATE OFFENSE COMMITTED 02/26/94		DATE CONVICTED 09/26/94		HOW JURY VERDICT		CUSTODY STATUS CUSTODY	
INVESTIGATING ARRESTING AGENCY _____			DATE INFO/COMPLAINT FILED 05/19/94		_____ SYSTEM NO.		
CII NO.		FBI NO.		ARREST REPORT NO.		_____ BOOKING NO.	

CONVICTED OF:

Count 1, PC 187(a), Murder, second degree;
Count 2, PC 273a(a), Child Abuse, felony

CODEFENDANT(S):

The codefendant, _____ , is scheduled for sentencing along with the defendant. The recommendation for the codefendant is 15 years to life on the instant case with four years in State Prison on her probation revocation case.

RECOMMENDATION: State Prison

THE OFFENSE:

SOURCES OF INFORMATION for this section

LMPD REPORTS, 2-26-94, 3-1-94, 3-2-94, 3-21-94; DA FILE

On 2-26-94 at approximately 7:56 a.m., _____ Fire Department, paramedics, and _____ police officers responded to a 911 call of a baby choking at ____ Upon arrival, the paramedics and fire officials found a one-and-a-half-year-old male child in a state of cardiac arrest. The child had blood around and in his mouth and several bruises on his chest. The father of the child, ____ was babysitting the three children. He told paramedics that he gave his son a glass of water and he started choking. The one-and-a-half-year-old victim was in the process of being transported to Children's Hospital when Officer _____ arrived at the scene. Officer ____ observed the victim, who had a distended stomach, a very pale appearance, and showed no outward signs of life. Paramedics told the officer where they were taking the child.

When officer ____ entered the apartment, he observed ____ taking a mattress from the living room to a bedroom. He seated at the victim had been watching TV while lying on the mattress. The officer asked him what happened, and ____ replied that his wife ____ left for work at about 7:30 a.m. A little after that, he gave his son a glass of water and he started choking. His son passed out, so he shouted for a neighbor to call 911, as he did not have a telephone. He then started CPR on his son by pushing on his son's chest and then checking for breathing. He said his son was not breathing, so he pinched his nose and blew in his mouth. He told the officer that he did not have any training in CPR. His wife was at work at the ____ and he had a neighbor telephone her to let her know what happened.

A Trauma Intervention Program volunteer arrived about that time and began entertaining ____ older daughter. The officer asked the last fireman as he was laving what he had seen. The fireman stated the child had blood around and in his mouth and bruises on his chest and was not breathing. They had the child on the floor and then placed him on the dining room table when the paramedics arrived. They established an airway and were getting air into the child, but it did not look like he would survive.

Officer ____ then notified his sergeant of the situation and investigators that there was a possible homicide.

The officer then continued to speak with ____ He asked him about his children, and ____ said he had three, a daughter, age 2-1/2 years, a son (the victim), age 20 months, and a daughter, age 2 month. The officer noted that ____ could not give him the dates of birth of any of his children and did not even know what month his two-month-old infant was born. He also was not sure of his wife's date of birth, and all the information concerning this was acquired later from his wife. ____ was not under any apparent stress at that time, as he though the paramedics would take care of his son and never asked about his son once. The officer asked him if he knew his son was going to Children's Hospital, and ____ said, "No, I thought he was going to _____ Hospital." He never asked if his son would be okay.

Officer ____ asked him if there had been any CPS involvement with his family in the past. ____ said, yes, his older daughter and the victim had been taken away them for over a year. He said they were under Court jurisdiction because his wife, ____ had been convicted of biting and abusing them. He then went into a bedroom and brough out a stack of court papers concerning these children. The ____ had an older daughter whom ____ had physically abused. ____ was also accused of abusing his wife several times, but that was never proven. The ____ second daughter and the victim had been taken away from them for over a year, and a lot of the papers concerned the ____ trying to get their children back. They finally got the victim back in June 1993 and their second daughter in September 1993. Their oldest daughter was permanently taken away from them. He also indicated that he used to work as a cook at the ____ in _____, but was fired because he had to go to court so much to get his children back. He had not worked in over a year, so he did the baby sitting. He also indicated that he got along well with his wife.

At that time, the officer received a radio call on the status of the victim. The victim was still alive, but was going through brain surgery and not expected tb survive. That information was relayed to ____ and he cried for a couple of minutes.

At approximately 10:00 a.m., ____ arrived at home. She stated she had gone to _____ Hospital, thinking her son was there. She then asked what was going on and what had happened. The officer told her what her husband had stated and that the victim was at Children's Hospital. The officer asked her how the victim was when she left the apartment for work, and she said he "seemed just fine." She had no idea how serious the victim's condition was and became almost hysterical. She cried uncontrollably for almost an hour and kept saying aver and over, "I want my baby, I want my baby." Her husband followed her around the apartment for awhile and tried to hold and comfort her, and he started crying again for awhile. Every now and then, ____ would stop her chant and say, "What did you do?" She did this as he held her.

_____ PD detectives arrived and took the ____ other two children into protective custody and transported them to Hillcrest Receiving Home. The ____ were informed of this.

Detective ____ then asked ____ if he would be willing to talk to him outside of the apartment and explain what had happened, ____ agreed. He stated he had been married to ____ for two years prior to their marriage They lived together for four years. They moved to their present apartment approximately nine months prior. Prior to that, they lived at the _____ Motel on _____ Drive in _____ for two year. He indicated he is an unemployed cook and had worked at the ____ in _____ for almost three years before he was fired because he was missing too much work. He has been unemployed for over a year.

____ is currently employed as a cook at the ____ in _____. She works between 10:00 a.m. and 5:00 p.m., five days a week. They do not have a vehicle, and she takes the bus to and from work. She leaves to catch the bus at 7:30 a.m. and usually arrives home between 7:30 p.m. and 8:00 p.m. For the last year, ____ has been babysitting his children while his wife works.

____ stated he has a total of four children. His oldest daughter is about five years old, and he could not remember her date of birth. This daughter was taken away from them when she was seven months old, and all parental rights were severed. This was because his wife was convicted of felony physical abuse on the child. This child has since been legally adopted by his wife's aunt in _____. Their second daughter is about three years old, the victim is about two years old, and their youngest daughter is about two months old. They have an active Social Services case, and both their second daughter and the victim had been taken away by Social Services at birth. They had just regained custody of them in the last eight months.

The detective asked ____ if the victim had ever had any broken bones of major health problems or illnesses. He stated that the victim was never sick and never had any broken bones.

Detective ____ then asked ____ to state what had happened with the victim, starting from the previous night. ____ stated that all of the children had eaten dinner at about 6:30 p.m. they had spaghetti, candy and chips. Between 7:30 p.m. and 7:45 p.m., he put the children in bed. Just after that, his wife came home from work. The children were all well and happy when he put them to bed, and there were no problems that he observed with any of his children. He and his wife slept on a mattress in the living room, because the living room was warmer than the bedrooms. At 7:25 a.m., he and his wife both woke up. They realized that she was running late for work. She got dressed and left for the bus at 7:30 a.m. He was awake when his wife left and, at 7:35 a.m., he heard the victim calling for his "baoa." He got up, walked into the southeast bedroom, and took the victim out of his crib. He set him on the floor, and they both walked into the kitchen. Once in the kitchen, the victim asked for a drink of water. He gave the victim a glass of water. As soon as he drank the water, the victim started choking. _____ ran outside and was able to get a neighbor to call 911. He then ran back into his apartment and placed his son on the kitchen floor and started mouth-to-mouth resuscitation and chest compressions. The detective asked him how his son sounded when he was choking, and _____ started that he could hear him gagging and gasping for air and that he was crying. He was then asked if he could feel a heartbeat before he started chest compressions, and _____ said, "Yeah, it was real fast." At that point, _____ said that he had a CPR course in high school, but that was it.

_____ stated that his son was accident prone. He would fall on his face a lot and cut his lips. He went on to say that the victim had several small bruises on the back of his legs, because he fell out of the crib three days prior.

Detective _____ then spoke with _____ She stated that she and _____ first started dating in April 1987. In October 1988, they began living together on and off for approximately three years. On 10-11-91, they got married.

_____ said she is currently on felony probation for a 1989 physical child abuse conviction. Her older daughter was taken away from her when she was seven months old. She had taken her to the hospital because of an infected toe. Upon examination, the doctors discovered human bite marks on the upper torso and back. The doctors also discovered old healing fractures of her limbs and ribs. The bite marks were matched to her teeth and she was convicted of child abuse.

_____ stated that she came home from work on Friday at about 5:30 or 6:00 p.m. They all had spaghetti for dinner. She did not remember what happened after that, but between 7:30 and 8:00 p.m., she noticed the children were in bed. She asked her husband about the children and he told her that he had put them to bed. The victim was fine and acting very happy all the time she was home and had no problems when he went to bed. She and her husband went to bed about 10:00 p.m. or 11:00 p.m. She said she woke up Saturday morning at 7:25 a.m. and realized she had to catch the bus at 7:40 a.m. She got dressed, went to check on the victim, and left the apartment at 7:30 a.m. They victim was asleep when she checked on him. She got to work at the _____ at about 8:30 a.m. She was told by the restaurant accountant to call her neighbor. When she did, her neighbor told her that her son had choked on some water and the police and ambulance came and took him to Grossmont Hospital. She then called her husband's best friend to come and take her to the hospital. When the friend arrived, he drove her to _____ Hospital. They told her that the victim was at Children's Hospital. The friend then drove her there. At Children's Hospital, she was told that the victim was in Radiology and it would be at least an hour before she could see him and find out about his injuries. The friend then drove her back to her apartment. Once she wars at the apartment, she asked her husband what happened. Her husband started crying. The officer who was at the apartment, Officer _____ then told her that her son was dead. Her husband told her that the victim had been drinking water and started choking.

She informed the detective that she and her husband have had physical fights in the past. The last one was over three years ago, and they had not been violent since. She stated she never saw her husband hit the victim or injure him in any way. She stated the victim has never had any broken bones and is usually pretty healthy. She did not have a pediatrician for him, but took the children to a clinic in _____. The interview was then terminated.

As Detective _____ walked back to the apartment, he was contacted outside by another officer. The other officer had just returned from Children's Hospital and stated that the victim had multiple bruises on his body, was unconscious, and had a subdural hematoma (swelling of the brain inside the skull). The doctor at Children's Hospital wanted to do brain surgery in an attempt to relieve the pressure on the brain. They could not do this until the victim's condition stabilized. At that point, the victim was in critical to grave condition and was not expected to live.

After discussion with the other officers about the injuries to the victim and the other information from the firefighters and paramedics at the scene, _____ was subsequently arrested for felony child abuse. He was then transported to the _____ Police Department for processing prior to being booked into County Jail.

After a Search Warrant was obtained for the _____ residence, a search was conducted. During the search, a pair of nunchakus, a green marijuana bong, a brass marijuana pipe, a metal tin containing 3.4 grams of marijuana and a scale were recovered.

At approximately 11:45 a.m., Detective _____ spoke with Child Protective Services Social Worker _____ she Indicated that they had an active case with her agency regarding the _____ family. There have also been several previous reports of suspected child abuse and neglect involving the _____ children. She told the detective the circumstances of their oldest daughter being removed from the family. She also indicated that _____ had been diagnosed having "disassociative disorder" and had been undergoing therapy.

The victim had been returned to the _____ in June 1993 by court order. Since December 1993, the social worker stated that she had not been able to see the victim. When she would go to their apartment, the _____ were never home or would not answer the door. Even when appointments were made with _____ to be home at specific times, no one would be there. The social worker also made several unannounced visits in the early evening hours in an attempt to catch the _____ at home. Even then, the _____ still pretended not to be home and did not answer the door.

At approximately 6:34 p.m., _____ PD detectives went to Children's Hospital and contacted _____ At that time she was taken into custody and transported back to the _____ Police Station for processing and interview.

Detective _____ reinterviewed _____ at the _____ Police Department. Detective _____ explained to _____ that his son had been examined by the doctors at children's Hospital. The injuries on the victim consisted of a subdural hematoma (swelling of the brain), retinal tears, bruising all over the body, and old rib fractures. These injuries were not consistent with his story as to what happened and that none of the injuries could have been caused by CPR. The detective then stated that he needed to know what and why this occurred _____ stated that the victim was accident prone and fell a lot. The victim falls out of his crib and is always falling outside. "I ain't ever touched him in all my life. I already know. If something happens, my kids are gone."

Detective explained to him that retinal tears are only caused by a severe shaking or sudden acceleration and deceleration of the head. He wanted to know how these injurias could have occurred and who caused them, if he did not. said, "It was just me and my wife there." He repeated that several times. The detective asked him if his wife was causing the injuries to the baby, and he said, "Not in my eyes." said, "I'm telling you the truth." He went on to say that the victim is always falling. He falls out of his crib a lot. "If we take him outside, he falls. There's a knot right here," pointing to his upper right forearm, "he got the other day, just walking to the car from the parking lot and bang."

_____ stated that he and his wife would argue over little things. When they did, he would yell and scream for several minutes and either ignore her or go for a walk. He denied ever seeing his wife hitting the children. He said, "I love my wife." After several more second, he stated "I've seen her snatch the kids before." He said he has seen _____ shake the victim in the past, and he continued to say, "I've done it too. Not physically, you know, _____ stop that. '" At that point, _____ raised his arms up in front of his face as though he was holding the victim by the upper arms and started to shake. He does this when he "gets into something. He knocks his bottle over. You know, little things." He then said, _____ no, don't do that," talking as though he was talking to the victim. "I didn't really get over and shake him, not to hurt him."

Detective _____ asked him if anything happened the previous night. _____ said nothing happened and that he really was not around. He went to the store and when he came back, the children were in bed. He got home about 7:00 or 8:00 p.m. He went to get potato chips and candy. When he came home, he ordered a pizza and the children were already in bed. The detective then asked him if there was anything he wanted to change about what happened that morning. _____ said no and then recited the same story as he had stated previously. He denied that anyone was upset about _____ getting up late or being late for the bus. He stated several minutes after _____ left, the victim asked for his "baba." "I picked him up and put him down. He followed me into the kitchen. I gave him a little glass of water and he started choking. He was gasping for air." He stated the victim was not crying, that he was just gasping for air. "I laid him down on the floor because he almost collapsed. I laid him down. I tipped his head back and started breathing and see if I can get him back. He had a heartbeat. His heart was still beating. I put him on the floor and started '1 , 1000, 2, 1000." _____ then demonstrated chest compressions. He did this for about ten minutes. "Then I noticed no signs of him waking back up. I got really scared. I started beating on the walls. That's when I saw the black dude walk up. I don't even know his name. I told him to call 911 for me. I ran back home and kept doing it until they got there."

Detective _____ asked him when was the last time he shook the victim. He said "It was last week or something. He got into something and I said, " _____ don't do that. I just grabbed his arm and shake him." He denied picking him up and shaking him. He said that _____ does the same thing and demonstrated it by using both hands as though he had a baby in his arms and was shaking it.

The detective had concerns about the old rib fractures and wanted _____ to explain how they occurred. "I can safely bet it was accidental. I didn't intentionally hit him. He had slipped out of the bathtub. Getting him out of the bathtub. There's a lot of things he's done. When he was small, he slipped everywhere."

In the eight months that the victim had been living with _____ and _____ stated that he shook the victim about ten times. _____ had only shaken him a couple of times. He also admitted to picking up the victim by the arm or the leg before and stated he picked him up and grabbed the other arm. _____ demonstrated this by placing his closed fist about 10 or 12 inches apart and holding them in front of his face. He then said, "Just to tell him to stop or that's not right and from fighting with his sisters."

The detective told him that some of the injuries on the victim had occurred within the last 12 hours. _____ said, "And I was the only one around him. The only thing I have a problem with is hollering at him." He indicated he was scared to discipline the children because of the situation. He usually makes them sit on the floor for as many minutes as they were old. The victim always cried when he sat him down, and he always scolded him for it.

_____ denied shaking the victim that morning or the previous night. He stated that a few days prior, he had fallen out of his crib and that he was always climbing out of his crib. The victim would try to get out of his crib, and he would fall on the floor and hit his head. The victim had been falling out of his crib for the past three months. He has also fallen out of the tub in the past. _____ would grab the victim by the arm and lift him out and, as he did, the victim would slip out of his grasp and would fall against the side of the bathtub.

The detective then asked him if he thought _____ could be doing any harm to the victim. _____ said, "I failed to report last time." He denied that his wife was Inflicting any injuries. He then said "yeah, I had a feeling" that something was going on, such as "whippings, scoldings, always in bed early, but she loves the kids, though." He said that she would just "holler at him before, just for no reason. Something his second daughter did. Physical. I never saw nothing in my eyesight. All I can say is we're both at fault. That's all I can say. "The detective asked him why he stated that, and _____ said, "Because it happened right in front of my eyes." He said, "I didn't do nothing."

"The children all act different around _____ than they do around me. They always go into their room and play when _____ come home. The kids seem scared of her. The victim is scared of me because I used to holler at him. He used to back away from me. The victim would always go to _____ but she was too strict with him." He then said, "I could have grabbed him too tight or something. I don't know. I used to pick him up, too, and throw him in the air." He did indicate that the victim never fell or was dropped when this was occurring. After several seconds of silence, _____ said, "He would always cry. Maybe I was picking him up too hard. Threw him up and grabbed him too hard. That's the only thing I can think of."

_____ admitted that he had "smoked just a little bit weed" within the past 24 hours. He said he and _____ smoked a joint the previous night around 10 p.m., sometime after the children went to bed. _____ only used marijuana. At that point, the interview with _____ was terminated.

Detective _____ then went to interview _____ He told her of the injuries to her son and wanted to know how they could have occurred. She stated that she had no idea. "I don't hardly take care of my son. My husband won't even let me touch him. He gets mad because I spoil them so much. _____ gets mad if my son comes by me." She stated that her son never cried out about anything or about his chest hurting. "No, he always wanted me. _____ would always send him to the other room to play. I have no idea. My husband won't even let me give him a bath."

The detective asked her why she stopped cooperating with Child Protective Services in August. She stated that her husband did not want them around. She said, "I don't know. He always said he didn't want them around. He didn't want anyone bugging us all the time, and he told them not to come back." She did not know why her husband was uncooperative, but felt "because of what he did to the victim." The detective then told her that her husband said he did not do anything to their son. _____ said, "Bull shit, I never hurt my baby and he never wanted to be around the victim." The detective asked her why her husband would say that the children were scared of her. She said, "He wants to cover his own butt because of what he did to the victim."

When asked what he did to the victim, she said, "Well, he practically killed him."

She denied ever striking her child, especially since June 1993. She stated she did not really discipline them and they were never really bad. She denied ever grabbing them or shaking them. She stated that her husband would go into the room where the victim's crib was located and would tell the victim to lie down. Her husband usually wanted to be with her. He would tell the victim to lie down and the victim would start crying. Her husband yells all the time. Her husband would put the children to bed and then pull the mattress out from the other bedroom into the living room for them to sleep on. She stated that he had gone to the store the previous night, but when he got back, he put the children to bed. It was between 7:30 and 8:00 p.m. and asked whether he put the children to bed. He told her that he had. She then stated she was home at that time, but her husband put the children to bed.

She admitted to having a "hit" of marijuana the previous night. "Barely a bong full. He smokes a lot." She did not know how much her husband smoked and she did not pay attention.

_____ said that her husband was verbally abusive to her and called her "white trash" and the victim "white boy" all the time because the victim had lighter skin than his.

The detective asked her how she would take out her anger, and she said, "I yell a lot. I cry a lot. I've learned to be strong." Her husband would do all of the discipline. He would yell at them. Her husband would get angry with the victim and would hit him. "It's so hard for me. I'm so happy I'm away from him now." The last time she believes her husband hit the victim was sometime the previous week. He would usually hit him in the mouth and tell him to shut up. She would get mad at her husband, and then her husband would get mad because she got mad. Her husband hits the victim in the mouth because he would be crying because he would want to be with her. He has said he does not like his son, and sometimes she has told him, "Why do you want to be like your father? You're mean to your son because your father was mean to you." She wanted to tell someone this, but did not know how.

_____ went on to say that her husband was always pushing the victim and that she saw her husband slap the victim sometime the previous week. She did not know how the victim sustained any physical damage to his bones. She said, "I know and I didn't even know what happened. I didn't realize it was this serious. I really didn't." However, she knew that her husband was hitting and yelling and screaming at the victim. She believed this was occurring while was at work. She did not want to work and wished that he would get a job. The victim would cry every time she would leave for work. She did not really want to believe something was happening, but did and did not know how to stop it. She admitted to seeing bruises on her son and when she asked her husband about it, he said that the victim had fallen down. She denied ever seeing any scrape marks on victim.

On one occasion, the victim was limping. Her husband had told her that he was running and got his foot caught in a door in the apartment.

She admitted that she has seen her husband picking up the victim and shaking him and also picking him up by one arm and carrying him around the house. She demonstrated this by grabbing a stuffed animal from a table. She grabbed it by both arms and said, "Be quiet, be quiet." At the same time, she slapped the stuffed animal in the mouth.

The detective asked her how the victim had dried blood around his mouth. She stated that the victim bit his lip a couple of days prior. She then said "I didn't even see the victim last night. When I got home, _____ already had the kids in bed. I didn't even know he was putting the kids in bed. We usually put them in bed around 8:00 p.m. It was before 8:00. I know that."

At that point, the detective asked her what her husband had told her when she got home that morning. She said, _____ told me he drank a glass of water and he started choking. I said, 'Yeah, right.' I didn't believe him. He wanted me to hug him and I kept pulling away." She thought that her husband had hurt her son. She further indicated that she was fearful that he was going to hurt the children for the last four months. Any time that the victim would have a mark or a bruise, her husband would put Desitin diaper rash medicine on it to cover it up.

Detective _____ asked her if there was anything else she wanted to say. She said, "No," and then said, "I know it's my fault, too."

The interview with ＿＿＿ was then concluded. Both ＿＿＿ and ＿＿＿ were subsequently transported to County Jail.

At 7:26 p.m., detectives received a telephone call from Dr. ＿＿＿ at Children's Hospital. Dr. ＿＿＿ stated that the victim, age 19 months, had died.

On 2-28-94, an autopsy was performed on the victim. The date and time of death was 2-26-94 at 6:30 p.m. The cause of death was determined as multiple blunt force injuries. The autopsy revealed on the victim's head, face and central nervous system there were multiple bruises on the right side of the head, right forehead and the right side of the face. There were multiple scalp bruises on the back of the head. There were multiple bruises, buccal mucosa with a chipped right incisor. There was subdural hemorrhage covering the convexities of the cerebral hemispheres and the base of the brain. There were bruises on the right cheek and chin and bilateral retinal hemorrhages and cerebral edema.

The victim also had neck injuries that consisted of soft tissue hemorrhage, posterior pharynx, and numerous abrasions, lacerations and bruises on the tip of the tongue. There were multiple bruises of the anterior chest wall and multiple recent and old healed fractures of the posterior ribs, 9th, 10th, 11th and 12th left and 8th, 9th, 10th and 11th right bilateral ribs. There were also healing of nondisplaced fractures of the clavicle.

The victim sustained skin bruises on the left side of the abdomen, hemoperitoneum, lacerations of the ligament of Treitz and mesentery, which was associated with soft tissue hemorrhage. He sustained multiple skin bruises to his back and had healing abrasions and fresh bruises of the sacrum and buttocks that were extensive. There were multiple skin and intramuscular soft tissue hemorrhages of the upper and lower extremities that were extensive.

On 2-28-94, Detective ＿＿＿ of the ＿＿＿＿＿＿ Police Department contacted ＿＿＿ at the ＿＿＿＿＿ Detention Facility. She started the conversation with what had happened on Friday morning. She stated that she had to be at work at 10:00 a.m. on Fridays. She left the apartment at 8:55 a.m. to catch the bus. When she left, the children were still asleep. Her husband was awake, but was still in bed. She arrived at work just prior to 10:00 a.m. She worked until 5:00 p.m. She received her paycheck during the day and, at 5:00 p.m., she walked over to a store around the corner from where she worked to get it cashed. At 6:00 p.m., she arrived at home. Her youngest daughter was in the bassinet. The other children were in their room. Her second daughter and the victim came out of their room to see her. The children were happy to see her. She did not remember having a conversation with her husband. As she did every payday, she gave her husband half of her paycheck. He went to the store and bought milk and candy bars. He then went to a friend's house around the corner and bought $20 worth of marijuana. Her husband was happy because it was Friday and she had gotten paid. Between 7:30 and 8:00 p.m., her husband put the children to bed. She was not really aware that he had done it.

At about 8:00 p.m., her 21-year-old brother came over. They all talked for awhile and smoked about four to five bongsfull of marijuana. Sometime between 10:00 and 11:00 p.m., her brother left and she went to bed. Her husband was still awake and watching television. Her husband had fed the children spaghetti before she arrived home from work. After he went to the store and got some milk, he ordered a pizza from Pizza Hut. He put the children in their bedroom and made them play there until he put them to bed. She usually never checked on the children, because that is what her husband did.

Several days prior, she found blood on the victim's mouth. She asked her husband about it, and he said that the victim bit his lip. She did not believe him, because she has seen him hit the victim in the mouth in the past.

The victim showed no signs of being in pain on Friday night or Saturday morning. About four months prior, her husband began yelling at the victim a lot. He began refusing to allow social workers to see or examine the children and refused to see his own therapist.

On Saturday, she woke up at 7:25 a.m. Realizing she was late, she got dressed and, as she did, she could hear the victim whining in his crib. As she was leaving out the door to catch the bus, her husband said, "Are you going to be late tonight?" She told him she would be home around 6:00 to 7:00 p.m. When she got to work about 8:30 a.m., she was told by a coworker that a neighbor called and said her son had choked and went to Grossmont Hospital. She was able to get a ride to Grossmont Hospital with a friend of her husband. She only knew his name as _____ Once at _____ Hospital, she was told that her son was at Children's Hospital. On the way to Children's Hospital, she said she told _____ _____ probably hurt the victim because he's mean to them. We will probably lose our kids. Don't tell _____ what I told you. He'll hurt me."

Once at Children's Hospital, she was told nothing about her son's condition. She was only told that he was in Radiology and would not be available for about an hour. She was then driven home by _____ .

When she got home to her apartment, she took her youngest daughter, age two months, away from her husband and walked away from him. She thought that her husband had hurt the victim somehow. When Officer _____ told her that her son had died, she thought _____ had killed him.

When the detective told her about the rib fractures, she said that for the last three to four months, her husband had been very mean to the victim and always had an excuse for all of the victim's bruises. Her husband would become physically violent with her about one to two times a week. Sometime during the last month when they were having an argument about hitting the victim, her husband said, "I wish you all were dead."

She stated that she always witnessed her husband shaking the victim and picking him up by one arm. The last four months, she did not want to work. She felt that her husband should work and that he was going to hurt the children. This was based on the physical violence she witnesses, including the shaking, hitting and pushing of the victim and the physical violence to her.

On Thursday or Friday, she saw makeup on the victim's face. She asked her husband about it, and he said that her second daughter had pushed him down. She did not remember seeing marks or bruises on the victim's body at all on. Thursday or Friday.

The interview with _____ was then concluded. Detectives then travelled to the Central Jail Facility to reinterview _____ During the interview, he reiterated the same story he stated previously. The detectives then asked him to explain all the injuries sustained by the victim. They told him that his son had numerous fractured ribs, some as old as four to five months and some as new as two to three days. The victim also had over 30 bruises on his body, some of which were bone deep. There was an abdominal injury and the subdural hematoma which the medical examiner felt killed him. These injuries occurred within a half hour of the paramedics arriving. The detective asked him if he caused those injuries. _____ thought for several seconds and began to cry. He then stated that he did not hurt his son. The detective asked him if his wife _____ had harmed his son. He continued to cry and rested his head in his arms. He then shook his head no. The detective stated that based on what he and _____ had stated previously, _____ was not at home when the injuries could have occurred aren't strong enough to injure the victim, who did" _____ said, "It only leaves me then. I can't tell you why I didn't do it."

_____ then wanted to speak with an attorney, and the interview was concluded.

During the continuing investigation, neighbors of the _____ were interviewed. Statements were made to the detectives that yelling and sounds of hitting were heard from the _____ residence almost every night. There were also sounds being heard of banging on the wall at least once a week.

On 4-15-94 at the request of _____ and his defense attorney, District Attorney _____ and his investigator requested a meeting in regard to making a statement about what had occurred. The defendant was interviewed at the Central Detention Facility and stated during the interview that, on the day the offense occurred, he woke up his wife and she was in a rush to get to work. The victim was up crying. She went into the room and he heard a little "ruckage." She told the victim to "lay down" and "your daddy's not ready to get up yet." He then heard some big crashes like someone was slamming something. She then hurried up and got dressed and left for work. The next thing he heard was the victim crying again, so he got up. He said, "What's wrong, buddy? You okay?" The victim kept saying, "Baba, baba." _____ changed the victim's diaper and put some cream on his buttocks. The victim had bruises. He then picked him up out of bed, put him behind him and said, "Come on, let's go get some, go get some baba." They went to the kitchen. He gave the victim a little cup of water in his favorite cup and then all of a sudden he collapsed. _____ felt the victim was choking and he started CPR. He performed the best he knew how for approximately five or ten minutes. He then ran out of the apartment and began knocking on a neighbor's door. He saw a black man walk up and told this individual to call 911.

Additionally, in the interview, he stated that his wife had a problem with the victim's color. The victim was not as dark as him _____. He also indicated that his wife had hit the victim in the mouth and had beat on him. This occurred prior to the instant offense.

DEFENDANT'S STATEMENT:

SOURCES OF INFORMATION for this section

INTERVIEW, _____ DETENTION FACILITY, 10–18–94;

The defendant elected not to submit a written statement on his probation questionnaire.

The defendant spoke in a very low and monotone voice during the interview. He displayed a very nonchalant and cold demeanor. He also did not shed any tears or get watery eyes when discussing his child's death.

The defendant stated that he woke up on the morning of the instant offense at 7:25 a.m. His son was crying. He woke up his wife because she had to go to work. She got dressed and went into their son's bedroom. The defendant heard a slamming noise in the room. She was in the room for approximately three to four minutes. He then heard one big slam, and then his wife ran out of the room, saying that she was late for work. She kissed him goodbye and then she left. His son was still crying, so he went into the room. The child wanted a bottle. He changed his son's diaper, set him down, and walked toward the kitchen with the child following him.

Once in the kitchen, the defendant began fixing him a bottle. He gave his son a glass of water. His son fell over, and he thought that his son was choking. He then began CPR and noticed that his son was not responding. His son was barely breathing. He had to leave him for a moment so he could get help. He left and began banging on people's doors. He saw a neighbor and told him to call 911. The defendant then ran back inside his apartment and continued giving his child CPR until the ambulance arrived.

The defendant indicated that his wife caused the bruises and broken ribs to their son. She would strike their son with her fists. He was present sometimes when the abuse occurred, and he tried to stop her a couple of times. His wife had a hard time with their son's skin color. She wanted him to be "darker."

When asked why this statement is inconsistent with a statement he told the patrol officers and detectives, he stated that police officers usually turn things around. He decided to tell his lawyer this story.

The defendant indicated that he was scared to contact the social worker regarding the abuse his son was subjected to by his wife. He did not want to lose his children since he had to fight to get them back for three years.

He indicated that his wife was in therapy while the abuse was going on. The defendant did not disclose this to the therapist. He also did not let the social worker in the home to see the children, because sometime the victim had bruises. The defendant was hiding and did not want the social worker to see the children. He also stated that the other children were not abused.

He denies ever striking his children. He loves his children very much. If they needed discipline, he would take a toy away from them or sit them down for five minutes.

The defendant believes he was convicted because of his size, color and the letters that he wrote to his wife while in custody. He would never have killed his son. His son was his heart, and he always wanted a son since his other children are girls.

He feels terrible that his son has died. He has never been in a situation like this before. He does not believe he will live through things if he goes to prison, because he is a convicted baby killer. He is scared to be incarcerated in State Prison.

In regard to an appropriate sentence, he would like the Court to know that it was wrong for him not removing his children from their home. However, he does not deserve a 15 year to life sentence. He was not aware he would be sentenced to State Prison.

CRIMINAL HISTORY:

SOURCES OF INFORMATION for this section
CII, 9–28–94; FBI, 9–28–94; LOCAL RECORDS, 10–19–94; PROBATION FILE

| 10-26-82 | Barstow PD | 496.1 PC; 488 PC | _____ 10–28–82: conv 488 PC, misd; 6 mos prob, 3 days j1 |
| 2-26-094 | LMPD | 187(a) PC; 273a(1) PC | _____ INSTANT OFFENSE |

PERSONAL HISTORY:

The following information was offered by the defendant. Unless noted otherwise it has not been verified.

Significant Family Information:

The defendant, is the youngest child in a family of six children. He has two brothers and three sisters. His parents divorced when he was young. His mother remarried. He believes his parents still reside in _____. He describes his childhood as fair, although his family had to struggle for food, clothing and rent. He reported no abuse.

Family Criminal History:

He indicated that one of his sisters, _____ has a history of drug abuse and arrests. She has been arrested in _____, _____ and _____.

Education:

The defendant graduated from _____ High School.

Employment History:

The defendant has been unemployed for approximately one and a half years. His prior employment was working as a cook for the _____ in _____. He worked for them for approximately two and a half years.

Source of Support:

Wife.

Financial Condition:

Broke.

Number of Dependents & Ages/Relationship to Defendant:

The defendant has an 11-year-old daughter from a previous relationship, a four-year-old daughter with his wife, a three-year- old daughter with his wife, the victim, who was 19 months, and a seven-month-old daughter.

Military Status:

None.

Marital Status:

The defendant married his wife, _____ on 10–11–92. She has sought a divorce from the defendant.

Psychological/Medical Problems:

The defendant stated that he has a cracked left shoulder which is separated.

Physical Health:

Healthy.

Substance Abuse History:

The defendant stated he occasionally consumes alcohol. In regard to drugs, he stated approximately three years ago, he began using crystal methamphetamine. He continues to the present and uses approximately one time per week, using a quarter gram. He also started using marijuana at age 16 and continues to the present. He was smoking marijuana every other day.

Gang Affiliation:

None.

COLLATERAL INFORMATION:

SOURCES OF INFORMATION for this section
TELEPHONE CONTACT WITH DEPUTY DISTRICT ATTORNEY;
TELEPHONE CONTACT WITH DEFENSE ATTORNEY; _____
TELEPHONE CONTACT WITH DEFENSE ATTORNEY _____ TELEPHONE CONTACT WITH CHILDREN'S SOCIAL WORKERS

Conversation with Deputy District Attorney:

The undersigned spoke with Deputy DA _____ on 10-18-94. He indicated that at the trial, the facts were presented virtually the same as the facts stated in the police reports. The doctors and a dental expert from defendant _____ case were brought in to testify regarding the abuse of the _____ first child. Also, the social worker for the family in 1993 testified.

Letters that _____ had written to his wife while in custody were brought in as evidence, including one that was very ambiguous and stated, "I know I killed my baby _____ but you know who really killed him." _____ also testfied and stated that he knew son was being abused by his wife, but he did not stop it.

A social worker for the Family Preservation Unit testified that _____ refused to sign a contract that would give them the "right to examine the body of the children." He refused to sign this contract in December 1993. Services were then not provided for the family since he refused to sign the contract. _____ had signed it.

The victim had bruises all over his body from his head to his toes. There was a bruise on the left leg that went from his skin all the way through to the bone. It was determined that bruise could only have been inflicted by a lot of force. Dr. _____ from Children's Hospital also testified that fingernail gouges were found on this victim and were the same as what was found on the _____ first child. Chest X-Rays were also examined from the _____ first child and this victim, and the rib fractures were very similar and in the same areas.

Conversation with Children's Social Workers on 10–18 and 10–19–94:

The undersigned spoke with Social Worker _____ on 10–18–94. She is the social worker for the _____ youngest child. She indicated that the child is doing fine and that she is currently in _____ with _____ maternal aunt. The child will eventually be adopted by this aunt. There were no physical injuries found on this child, although the child is developmentally delayed.

On 10–19–94, the undersigned a spoke with Social Worker _____ the social worker for the _____ second child. She indicated that she is in a confidential foster home and doing pretty well. She is attending counseling one time per week and is also in preschool two times per week. This child, who is approximately three years of age, is still attached to a bottle and a pacifier. She does not sleep by herself and sleeps with her older foster sister. She also still has nightmares and is not eating well.

The child never asks about her parents and, when the therapist brings it up, she does not want to talk about it.

The parental rights were terminated for this child on 9–27–94. The foster parents intend to adopt this, child. This child is very attached to the foster parents.

Conversation with Foster Parents:

The foster father indicated that they had the _____ second child for quite some time prior to her being returned to her parents. Since they have had her returned to them after the instant offense, they took her to their pediatrician for an examination. The pediatrician indicated there were significant bruises on the child's back and a bite mark on the arm. There is also some scarring on the back of her neck under her hair. These marks could be from cigarette burns or the gouging of fingernails. They are deep pockmarks which are still prominent. The pediatrician did not conduct a more thorough examination since the child was traumatized and he did not want to do anything to further traumatize her.

When the foster parents picked up the child from _____, she was stiff and stoic. It was approximately three or four days before she began speaking again. For quite some time, she was afraid of the foster father and for one month she did not speak to him. When she wanted to speak to him, she would whisper to the foster mother to tell him whatever she wanted him to know. Last month, she began speaking normally and directly to the foster father.

On one occasion, she saw a picture of the foster mother's father and brother playing. The first comment she made was that the man was hurting the child. This child has had a definite reaction to male figures, which has not been positive. She is currently working with a therapist, and the therapist is trying to see what the child will disclose.

There has been a great deal of anxiety since the child was returned to the foster parents. The child had bonded with the foster parents prior to her being returned to her natural parents. Since she has been returned, when the foster mother leaves the home to run an errand or go to an appointment, the child becomes very angry that she went and acts out her anger.

Telephone Contact with Defense Attorney _____

The undersigned spoke with defense attorney _____ on 10−20−94. She indicated that the codefendant, _____, testified at trial. Evidence was also presented that the loss of consciousness to the victim would have been immediately after the blow was inflicted, which would indicate that _____ was responsible for inflicting the injury since his wife was not at home. She also indicated that two psychologists diagnosed the defendant and stated that her previous diagnosis of "disassociative disorder" was incorrect and that she was misdiagnosed.

Telephone Contact with Defense Attorney _____

The undersigned spoke to _____ on 10−21−94. He indicated that the facts stated at trial were the same as those on the police reports.

SENTENCING DATA:

As to Count 2:

Possible Circumstances in Mitigation:

Rule 423(b)(1): The defendant's prior record of criminal conduct could be considered insignificant in that it consists of no prior felony convictions.

Possible Circumstances in Aggravation:

Rule 421(a)(3): The victim, who was 19 months old, was particularly vulnerable. He was not able to verbalize the abuse that was being inflicted upon him to anyone or seek help for himself.

Rule 421(a)(11): The defendant took advantage of a position of trust or confidence to commit this offense. The 19-month-old victim depended upon his parents to care and provide for him along with nurturing and loving him in a proper environment. They violated this trust when they continuously abused this victim.

Prison Term Analysis:

The circumstances in aggravation dominate and suggest imposition of the upper term be set. The possible prison terms for 273a(1) PC, Count 2, are two years, four years or six years.

The sentencing scheme proposed by the Probation Officer will involved a "two box" system, one "box" for the indeterminate term (Count 1, 187(a) PC, Murder, second degree) and one "box" for the determinate term in Count 2.

Count 1, 187(a) PC, Murder, second degree, carries a penalty of 15 years to life. If the Court finds the second degree murder conviction on Count 1 was based upon the felony murder rule, murder was committed in the course of the child abuse in Count 2, then 654 PC would bar punishment on Count 2. The undersigned is recommending a stay of punishment on Count 2 under 654 PC per People v. Boyd 222 Cal.App.3d 575.

EVALUATION:

As to both counts unless otherwise specified:

Circumstances Supporting a Grant of Probation:

Rule 413(a): The defendant appears eligible for a grant of probation.

Rule 414(b)(1): The defendant's prior record of criminal conduct could be considered insignificant, in that it consists of no prior felony convictions.

Circumstances Supporting a Denial of Probation:

Rule 414(a)(1): The nature, seriousness and circumstances of the crime are extremely brutal and vicious and warrant a State Prison commitment. The defendants abused their 19-month-old son to the point of causing his death. He had over 30 bruises on his body, several broken ribs, and both clavicles were broken, with all broken bones in different stages of healing, and a cerebral hematoma, which ultimately caused his death.

Rule 414(a)(3): The victim was particularly vulnerable in that he was only 19 months old and unable to verbalize and inform anyone of the abuse that was being inflicted upon him.

Rule 414(a)(4): The defendant caused the death of his 19-month-old son.

Rule 414(a)(6): The defendant was an active participant.

Rule 414(a)(9): The defendant took advantage of a position of trust and confidence to commit this offense. The defendant, being the natural father of the child, was responsible for the care, custody and control, along with the loving and nurturing of the child. The defendant relied on him to provide for him and satisfy these natural needs without abusing him. He violated his position as a father when he abused his child and failed to protect him.

Rule 414(b)(3): The defendant did not express a willingness to comply with the terms of probation.

Rule 414(b)(4): The defendant does not appear able to comply with reasonable terms of probation, as is indicated by his lack of willingness to comply with the terms of probation, his lack of employment, and his substance abuse. The nature of the offense does not warrant a grant of probation.

Rule 414(b)(7): The defendant is in denial regarding inflicting any abuse upon his child. He is sorry that he died and that he failed to protect him.

Rule 414(b)(8): There is a likelihood that, if not imprisoned, the defendant will continue to be a danger to his other children.

The 30-year-old defendant is appearing before the Court today for sentencing on a guilty jury verdict on Count 1, 187(a) PC, Murder, second degree, and Count 2, 273a(1), Child Abuse, a felony. A 911 call was received of a baby choking at a residence on _____ Lane. Paramedics and La Mesa fire officials responded and found a 19-month- old child in a state of cardiac arrest. The child had blood around in the mouth and several bruises on his chest. The mother had left for work a half hour earlier, and the father, _____,

was babysitting the three children. _____ said he gave the defendant a glass of water and he started choking. The child was taken to Children's Hospital, where he ultimately died. An autopsy was performed which disclosed over 30 bruises on the victim's body from his head to his toes, multiple rib and clavicle fractures in various stages of healing, and a cerebral hematoma. The coroner stated the cause of death was multiple blunt force injuries.

The defendant has a prior record that consists of a misdemeanor petty theft that occurred in 1982. The defendant admitted to using marijuana and crystal methamphetamine and stated he has been unemployed for approximately one and a half years. He has been the caretaker of his three children while his wife worked.

In regard to the instant offense, the defendant denied inflicting any abuse to any of his children. He stated that he witnessed his wife strike the victim and, on a couple of occasions, attempted to stop her. He never reported any incidents to authorities or the social worker, because he did not want his children taken away from him.

It is hard to believe that this defendant, 5'8", 175 lbs., could not atop his 5'4", 90 lb. wife from striking their son. This 19-month- old child suffered and was treated in a very brutal fashion at the hands of his parents. These people were the individuals responsible to love and nurture this child and, instead, they violated their parental rights by committing this cold, callous, heartless and vicious crime. This child sustained significant blows to his body, which ultimately caused his death. This defendant had a very nonchalant attitude about this offense and showed absolutely no remorse for what has occurred. His only concern was that he was "scared" of being sentenced to State Prison and what might happen to him while being housed there. He shed no tears for his son who was his "heart." He has displayed nothing but a blatant disregard to his son's life and life in general.

Although this defendant is eligible for a grant of probation, to grant probation to such an individual would not be acceptable. He deserves to be incarcerated in State Prison for as long a period as possible. Therefore, considering all the factors presented, the Probation Officer recommends a 15 year to life sentence in State Prison.

CUSTODY DATA:

Date Confined	Date Released	Place	Custody Days
2–26–94	11–3–94 (In custody)	County Jail	251
		4019 PC Credits	124
		Total CTS	375

RECOMMENDATION:

That probation be denied and the defendant be committed to the Department of Corrections for the indeterminate term of 15 years to life, with credit for time served of 251 actual days and 124 days 4019 PC credits, a total of 375 days credit; further, that the defendant pay a restitution fine pursuant to 13967 Government Code in the amount of $10,000 to be paid forthwith or as provided in 2085.5 PC.

Term recommendation breakdown is as follows:

Crime	Suggested Base Term	Recommended Term	Recommended Stay
Indeterminate Term:			
187(a) PC, second degree, Count 1	15 years to life	15 years to life	0
Determinate Term:			
273a(a)(1) PC, Count 2	Upper—6 years	0	6 years barred per 654 PC
	TOTAL TERM	15 years to life	

Respectfully submitted,

_____

Chief Probation Officer
By:

Approved _____

_____

I have read and considered the foregoing report.

Deputy Probation Officer

_____

JUDGE OF THE SUPERIOR COURT

_____ /10–26–94

PROB. 2185 (6–19–91)

Performance Evaluation

EMPLOYEE LAST NAME	FIRST NAME	CVPD ID #
Wayne	John	

POSITION / JOB TITLE	RATING PERIOD FROM (DATE)	TO (DATE)
Police Agent		

RATING SUPERVISOR LAST NAME	FIRST NAME	CVPD ID #

Overall Appraisal of Employee Performance:

- ☐ **Above Standards**
- ☒ **Meets Standards**
- ☐ **Improvement Needed** (see Professional Development Plan, included)

Rater:

I have explained this report to the rated employee. I attest that the information contained herein is accurate and is based upon my observation and/ or knowledge of the facts.

Signature:　　　　　Date:

Employee: Agent John Wayne

- ☐ I have discussed my evaluation with my supervisor.
- ☐ I would like to discuss my evaluation or other matters with someone other than my supervisor.
- ☐ See comments section for my input.

Signature:　　　　　Date:

Lieutenant: Lt. Bongo Banger

I have reviewed this report for accuracy and completeness and I approve.

Signature:　　　　　Date:

Department Head: Captain John Depp

I have reviewed this report for accuracy and completeness and I approve.

Signature:　　　　　Date:

Performance measures included herein are based, in part, on the overall expectation of the employee performance by the department (to include subordinates, peers, supervisors and managers). Standards are based on the employee's knowledge and application of the Department Procedure Manual, any Training Bulletins, standard operating procedures, and the orders and commands of supervisors, to include written directives such as the "State of the Watch" expectations.

The following ratings will be used to document the department's rating of your performance in each anchor:

O	Outstanding
AS	Above Standard
MS	Meets Standard
SS	Sub-Standard (improvement needed)
U	Unsatisfactory
NA	Not Applicable

The employee should expect written comments for any rating of "SS" (Sub-Standard) or "U" (Unsatisfactory). The purpose of these comments is to identify deficiencies and to recommend corrective measures. The supervisor is also encouraged to include written comments for any ratings of "AS" (Above Standard) and "O" (Outstanding).

A. ENFORCEMENT

#		Rating	Comments
1	Maintain beat integrity by patrolling in your assigned area unless cleared to leave by your dispatcher, or for emergency response. Exception to be cleared through your supervisor. (Meets Standards is the highest rating possible.)	☐ ☐ ☒ ☐ ☐ ☐	
2	Take the most expeditious route to assigned calls, and do not delay your response unless cleared first with dispatch and/or your supervisor. When assigned by radio, give your location.	☐ ☐ ☒ ☐ ☐ ☐	
3	Monitor your radio, MDC, and any other communication devices at all times. Acknowledge transmissions when called, and keep your status updated. Use the radio only for work related matters and maintain the highest levels of professionalism when broadcasting.	☐ ☐ ☒ ☐ ☐ ☐	
4	Handle all activities per Law, Policy and Procedures Manual, and Standard Operating Procedures.	☐ ☐ ☒ ☐ ☐ ☐	
5	Apply problem solving techniques to identified crime and disorder problems in area of responsibility and initiate appropriate steps to resolve them by utilizing available resources, i.e. Supervisors, Tough on Crime, other Department methods or strategies, etc. *Note: This rating will be based on effort and outcomes. A "meets standards" rating is earned by identifying problems and applying basic techniques. An "above standard rating" is earned by demonstrating advanced techniques. An "outstanding rating is earned by using advanced techniques and having a positive impact on the problem*	☐ ☐ ☒ ☐ ☐ ☐	
6	Your activity levels should be comparable to your peers in like conditions as considered over the previous 12 months. The following will be considered: arrests, traffic contacts, FI cards, hours worked, and citizen/business contacts. *Note: Your activity is to be quality work, which is problem oriented, proactive and addresses the priorities identified in your assigned beat. If you cannot maintain an adequate activity level with quality work, which is problem oriented, you must advise your supervisor immediately. Activity for the sake of activity is not considered quality work.*	☐ ☒ ☐ ☐ ☐ ☐	Agt John Wayne is generally more proactive than other Field Agents I have worked with in the past. His proactive activities, however, do not interfer with the expected duties and responsibilities of his Rank.

B. JOB KNOWLEDGE

1	Crime and arrest reports will have the most appropriate charge.	☐ ☐ ☒ ☐ ☐ ☐
2	Officers will know the elements of crimes, traffic violations, and other offenses and be able to articulate them.	☐ ☐ ☒ ☐ ☐ ☐
3	Officers will know the most current case law regarding laws arrest, search and seizure and other pertinent topics.	☐ ☐ ☒ ☐ ☐ ☐
4	Officers will know of resources outside the Police Department that may assist them in resolving crime and disorder problems.	☐ ☐ ☒ ☐ ☐ ☐
5	Officers will know the most common crime types, crime locations, calls for service types, and important crime/disorder information.	☐ ☐ ☒ ☐ ☐ ☐
6	Officers will comply with the Department policies and procedures regarding court appearances. This includes but is not be limited to: arriving in court as scheduled, reviewing reports prior to court appearances, presenting evidence, wearing proper attire, contacting the DA's Office as instructed, and providing credible, complete, and courteous testimony.	☐ ☐ ☒ ☐ ☐ ☐
7	Officers will conduct thorough investigations. This will include attempts to locate and interview all involved parties and attempts to locate and properly document evidence.	☐ ☐ ☒ ☐ ☐ ☐

INTERPERSONAL SKILLS

You are required to conduct yourself in a manner, which supports teamwork and enhances the City/Department in the accomplishment of our stated missions and objectives. You will also conduct yourself in a manner that promotes a good public image, promotes customer service, and brings credit to the City. This includes the following areas:

C. Teamwork

		Rating
1	Perform your job so that others are not burdened with additional work. Help others when the need is apparent. Promote teamwork by sharing information useful to achieving desired results. *Note: This rating will be based on the teamwork displayed by the employee. Patterns of abusing time off may also be addressed in this section. It will pertain to the overall pattern or behavior displayed and may coincide with rating anchors addressed in other portions of the evaluation.*	☐ ☒ ☐ ☐ ☐ ☐ — Agent John Wayne is a complete team player. He offfers information, assistance and is an active participant when appropriate and needed. This is a quality that subordinates and peers admire.

D. Relationship with Fellow Employees

		Rating
1	Treat others with respect.	☐ ☐ ☒ ☐ ☐ ☐
2	Find constructive ways to handle differences. Do not allow differences with others to disrupt your work or the work of others.	☐ ☐ ☒ ☐ ☐ ☐
3	Attempt to resolve issues at the lowest possible administrative level.	☐ ☐ ☒ ☐ ☐ ☐
4	Conduct yourself in a manner which makes you part of the solution, not part of the problem. Demonstrate initiative by suggesting practical, constructive alternatives and be willing to contribute to realistic solutions. Introduce ideas in ways that aid understanding and produce results to your team.	☐ ☒ ☐ ☐ ☐ ☐ — Agent John Wayne often times participates in group settings such as Roll call, to offer senarios or suggestions, to teach and develop his team mates.
5	Recognize, formally and informally the good work of peers and co-workers.	☐ ☐ ☒ ☐ ☐ ☐

E. Acceptance of Supervision

		Rating
1	Discuss your complaints with your supervisor in a constructive and respectful manner.	☐ ☐ ☒ ☐ ☐ ☐
2	Be receptive and respond properly to instruction and direction.	☐ ☐ ☒ ☐ ☐ ☐
3	Report to your supervisor any citizen contacts that may generate a complaint.	☐ ☐ ☒ ☐ ☐ ☐
4	Comply with the City harassment policy.	☐ ☐ ☒ ☐ ☐ ☐

F. Public Relations

1. Behave and act in a manner consistent with the City and Department's Mission Statement, values, and policies. Interact with the public in a manner that is service-oriented as exhibited by courtesy, integrity, respect, fairness, excellence and professionalism. ☐ ☐ ☒ ☐ ☐ ☐

G. REPORT WRITING

1. Reports must be in accordance with Law and Policy and Procedures Manual. ☐ ☐ ☒ ☐ ☐ ☐

2. 90% of your reports should be useable on first submittal. No more than 10% should have to be returned to you for errors, omissions, missing elements, incomplete preliminary investigation or lack of corpus, spelling, grammar, sentence structure, format, illegibility, etc. ☐ ☐ ☒ ☐ ☐ ☐

   Note: A "useable" report is one that does not require further work by the officer and it accurately reflects the preliminary investigation conducted by the officer. Differences in writing style may be tolerated if they do not impair prosecution or accurate record keeping. If the reviewer or others have to do work the officer should have done, the report is not useable when first submitted.

3. Take reports and submit them as soon as possible during the shift as required by Department Policy and Standard Operating Procedures. ☐ ☐ ☒ ☐ ☐ ☐

H. SAFETY

You are expected to conduct your work in a manner, which protects you, your coworkers, and others from harm; and which protects equipment and facilities from damage.

1. Follow applicable Laws, City/Department Policies, Procedures, and Standard Operating Procedures pertaining to, but not limited to: approved field tactics, arrest and handcuffing techniques, communicable diseases, firearms, hazardous substances and materials, pursuits/driving, radio, use of Force, vehicles and equipment, and work places. ☐ ☐ ☒ ☐ ☐ ☐

2. Use and maintain all required safety equipment per City/Department policy. ☐ ☐ ☒ ☐ ☐ ☐

3. Practice safe behavior in order to prevent accidents, injury, or damage and participate in and comply with City/Department-provided safety training. ☐ ☐ ☒ ☐ ☐ ☐

| 4 | Take immediate action to correct and/or report unsafe acts and conditions of which you become aware. | ☐ ☐ ☒ ☐ ☐ ☐ |
| 5 | Report all accidents, injuries, incidents, threats, or threatening behavior per City/Department policy. | ☐ ☐ ☒ ☐ ☐ ☐ |

I. WORK HABITS

You are expected to be productively engaged in the Department's tasks while on paid time. Organize your time and focus your attention on the priorities assigned.

1	Begin shift at the time established prepared to perform your assigned duties, in appropriate attire (per policy), and with all necessary equipment.	☐ ☐ ☒ ☐ ☐ ☐
2	Be in the field and available for calls within 10 minutes after briefing, unless otherwise directed by your supervisor.	☐ ☐ ☒ ☐ ☐ ☐
3	Remain in service and available until the end of shift, unless directed otherwise by your supervisor.	☐ ☐ ☒ ☐ ☐ ☐
4	Demonstrate the ability to establish priorities by completing assignments by established times, unless prior authorization is secured from your supervisor for an extension.	☐ ☐ ☒ ☐ ☐ ☐
5	Comply with City/Department policies for meal breaks.	☐ ☐ ☒ ☐ ☐ ☐
6	Comply with Department overtime and leave policy (i.e. vacation, sick leave, compensatory time, FMLA, etc.). Avoid patterns of short-term (one or two days) sick leave use in conjunction with days off, vacations, holidays, and special events.	☐ ☐ ☒ ☐ ☐ ☐
7	Know and comply with all City/Department policies and procedures.	☐ ☐ ☒ ☐ ☐ ☐
8	Display ability to multi-task. This will include delegation of duties and the management of various tasks most commonly associated with the type of call for service, investigation, or assignment the Officer is involved in.	☐ ☐ ☒ ☐ ☐ ☐
9	Attend scheduled training as required. *Note: Consideration for an above-standard or outstanding rating in this area may include seeking and obtaining additional training (to include formal training, informal training, and self-initiated learning) relevant to law enforcement that will enhance the Officer's professional development.*	☐ ☐ ☒ ☐ ☐ ☐

J. EQUIPMENT USE, MAINTENANCE, AND PROFICIENCY

You are expected to use, maintain and be proficient with equipment in a manner that will promote its function/purpose and remain in good working order and appearance.

1	Maintain all Department issued equipment in clean, working condition. Immediately report damage or malfunction to your supervisor.	☐	☐	☒	☐	☐	☐
2	Conduct vehicle checks per Standard Operating Procedures. Check vehicle at the beginning and the end of shift and replenish supplies. Immediately report damage or deficiencies to supervisor and complete vehicle damage form.	☐	☐	☒	☐	☐	☐
3	Check out and return all equipment to its proper place at the end of shift.	☐	☐	☒	☐	☐	☐
4	Immediately report damage to any equipment to your supervisor and complete necessary paperwork.	☐	☐	☒	☐	☐	☐
5	Keep vehicles clean and free of contraband, evidence and debris. Fuel vehicle at the end of shift unless otherwise directed.	☐	☐	☒	☐	☐	☐
6	Demonstrate proficiency in the use of ALL Department issued equipment that is required. Note: Proficiency will be demonstrated in the equipment the Officer is expected to carry and/or use including, but not limited to: firearms; less lethal options such as air tasers, bean-bag shotgun; intermediate weapons such as baton or O.C. Other equipment considered for this rating will be vehicles; MDC; police radio; recording devices such as M.V.R.'s and personal recording devices; Intoximeter; P.A.S. device; computers (booking and report writing); digital cameras; etc.	☐	☐	☒	☐	☐	☐

K. APPEARANCE

1	Maintain a clean, well-groomed, professional appearance. Present yourself in a manner most likely to inspire public confidence and respect. Comply with the standards set forth in the department uniform and grooming policy, including exercising good personal hygiene and maintaining a neat and orderly appearance.	☐	☐	☒	☐	☐	☐

ADDITIONAL COMMENTS: *(List any additional comments or recommendations. Include any and all attaways, awards, commendations, or specialized training received during this rating period.)*

Agent John wayne was promoted to Agent in October of 2011. He was assigned to Swing Watch, as a new Agent on November 24, 2011. He has brought a fresh, safety first, investigator's prospective to his subordinates that he routinely demonstrates in his daily functions. Agent John Wayne has demonstrated that he is extremely approachable, while maintaining the role of his new rank. These qualities have provided a Mentoring based, broader approach and visible example for subordinate's professional thought, development and actions.

PROFESSIONAL DEVELOPMENT PLAN:

Agent John Wayne already has a good grasp of the responsiblities of his new Rank. I recommend that as he begins his new assignment in Patrol, he expand his credentialed knowlege and experience in supervision models and theories. He can do so by exposing himself to reading resources or formal classes that examin leadership styles and functions. I suggest Agent John Wayne to contact Training to clarify the Department's Training Plan for his rank so he is aware of future opportunities and requirements.

EMPLOYEE COMMENTS:

A-2

Affidavit for Search Warrant

IN THE SUPERIOR COURT OF THE STATE OF CALIFORNIA,
COUNTY OF SAN DIEGO

STATE OF CALIFORNIA,)

(ss.

COUNTY OF SAN DIEGO)

AFFIDAVIT FOR SEARCH WARRANT

No. _____

I, John Smooth, do on oath make complaint, say and depose the following on this day of _____ January, 2000: That I have substantial probable cause to believe and I do believe I have cause to search:

LOCATION, PROPERTY, AND/OR PERSON[S] TO BE SEARCHED

A. The premises and all parts therein, including all rooms, attics, basements, cellars, crawl spaces, safes, mail receptacles, storage areas, containers, grounds, trash areas, garages and outbuilding assigned to or part of the residence located at **1234 Busy Street, City of Best, County of San Diego**; the residence is contained in a two story single family residence, having a primarily white wood exterior with green wood trim, and having the numbers **"1234"** in white on the left side of the door;

B. And for any vehicles including all vehicle compartments, containers and trunks identifiable as being registered to or belonging to person(s) residing at the residence via keys, admissions and documentation;

ITEMS TO BE SEIZED

For the following property, to wit:

1. Controlled substances methamphetamine and derivatives of methamphetamine;
2. Paraphernalia for the use, sale and transfer of cocaine including baggies, tinfoil wrapping, bottles, razor blades, mirrors, and scales;
3. Evidence of the transfer and sales of cocaine including scales and other weighing devices, articles of personal property tending to establish and document sales of methamphetamine, including United States currency, gold, precious metals, jewelry, works of art, precious collectible items such as stamps, trading cards, coins, celebrity autographs, and financial instruments including stocks and bonds which are the fruits, instrumentalities and/or evidence of controlled substance trafficking, buyer lists, seller lists, recordation of sales, address and telephone lists;

4. Other documentation reflecting the receipt or sales of controlled substance including to seize, view, and forensically examine all computers, computer hard drives, discs, "zip" drives, hand held computers commonly referred to as "palm pilots" and cellular telephones;

5. Firearms and ammunition;

6. And papers, documents and effects tending to show dominion and control over said premises, including keys, fingerprints, clothing, handwritings, prescription bottles, photographs, documents and effects bearing a form of identification such as a person's name, photograph, Social Security number or driver's license number; and to intercept incoming phone calls both land line and cellular during execution of the warrant.

AFFIANT'S QUALIFICATIONS

I am a peace officer employed by the Best City Police Department (BCPD) and have been so employed for about 20 years. I am currently assigned to the Narcotics Unit and have been so assigned for about 19 years. Prior to my current assignment, I previously worked as a patrol officer at Northern and Northwestern Divisions. During this time, I have investigated illicit controlled substance trafficking in Best City and surrounding areas. I have had formal training and experience in controlled substance investigations and I am familiar with the manner in which controlled substances, including methamphetamine, are packaged, marketed, and consumed.

I have received training in the identification of all types of controlled substances by sight and odor, including methamphetamine. I have made and/or assisted in an excess of 2000 arrests for violations involving such substances. In the course of my employment, I have become familiar with the ordinary meaning of controlled substance slang and jargon, and I am familiar with the manners and techniques of traffickers in cocaine as practiced locally.

PROBABLE CAUSE

Within the past ten days, in the course of my duties, I have received information that controlled substances, including cocaine were currently being sold at **1234 Busy Street in Best City, CA.** Based on that, Narcotics Detectives and I decided to conduct surveillance at the location and then try to make a controlled buy from said person using a cooperating and reliable individual (CI).

I desire to keep said CI confidential because the CI has requested me to do so, because it is my training and experience that such informants suffer physical, social and emotional retribution when their identities are revealed, because it is my experience that to reveal the identity of such informants seriously impairs their utility to law enforcement, and because it is my experience that revealing the identity of such informants dissuades other citizens from disclosing confidential information about criminal activities to law officers.

I believe the CI to be credible and reliable for the following reasons. I know from my personal interactions with CI and my conversations with officers and other members of the BCPD Narcotics Section who have worked with CI that CI has worked with members of the BCPD Narcotics Section for a number of years. CI has, in the past, given us information that controlled substances, including cocaine, was to be found at specified locations and on persons who were named and described by CI. Members of the Narcotics Section subsequently investigated the locations and persons named by CI and determined that the information was correct in all respects. CI has not given me or members of the Narcotics Section misleading information to my knowledge, nor has the CI given reason me reason to doubt the CI's ability to identify controlled substances, including cocaine. CI has previously correctly identified cocaine to me, and other detectives have told me CI has correctly identified cocaine to them. I know from my conversations with CI and officers who have spoken with CI that CI is familiar with the methods of packaging, consumption and transfer of that substance. CI is not working for consideration of a criminal case, but CI receives monetary consideration for this information. CI has no known criminal history for acts of dishonesty.

Detectives and I conducted surveillance of the property located at **1234 Busy Street.** I then conducted a controlled buy at described location using CI Detectives searched the CI prior to having the CI go to the location to make the controlled buy, for money and contraband with negative results. I provided CI with a certain amount of money and maintained surveillance as I saw CI go to **1234 Busy Street.** Detectives saw CI approach the location, make contact with a white male at the door of the location who allowed CI into the residence. Detective's maintained constant surveillance of location and after a few minutes saw CI leave the location. Detective's maintained constant surveillance of CI as CI then went to a pre-designated meeting spot to meet with Detectives and me.

CI told me that when CI entered the location, CI met with a white male. CI provided the male, with a certain amount of money and in return the male handed CI a bindle containing a powdery substance. CI handed me the substance CI stated CI received from the male, which appeared to be consistent with cocaine. CI told me he gave the male the money provided to CI in exchange for the cocaine CI gave to me. CI stated the powdery substance was "coke" (Cocaine). Detectives searched CI again for money and contraband and neither was found.

The substance was analyzed by a trained expert in such examinations employed by the BCPD and assigned to the crime laboratory, who indicated that according to the analysis, which was performed following recognized scientific procedures, the substance contained within the package is cocaine. Furthermore, the amount of substance CI gave me was consistent with the amount of money paid for it based upon local current prices for such contraband. My experience indicates that disclosure of the precise quantity purchased might tend to disclose the identity of the CI.

OPINIONS AND CONCLUSIONS

Based on my training and experience and my investigation I believe that persons are currently engaged in the sales of cocaine at the residence located at **1234 Busy Street, City of Best, County of San Diego.**

Based on my training and experience, I know person(s) engaged in the illegal sales of cocaine often times use their residence to manufacture, process and store the cocaine. Based on my training and experience, I know that persons who possess and sell cocaine frequently are users of same and will possess paraphernalia for the packaging and use of same as such paraphernalia can be used on a continuing basis and will commonly have said contraband on hand, secreted at their premises or on their person or in their vehicle, in order to maintain the confidence of their customers as well as to satisfy their own habits; and, that the selling of such contraband is an ongoing type of business because it takes time to develop "clientele", the nature of drug abuse requires a steady supply, and the business tends to be too lucrative to abandon. They also have "fruits" of their illegal sales on hand including United States currency and other valuables.

Furthermore, my training and experience indicates persons dealing in controlled substance trafficking frequently arm themselves with firearms and ammunition and keep them available either in their premises, in their vehicles or on their person. This phenomenon is primarily due to the large amounts of cash or valuable contraband involved in the drug trade and the fact that people so inclined tend to resort to violence to resist robbery, settle disputes or thwart capture by law enforcement. Accordingly, presence of firearms, along with the other described evidence, will tend to circumstantially establish sales and provide a basis for alleging additional allegations and violations under the Penal Code.

NIGHT SERVICE REQUEST

Based on my training and experience, I know persons involved in drug trafficking fear detection by police and usually go to great lengths to conceal their contraband. The sale of controlled substance frequently takes place late at night. I know police have a better chance of finding the contraband if they have option of conducting their search during a time of high activity. A drug dealer's supply may run out at any time. The heaviest activity usually occurs after their supply has been replenished. I also know drug dealers will flush contraband down the toilet or otherwise destroy evidence if they are alerted in advance and that early morning hours often provide the best opportunity to insure evidence is not destroyed.

Experience has taught me that execution of a search warrant during the early morning hours often provides the best opportunity to insure evidence is not destroyed in such a manner. So, the flexibility of searching day or night, with only short notice, is necessary in order to seize as much of the dangerous drugs as possible before it can either be sold and distributed in the community or destroyed. Prior to executing the warrant attempts will be made, either through informant information or surveillance of the premises, to attempt to execute the warrant when the most contraband and evidence is present. Based on these reasons I respectfully request the court grant my **night service request.** Therefore, based on my training, experience, and the above facts, I believe I have substantial cause to believe the above-described property or a portion thereof will be at the described premises when the warrant is served.

Based on the aforementioned information and investigation, I believe grounds for the issuance of a search warrant exist as set forth in Penal Code section 1524.

I, the affiant, hereby pray a search warrant be issued for the seizure of said property, or any part thereof, from said premises at any time of the day or night, good cause being shown therefore, and the same be brought before this magistrate or retained subject to the order of this Court as provided by law "unless seized under federal asset forfeiture laws pursuant to Title 21 United States Code section 881."

This affidavit has been reviewed for legal sufficiency by Deputy District Attorney Tu Goode.

Given under my hand and dated this _____ day of January, 2000.

_____

John Smooth

Subscribed and sworn to before me

this _____ day of January, 2000,

at _____ a.m./p.m.

_____

Judge of the Superior Court

A-3

Search Warrant

IN THE SUPERIOR COURT OF THE STATE OF CALIFORNIA,

COUNTY OF SAN DIEGO

SEARCH WARRANT

No. _____

The People of the State of California, to any peace officer in the County of San Diego:

Proof, by affidavit, having been this day made before my by John Smooth, a peace officer employed by the Best City Police Department, that there is substantial probable cause pursuant to Penal Code section 1524 for the issuance of the search warrant, as set forth in the affidavit attached hereto and made a part hereof as is fully set forth herein, you are, therefore, commanded to make search at any time of the day **or night,** good cause being shown therefore,

LOCATION, PROPERTY, AND/OR PERSON [S] TO BE SEARCHED

A. The premises and all parts therein, including all rooms, attics, basements, cellars, crawl spaces, safes, mail receptacles, storage areas, containers, grounds, trash areas, garages and outbuilding assigned to or part of the residence located at **1234 Busy Street, City of Best, County of San Diego**; the residence is contained in a two story single family residence, having a primarily white wood exterior with green wood trim, and having the numbers **"1234"** in white on the left side of the door;

B. And for any vehicles including all vehicle compartments, containers and trunks identifiable as being registered to or belonging to person(s) residing at the residence via keys, admissions, and documentation;

ITEMS TO BE SEIZED

For the following property, to wit:

1. Controlled substances cocaine and derivatives of cocaine;

2. Paraphernalia for the use, sale and transfer of cocaine including baggies, tinfoil wrapping, bottles, razor blades, mirrors, and scales;

3. Evidence of the transfer and sales of cocaine including scales and other weighing devices, articles of personal property tending to establish and document sales of cocaine, including United States currency, gold, precious metals, jewelry, works of art, precious collectible items such as stamps, trading cards, coins, celebrity autographs, and financial instruments including stocks and bonds which are the fruits, instrumentalities and/or evidence of controlled substance trafficking, buyer lists, seller lists, recordation of sales, address and telephone lists;

4. Other documentation reflecting the receipt or sales of controlled substance including to seize, view, and forensically examine all computers, computer hard drives, discs, "zip" drives, hand held computers commonly referred to as "palm pilots" and cellular telephones;

5. Firearms and ammunition;

6. And papers, documents and effects tending to show dominion and control over said premises, including keys, fingerprints, clothing, handwritings, prescription bottles, photographs, documents and effects bearing a form of identification such as a person's name, photograph, Social Security number or driver's license number; and to answer incoming phone calls both land line and cellular during execution of the warrant;

and if you find the same, or any part thereof, to bring it forthwith before me at the Superior Court of the State of California for the County of San Diego, or to any other court in which the offense in respect to which the property or things is triable, or retain such property in your custody, subject to the order of this Court, pursuant to section 1536 of the Penal Code unless seized under federal asset forfeiture laws pursuant to Title 21 United States Code section 881 and to dispose of said property pursuant to law when the property is no longer of evidentiary value.

Given under my hand and dated this _____ day of January, 2000.

_____
Judge of the Superior Court

B-1

1000 Most Commonly Misspelled Words in Criminal Justice

SPELLING LIST # 1

1. Euphoria
2. Erratic
3. Epilepsy
4. Emergency
5. Embezzlement
6. Convenience
7. Committed
8. Circumstantial
9. Caliber
10. Disheveled
11. Depression
12. Deceased
13. Dangerous
14. Counterfeit
15. Corpus Delicti
16. Baggage
17. Accomplice
18. Accidental
19. Abandon
20. Belligerent
21. Beginning
22. Barrel
23. Barbiturate
24. Bandanna
25. Bailiff

SPELLING LIST # 2

1. Hemorrhage
2. Handkerchief
3. Hallucination
4. Gauge
5. Fraudulent
6. Forcible
7. Fluorescent
8. Flammable
9. Feces
10. Jewelry
11. Knuckles
12. Laceration
13. Latent
14. Lenses
15. Lens
16. Loitering
17. Location
18. Lieutenant
19. License
20. Intoxication
21. Interrogation
22. Identification
23. Hypodermic
24. Hydraulic
25. Horizontal

SPELLING LIST # 3

1. Terrorist Threats
2. Sodomy
3. Self – Incrimination
4. Robbery
5. Polygraph
6. Mayhem
7. Domestic Violence
8. Deoxyribonucleic Acid
9. Criminalistics
10. Counterfeit
11. Conspiracy
12. Burglary
13. Bribery
14. Bigamy
15. Bestiality
16. Assault
17. Abuse
18. Forgery
19. Fraud
20. Harassment
21. Homicide
22. Incest
23. Loitering
24. Malicious Mischief
25. Manslaughter

SPELLING LIST # 4

1. Pedestrian
2. Marriage
3. Intimidated
4. Fascinated
5. Exaggerate
6. Drunkenness
7. Controversial
8. Apparatus
9. Accessories
10. Truancy
11. Accelerated
12. Warrant
13. Testimony
14. Transferred
15. Technique
16. Suspicious
17. Surrender
18. Studying
19. Sabotage
20. Prominent
21. Procedure
22. Privilege
23. Premises
24. Personal
25. Performance

SPELLING LIST # 5

1. Guitar
2. Habitual
3. Hallucinogen
4. Imitation
5. Heroin
6. Identifiable
7. Gymnasium
8. Narrative
9. Negligence
10. Glancing
11. Fictitious
12. Fatality
13. Faded
14. Facsimile
15. Participant

16. Gratification
17. Nickel
18. Oxygen
19. Noisy
20. Overt
21. Offensive
22. Parcel
23. Occupation
24. Obscene
25. Obnoxious

SPELLING LIST # 6

1. Separately
2. Sheath
3. Sheriff
4. Signaled
5. Silhouette
6. Specific
7. Strangulation
8. Straight
9. Subdued
10. Surveillance
11. Scissors
12. Warehouse
13. Wrestle
14. Infraction
15. Misdemeanor
16. Zigzag
17. Quarrel
18. Questioning
19. Racial
20. Realize
21. Receipt
22. Recognize
23. Revoked
24. Rigor Mortis
25. Schizophrenia

SPELLING LIST # 7

1. Amnesia
2. Addicted
3. Amphetamine

4. Bookkeeping
5. Brassiere
6. Breathalyzer
7. Codeine
8. Disease
9. Disguise
10. Corpse
11. Decomposition
12. Detained
13. Diabetic
14. Diarrhea
15. Dilated
16. Concealed
17. Complexion
18. Disperse
19. Cocaine
20. Ceiling
21. Caucasian
22. Cartridge
23. Alias
24. Altercation
25. Acquaintance

SPELLING LIST # 8

1. Fetal
2. Fiber
3. Forcibly
4. Foreign
5. Fracture
6. Frequency
7. Genuine
8. Habitually
9. Hazard
10. Incendiary
11. Idiosyncrasy
12. Interpret
13. Intestine
14. Investigation
15. Epileptic
16. Equipped
17. Erratically
18. Evidence
19. Exhaust
20. Explanation
21. Expose

22. Extortion
23. Extremely
24. Injection
25. Fatal

SPELLING LIST # 9

1. Wrist
2. Wounded
3. Witnesses
4. Width
5. Visible
6. Vicious
7. Vengeance
8. Vertebrae
9. Vial
10. Unnecessary
11. Urinate
12. Urine
13. Trespassing
14. Turquoise
15. Through
16. Tobacco
17. Transferred
18. Transient
19. Translator
20. Unconscious
21. Throat
22. Threatened
23. Tenant
24. Tattoo
25. Postmortem Lividity

SPELLING LIST # 10

1. Prostitution
2. Poisonous
3. Prohibited
4. Proceeded
5. Pursuit
6. Presumptive
7. Patrolling
8. Pneumatic
9. Possession

10. Pressure
11. Partial
12. Pavement
13. Passenger
14. Parallel
15. Permanent
16. Preliminary
17. Paraphernalia
18. Promissory
19. Phlegm
20. Perspiration
21. Prescription
22. Permission
23. Prejudice
24. Possibly
25. Pregnant

SPELLING LIST # 11

1. Confession
2. Confidential Informant
3. Consent
4. Contagious
5. Contraband
6. Contusion
7. Counselor
8. Cooperate
9. Convulsion
10. Credibility
11. Criminalist
12. Cruelty
13. Cursory
14. Cadillac
15. Canvass
16. Careful
17. Characteristic S
18. Chevrolet
19. Chrysler
20. Citation
21. Classification
22. Clothes
23. Coercion
24. Combustible
25. Commercial

SPELLING LIST # 12

1. Mannequin
2. Mantel
3. Margarine
4. Marijuana
5. Marshal
6. Measurement
7. Movable
8. Molested
9. Moccasin
10. Narrow
11. Narcotic
12. Murdered
13. Multiple
14. Muffler
15. Mucus
16. Mustache
17. Maneuver
18. Nephew
19. Felony
20. Criminologist
21. Niece
22. Nervous
23. Malicious
24. Neighbor
25. Neglect

SPELLING LIST # 13

1. Canister
2. Complaint
3. Carburetor
4. Comparison
5. Cardiac
6. Commit
7. Civil
8. Collision
9. Coincidence
10. Concussion
11. Constitution
12. Condition
13. Continuous
14. Daughter
15. Correspondence

16. Hemophilia
17. Height
18. Headache
19. Guttural
20. Divert
21. Discrepancies
22. Diesel
23. Diagram
24. Description
25. Decision

SPELLING LIST # 14

1. Suffocation
2. Stomach
3. Specimen
4. Siphoned
5. Sheriff
6. Sexual
7. Severed
8. Seizure
9. Oriental
10. Ordnance
11. Ordinance
12. Opposite
13. Omitted
14. Odor
15. Occurred
16. Magazine
17. Maintain
18. Material
19. Minimum
20. Monetary
21. Obstacle
22. Obtained
23. Obvious
24. Occasion
25. Occupant

SPELLING LIST # 15

1. Verified
2. Verify
3. Version

4. Violated
5. Violation
6. Volume
7. Volunteer
8. Waive
9. Warning
10. Weapon
11. Zealous
12. Weight
13. Whorl
14. Willful
15. Willfully
16. Wiry
17. Witness
18. Vein
19. Velocity
20. Voluntary
21. Warrant
22. Writ
23. Writing
24. Witnessed
25. Written

SPELLING LIST # 16

1. Impact
2. Safety
3. Salvage
4. Satisfactory
5. Scales
6. Schedule
7. Search
8. Seduce
9. Seize
10. Sergeant
11. Similar
12. Signature
13. Skeletal
14. Skidded
15. Smolder
16. Sobriety
17. Stationary
18. Stimulant
19. Stopped
20. Strategy
21. Subpoena

22. Successful
23. Suicide
24. Supervisor
25. Surprise

SPELLING LIST # 17

1. Raid
2. Rattan
3. Reasonable
4. Receding
5. Receive
6. Recognizance
7. Routine
8. Ripped
9. Rigid
10. Rifle
11. Revolver
12. Resuscitation
13. Restrained
14. Restaurant
15. Responsible
16. Resistance
17. Reputation
18. Receiving
19. Repossession
20. Released
21. Registration
22. Reduce
23. Registered
24. Refuse
25. Referred

SPELLING LIST # 18

1. Damage
2. Deadly
3. Debris
4. Defecate
5. Deliberate
6. Delinquent
7. Describe
8. Deposition
9. Denied
10. Diagnosed
11. Develop
12. Detrimental
13. Deterrence
14. Destination
15. Desperate
16. Dying
17. Doubtful
18. Disturbance
19. Distinction
20. Disposition
21. Dispatched
22. Dislocation
23. Disk
24. Discrepancy
25. Disappearance

SPELLING LIST # 19

1. Cylinder
2. Counseled
3. Corrective
4. Corporation
5. Coroner
6. Conviction
7. Continuation
8. Construction
9. Consequently
10. Comfortable
11. Compensate
12. Complainant
13. Compliance
14. Concussion
15. Consciousness
16. Cafeteria
17. Canceled
18. Carrying
19. Cartilage
20. Cashier
21. Catsup
22. Certificate
23. Choose
24. Cigarette
25. Citable

SPELLING LIST # 20

1. Incompetent
2. Inconsistent
3. Indecent
4. Incorrigible
5. Ingenious
6. Infraction
7. Indictment
8. Immediately
9. Impede
10. Implement
11. Implied
12. Impossible
13. Impounded
14. Inquiry
15. Impression
16. Inadmissible
17. Interrogate
18. Intermittent
19. Intercept
20. Insane
21. Interrupted
22. Intersection
23. Intoxication
24. Irritated
25. Issued

SPELLING LIST # 21

1. Passenger
2. Plymouth
3. Pump Action
4. Rolls-Royce
5. Ruger
6. Subaru
7. Saab
8. Shotgun
9. Silencer
10. Smith & Wesson
11. Suzuki
12. Triumph
13. Volkswagen
14. Volvo
15. Automatic

16. Binoculars
17. Browning
18. Colt
19. Continental
20. Ford
21. Harley Davidson
22. Honda
23. Lexus
24. Lincoln
25. Mercedes Benz

SPELLING LIST # 22

1. Arch
2. Cross Dresser
3. Deportation
4. Exhibitionist
5. Extradite
6. Fetish
7. Foreigner
8. Furtive
9. Incarceration
10. Interview
11. Unlawful
12. Trickery
13. Transvestite
14. Transgender
15. Tourist
16. Statue
17. Shining
18. Restraining Order
19. Principle
20. Principal
21. Pervert
22. Loop
23. Library
24. Jamaican Switch
25. Intimidation

B-2

Homonyms and Other Commonly Mistaken Words in Criminal Justice

Homonym / Homophone / Homograph

This word set can be confusing, even for word geeks. Let's start with the basics. A *homograph* is a word that has the same spelling as another word but has a different sound and a different meaning:

lead (to go in front of)/*lead* (a metal)
wind (to follow a course that is not straight)/*wind* (a gust of air)
bass (low, deep sound)/*bass* (a type of fish)

A *homophone* is a word that has the same sound as another word but is spelled differently and has a different meaning:

to/two/too
there/their/they're
pray/prey

Not so bad, right? The ending *–graph* means drawn or written, so a homograph has the same spelling. The *–phone* ending means sound or voice, so a homophone has the same pronunciation. But here's where it gets tricky. Depending on whom you talk to, *homonym* means either:

A word that is spelled like another but has a different sound and meaning (homograph); a word that sounds like another but has a different spelling and meaning (homophone)
OR
A word that is spelled and pronounced like another but has a different meaning (homograph *and* homophone)

So does a homonym have to be both a homograph and a homophone, or can it be just one or the other? As with most things in life, it depends on whom you ask.

In the strictest sense, a homonym must be both a homograph and a homophone. So say many dictionaries. However, other dictionaries allow that a homonym can be a homograph or a homophone.

With so many notable resources pointing to the contrary, are we losing this strict meaning? What then will we call a word that is spelled and pronounced the same as another but has a different meaning? If *homonym* retains all these meanings, how will readers know what is actually meant?

The careful writer would do well to follow the strict sense, ensuring his meaning is understood immediately.

More Choose your Words

abhorrent / aberrant

accept / except

ado / adieu

adopt / adapt

adverse / averse

affect / effect

afflict / inflict

aggravate / irritate

allude / elude

allusion / illusion / delusion

alternate / alternative

ambiguous / ambivalent

amicable / amiable

amoral / immoral

amuse / bemuse

anecdote / antidote

appraise / apprise

assume / presume

assure / ensure / insure

aural / oral / verbal

bare / bear

bazaar / bizarre

breach / breech

bridal / bridle

capital / capitol

censor / censure

cite / site / sight

climactic / climatic

complement / compliment

compose / comprise

concurrent / consecutive

confident / confidant(e)

connotation / denotation

connote / denote

conscious / conscience

contemptible / contemptuous

continual / continuous

correlation / corollary

council / counsel

decent / descent / dissent

definitely / definitively

demur / demure

didactic / pedantic

disassemble / dissemble

discomfit / discomfort

discreet / discrete

disillusion / dissolution

disinterested / uninterested

dual / duel

economic / economical

elusive / illusive

emigrate / immigrate / migrate

eminent / imminent

eminent / imminent / immanent

empathy / sympathy

endemic / epidemic

entitle / title

entomology / etymology

envelop / envelope

envy / jealousy

epigram / epigraph

epitaph / epithet

especially / specially

exalt / exult

exercise / exorcise

expedient / expeditious

extant / extent

facetious / factious / fatuous

farther / further

faze / phase

ferment / foment

fictional / fictitious / fictive

figuratively / literally

flair / flare

flaunt / flout

flounder / founder

formerly / formally

formidable / formative

fortunate / fortuitous

gibe / jibe

gig / jig

gorilla / guerrilla

grisly / gristly / grizzly

hale / hail

healthful / healthy

hero / protagonist

historic / historical

hoard / horde

homonym / homophone / homograph

hone / home

imply / infer

incredible / incredulous

indeterminate / indeterminable

indict / indite

inflammable / inflammatory

ingenious / ingenuous

insidious / invidious

instant / instance

intense / intensive / intent

introvert / extrovert

irony / satire / sarcasm

it's / its

laudable / laudatory

lay / lie

loath / loathe

lose / loose

luxuriant / luxurious

marital / martial

mean / median / average

medal / meddle / mettle

metaphor / simile

moral / morale

morbid / moribund

nauseated / nauseous

naval / navel

objective / subjective

optimistic / pessimistic

palate / palette / pallet

paradox / oxymoron

parameter / perimeter

parody / parity

peak / peek / pique

peddle / pedal / petal

persecute / prosecute

personal / personnel

pitiable / pitiful / piteous / pitiless

pore / pour

practical / practicable

pragmatic / dogmatic

precede / proceed

precedent / president

predominate / predominant

premier / premiere

prescribe / proscribe

pretentious / portentous

principal / principle

prophecy / prophesy

prostate / prostrate

quote / quotation

rebut / refute

regrettably / regretfully

reluctant / reticent

respectfully / respectively

sac / sack

scrimp / skimp

sensual / sensuous

simple / simplistic

stationary / stationery

statue / statute

than / then

that / which

their / there / they're

tortuous / torturous

turbid / turgid

unconscionable / unconscious

unexceptional / unexceptionable

venal / venial

veracious / voracious

wave / waive

weather / whether / wether

who / whom

who's / whose

your / you're

Index